THE NOVELS OF *August Strindberg*

THE NOVELS OF

August Strindberg

A STUDY IN THEME AND STRUCTURE

by Eric O. Johannesson

UNIVERSITY OF CALIFORNIA PRESS

BERKELEY AND LOS ANGELES · 1968

University of California Press
Berkeley and Los Angeles, California
Cambridge University Press
London, England

© 1968 by The Regents of the University of California
Library of Congress Catalog Card Number: 68-29156
Designed by James Mennick
Printed in the United States of America

To Suzy

Preface

The primary purpose of this book is twofold: to trace in the novels of August Strindberg the development of a psychological theme, and to show how this theme is reflected in the shifting patterns of his narrative art. The theme on which I have chosen to concentrate, the quest for identity, is admittedly broad, but it is the only theme that appears sufficiently general and inclusive to encompass this contradictory, metamorphic, and experimental novelist. It should, I hope, afford us the perspective that will enrich our experience of the novels, their meaning and significance not only as psychological documents but also as works of fiction.

Now Strindberg is an autobiographical novelist, and such novelists pose particular problems for the literary critic, chief among them the difficulty of separating the life from the work. I cannot claim that I have succeeded in solving this problem, but I should like to emphasize at the outset that it has not been my intention to write a psychological study of Strindberg's life and mind as reflected in his novels; I have concentrated, instead, on the study of a psychological theme in his novels.

Similarly, while the approach to the study of the novel in this book may be labeled psychoanalytic in some instances, I have not sought to write a psychoanalytic study of Strindberg, a task for which I am poorly equipped. What I have sought to demonstrate is how his novels explore the self and the forces that condition it, in a manner that anticipates the concepts and methods of psychoanalysis.

We already know that Strindberg's novels are closely based on his life, and the man behind them will undoubtedly never cease to attract our curiosity, but to the critic of fiction other questions plead for an answer. We know that the novels have much to tell us about Strindberg, but what do they have to tell us about the nature and quality of human experience? In concentrating on the quest for identity as the major theme, I have sought a vantage point from which we might be able to determine the extent to which Strindberg has succeeded in integrating his experiences into significant art and in projecting his personal quest onto the more objective plane of the life of the psyche. For the quest for identity is a problem of general significance and a central theme in much modern literature.

The secondary purpose of this book is to establish a basis for the evaluation of Strindberg's significance as a novelist. His dramas, we know, have had a strong influence on the development of the modern theater. What contribution, if any, have his novels made to the development of the modern novel? The assumption of this book is that although they have been largely overshadowed by the dramas, Strindberg's novels are, at their best, vital and important works of fiction which are not to be disregarded, and which anticipate or mirror the development of the modern psychological novel. Here the major theme again ought to serve as the vantage point from which our experience of the novels is enriched in meaning and significance, since Strindberg's progressive tendency to transcend the limitations of the realistic novel and to experiment with new narrative forms, with symbolism and myth, is, basically, a reflection of his progressive exploration of the self.

I have not confined myself to a single critical approach in this study. Both as a dramatist and as a novelist, Strindberg was an improvisator and an experimenter. Every work represents a departure. In each essay, consequently, I have sought to use the method best suited to reveal the particular mode of artistic integration, of structure, while simultaneously tracing the general theme. In other words, I have sought to treat each novel as a unique work of literature, evaluating it on its own merits, as well as in terms of its significance with reference to the development of the major theme.

The emphasis on Strindberg as a psychological novelist has obviously necessitated certain limitations. Some important facets of his art of fiction have been neglected. Those who value his novels mostly for their vitality of language, for their vivid and impressionistic treatment of the milieu, or for their biting social satire and criticism, are likely to register disappointment, as are undoubtedly those who regard *The People of Hemsö* as his major achievement.

Owing to the broad scope of the study, I have made no systematic effort to trace the numerous influences by various writers on the novels, nor have I tried to demonstrate affinities between Strindberg and other novelists, except for the purpose of illustrating a specific point under discussion. For the same reason I regret that I have not been able to consider in detail the relationship between the novels and the dramas, a major task well worthy of a separate volume.

In my choice of novels, I have been guided by the two purposes of the book, as well as by my own critical taste. I have therefore included all the major novels, except *Legends* and *The Gothic Rooms* (both of which add little to the development of the theme and are inferior works of literature), and the short novels and tales that serve to shed light on the major theme or on the development of Strindberg's narrative art. Again, it ought to be emphasized that a large body of short fiction remains outside the purview of this book.

Although there is as yet no general critical study of Strindberg's novels in Swedish, I am deeply indebted to the works of many Swedish scholars, chief among them the brilliant contributions of Gunnar Brandell, Torsten Eklund, Staffan Björck, Sven Rinman, Walter A. Berendsohn, Göran Printz-Påhlsson, and Karl-Åke Kärnell. Without the labors of these men and others, whose works are listed in the bibliography, this book would never have been written.

I also wish to thank all those who have given generously of their time and advice during the preparation of the manuscript, and, in particular, Walter Johnson, without whose unfailing encouragement and friendly support I would never have completed the book. I am also indebted to the American Council of Learned Societies for a grant in 1960–61, and to the University of California for a grant in lieu of summer teaching.

Contents

xii · CONTENTS

Chronology

*Titles in capital letters refer to
novels discussed in this book.*

1849 January 22. Strindberg born in Stockholm.
1862 Mother dies.
1867 Studies at Uppsala University.
1870 *Fritänkaren (The Freethinker)*, first drama. Returns
      to Uppsala.
1872 Leaves Uppsala. *Början av Än Bogsveigs saga (The
      Beginning of Än Bogsveig's Saga)*, first prose work.
      *En berättelse från Stockholms skärgård (A Tale
      from the Archipelago)*, a fragment. Writes *Mäster
      Olof (Master Olof)*, first major historical drama.
1874 Assistant in the Royal Library.
1875 Meets Siri von Essen.
1876 First Parisian journey.

1877   Marries Siri von Essen. *Från Fjärdingen och Svart-bäcken* (*Uppsala Stories*).

1879   RÖDA RUMMET (THE RED ROOM).

1881   First performance of *Master Olof*.

1882   *Det nya riket* (*The New Kingdom*), a collection of social satires. *Svenska öden och äventyr* (*Swedish Destinies and Adventures*), first historical tales. Leaves position in the Royal Library.

1883   Leaves Sweden and settles in France. *Dikter* (*Poems*). UTVECKLING (PROGRESS).

1884   Moves to Switzerland. Visits Italy. Returns briefly to Sweden to stand trial for blasphemy after the publication of *Giftas* (*Married*), the first volume of stories devoted to the subject of marriage.

1885   Returns to France. *Utopier i verkligheten* (*Utopias in Reality*), stories with socialism and pacifism as their theme.

1886   Moves to Switzerland and to Bavaria. *Married*, Vol. II. TJÄNSTEKVINNANS SON (THE SON OF A SERVANT), Vols. I and II.

1887   Seeks to establish a theater in Copenhagen. Essay on "Själamord ("Psychic Murder"). *Fadren* (*The Father*), naturalistic drama. HEMSÖBORNA (THE PEOPLE OF HEMSÖ). THE SON OF A SER-VANT, Vols. III and IV (Vol. IV, pub. 1909).

1888   *Fröken Julie* (*Miss Julie*), and *Fordringsägare* (*Creditors*), plays. LE PLAIDOYER D'UN FOU (THE DEFENSE OF A FOOL), completed. DEN RO-MANTISKE KLOCKAREN PÅ RÅNÖ (THE ROMANTIC ORGANIST), included in *Skär-karlsliv* (*Life in the Archipelago*). TSCHANDALA, written.

1889   Returns to Sweden.

1890   *I HAVSBANDET (BY THE OPEN SEA). EN HÄXA (A WITCH).*

1891   Marriage dissolved.

1892   Visits Berlin and meets Frida Uhl.

1893   Marries Frida Uhl.

1894   Returns to France and settles in Paris after separation from Frida. Brief visits to Austria, the home of his wife's parents, and to Sweden during the following three years, the period of the so-called Inferno crisis.

1896   Settles in Lund, Sweden.

1897   Begins last stay in Paris. *INFERNO.*

1898   *Legender (Legends). Till Damaskus (To Damascus),* Part I.

1899   Return to Stockholm. Returns to the historical drama in *Gustav Vasa* and *Erik XIV.*

1901   Marries the actress Harriet Bosse. *Dödsdansen (The Dance of Death).*

1902   *Ett drömspel (A Dream Play).*

1903   New Historical dramas: *Kristina (Queen Christina),* and *Gustav III. ENSAM (ALONE). Sagor (Fairy Tales).*

1904   Marriage to Harriet Bosse dissolved. *Götiska Rummen (The Gothic Rooms).*

1905   *Ordalek och småkonst,* poems.

1907   Establishment of the Intimate Theater. *Spöksonaten (The Ghost Sonata),* and other Chamber plays. *SVARTA FANOR (BLACK BANNERS). TAKLAGSÖL (THE ROOFING FEAST). SYNDABOCKEN (THE SCAPEGOAT). En blå bok (A Blue Book),* begun.

1909   *Stora landsvägen (The Highway),* last drama.

1912   May 14. Strindberg dies.

A Note on the Text

Unless otherwise indicated, all the references to Strindberg's works are to *Samlade skrifter*, ed. John Landquist (55 vols.; Stockholm, 1912–1927). The volume number appears in italics, the page numbers in roman (i.e., *22*, 77, means volume 22, page 77).

The translations are my own with two exceptions. In chapter v, *"The People of Hemsö,"* in which matters of style are elaborated upon, I have used Elspeth Harvey Schubert's beautiful translation with its remarkable fidelity to the original (Stockholm: Bonniers, 1959), cited as EHS in the text. In chapter xi, *"Inferno,"* I have used Mary Sandbach's excellent translation because it is based on both the French and Swedish texts, an admirable compromise in my estimation (London: Hutchinson, 1962); cited as MS in the text.

In chapter vi, *"The Defense of a Fool,"* my translations are based on Tage Aurell's Swedish version *En dåres försvar-*

stal (Stockholm: Bonniers, 1962), cited as TA in the text. Had Evert Sprinchorn's *A Madman's Defense* (New York: Anchor Books, 1967) been available at the time of writing, I would have used it in this chapter as the novel poses textual problems similar to those of *Inferno* and it is a fine translation of Strindberg's original *Le plaidoyer d'un fou.*

Brev in the notes refers to August Strindberg, *Brev,* ed. Torsten Eklund (9 vols.; Stockholm: Bonniers, 1947–1966).

⟶ 1. Strindberg and the Novel

THE SERIOUS STUDENT of modern literature is likely to be familiar with the name August Strindberg. If the student is not a Scandinavian, or particularly interested in Scandinavian literature, he will in all likelihood think of Strindberg exclusively in his role as one of the progenitors of the modern drama, as the author of *The Father, Miss Julie, The Dance of Death, A Dream Play,* and *The Ghost Sonata.* If told that Strindberg was also a novelist of considerable stature, he is likely to register surprise and a measure of incredulity, for the reason that outside Scandinavia, Strindberg has received scant critical recognition as a writer of fiction. Nevertheless, he produced a large body of fiction: about a dozen novels and an equal number of volumes containing short stories and tales.

It is true, of course, that Strindberg never seriously cultivated the novel as a mode of literary expression. On the contrary, he often tended to dismiss it in an arbitrary fashion, as therapy, as pamphleteering, as a way to make money when the theaters were closed to him. Unlike a Flaubert or a Henry James, he did not consciously pursue the craft of fiction, in part because he disliked the well-made, the constructed, the artificial. Impatient and tempestuous, he worked hurriedly, often in the heat of passion or in the whirlwind of inspiration. When the passion was spent, he showed little interest in revision. He regarded repetition, even of a successful experiment, with disfavor, so that every novel he wrote denotes a fresh departure. The diversity of forms is also extraordinary, almost every type of narrative being represented in his production: *Bildungsroman*, Gothic romance, fable, myth, journal, monologue. The novel, it seems, appealed to Strindberg primarily as a loose-jointed form that placed a minimum of restraint on his persistent need to project and to explore the self.

Nevertheless, Strindberg produced some remarkable novels and an excellent body of short fiction, and there are indications that had he so desired he might have become a major novelist. While most of his novels tend to be somewhat static as far as the action is concerned, concentrating on psychological analysis or reflection, they do give evidence of his gift for storytelling. He has the novelist's love of the concrete, an unmatched skill in the handling of the Swedish language,[1] a dramatist's knack for dialogue, and a remarkable degree of

---

[1] Although not all Swedish critics are equally impressed by the more experimental aspects of Strindberg's works, they are, in the words of Alrik Gustafson, "without exception in agreement that his handling of language is one of the chief miracles of Swedish literature. No Swedish author has the stylistic variety and range, the spontaneity, directness, and economy of phrasing that Strindberg commands. He shook Swedish prose completely loose from its earlier ceremonious, rhetorical propensities, bringing to it a pulsing aliveness and intensity which have provided the point of departure for all modern developments in Swedish prose style" (*A History of Swedish Literature* [Minneapolis: University of Minnesota Press, 1961], pp. 254–255).

psychological insight, based partly on intense self-analysis, partly on his readings in psychology. His first novel, *The Red Room*, and, above all, *The People of Hemsö*, with its objective presentation of life in the Stockholm archipelago and of characters who possess independent life and are molded by the world in which they live, show that Strindberg might well have made a successful bid to become a major novelist within the tradition of the realistic novel, the tradition of Balzac, Dickens, Flaubert, and Zola. But then *The Red Room* found no sequel despite the entreaties of friendly critics, and *The People of Hemsö* remained an "intermezzo scherzando." What prevented Strindberg from continuing within this tradition of the novel and made him fail to realize his promise was, above all, the fact that his main ambition was to become a dramatist, not a novelist, but also, most significantly, his interest in psychology, his desire to explore the self and the forces and things that condition its existence, a desire that led him to turn within himself for the new reality with which to forge his art, made him transcend the limitations of the realistic novel, and forced him into experiments with new forms of expression.

The fact is that Strindberg is undoubtedly one of the most persistently autobiographical writers in the history of modern literature, irrespective of the form of literary expression he used: fiction, drama, or poetry. In the sense that he tends to depict characters who represent facets of himself in narratives that have an open-ended, biographical structure and often derive their unity from the protagonist rather than from the action, Strindberg is an autobiographical novelist and belongs in the company of Stendhal, D. H. Lawrence, Gide, Proust, and Henry Miller. Nevertheless, from this it would be rash to conclude that his novels are of interest mainly to the biographer and to the psychologist and not to the critic of fiction. To read Strindberg's novels as autobiographical documents alone, as has often been done, is to miss their subtlety, their complexity, and their general significance, both as contributions to our knowledge of the workings of the psyche and as narrative art.[2] What is important to recognize is that although Strindberg, like most autobiographical novelists from Goethe to Henry Miller, used the novel as an avenue to self-discovery, he also, like all significant artists, aimed at truth-telling of a higher order, arranging and synthesizing his experiences, thereby investing them with the general significance and relevance of art. Like his dramas, his novels are imbued with a Faustian spirit, an unrelenting quest for knowledge and for truth, regardless of the consequences, a quest in pursuit of which he used his own life and experience as foundation. Thus, although his novels are self-explorations, they constitute, above all, a profound exploration of the self, and although the protagonist in most of them tends to bear the author's own features, he is not to be identified with Strindberg.

While the biographer and the psychologist will undoubtedly continue to focus their attention on the facts behind the fiction, on the person behind the mask, the critic who is to determine the originality and the achievement of Strindberg the novelist must therefore search elsewhere. He must search instead for Strindberg's unique ways of perceiving and telling the facts of his experience, for those aspects of his mind and art which serve to transform his self-exploration into an exploration of the self. Above all, he must try to grasp the major themes that form the integrated patterns in these autobiographical narratives.

In considering Strindberg the novelist, two aspects of his mind are of particular significance. One is his profound scien-

---

[2] For an excellent article on the general tendency among Swedish Strindberg scholars to favor the biographical approach, as well as on some new trends, see Göran Lindström, "Strindbergforskning 1915–1962," *Svensk litteraturtidskrift,* 2 (1962), 60–81.

tific and empirical bent, best manifested in his deep interest in the young science of psychology. The other is his dialectic attitude to thinking, to the search for truth, primarily expressed in his so-called experiments with standpoints.

Few modern writers have been as scientifically oriented as Strindberg. Among his contemporaries in Scandinavia, only J. P. Jacobsen, the author of *Niels Lyhne*, reveals a similar interest in science. If we disregard the aged Strindberg's intemperate attacks on Darwin and the theory of evolution, the hostility to science so characteristic of much modern literature is remarkably absent. During a good part of his career Strindberg did in fact aspire to become a scientist rather than a writer, and it is characteristic that although the artist-hero is the protagonist in most of his novels, in no fewer than four of them—*Tschandala, By the Open Sea, Inferno,* and *The Roofing Feast*—the hero is a scientist. We thus find Strindberg in the 1880's, after having already earned a reputation as a Sinologist as a young man, seriously devoting himself to the study of history, producing an interesting cultural history of Stockholm, and then proceeding to sociology, gathering material for a study of the French peasant during a tour in southern France.[3] In the 1890's he gave up his writing altogether for a number of years in order to concentrate on his experiments in chemistry, ostensibly for the purpose of making a name for himself as a natural scientist as he had already done as a playwright.

Despite this interest in the natural and social sciences, it was the science of psychology, then in its infancy, that absorbed his attention more than anything else, at least from the middle of the 1880's on. In retrospect, even his chemical experiments in Paris during the 1890's may in fact, at least

---

[3] The latter study, entitled *Bland franska bönder* (*Among French Peasants*), first printed in 1889, is included in *Samlade skrifter*, vol. 20.

to those who have read Jung's writings on alchemy, appear to be an effort at the transmutation of the self rather than of base metals. Always excessively self-conscious and given to self-analysis, qualities he ascribed to his Christian upbringing, Strindberg discovered in the new psychology the tools and the theoretical framework to penetrate the as yet relatively uncharted regions of the psyche. Never above the desire to be in the mainstream and a member of the avant-garde, he was, like Nietzsche, convinced that psychology was the science of the future, the path to more fundamental problems, and, most important, the potential source of an infusion of new vitality and significance into literature.[4]

The impact of this psychological interest on Strindberg's fiction is manifold, but it may be summarized roughly as follows. To the extent that his novels are autobiographical, they are not written from an autobiographical point of view, for although the insights into the workings of the psyche which they convey are based on self-analysis, they also manifest a conscious desire to make these insights conform to scientific thought. Or, put in different terms: although Strindberg writes about himself and his experiences, this autobiographical foundation is irrelevant, because the schemes of meaning underlying his constructed plots are clearly designed to illustrate psychological theories concerning the nature of the self, theories that are either derived from the author's knowledge of contemporary psychology or serve to anticipate the subsequent codifications of psychoanalysis.

Thus when Strindberg in the autobiographical *The Son of a Servant* depicts his hero Johan as "characterless," sub-

---

[4] In the introduction to his fine study *Hjärnornas kamp: Psykologiska ideer och motiv i Strindbergs åttiotalsdiktning* (Stockholm: Natur och Kultur, 1952), Hans Lindström has analyzed the development that led to this turning point in Strindberg's literary career and the reasons for Strindberg's new and more positive attitude to literature.

stituting the notion of a multiplicity of selves for the traditional concept of identity, this self-portrayal was aided by, and largely formulated in terms of, his reading of contemporary psychology, chiefly the works of Sir Henry Maudsley and Théodule Ribot.

Similarly, the novel *Tschandala*, based on the harassing experiences Strindberg had in the small town of Skovlyst north of Copenhagen in the year 1888, though often regarded as an obvious manifestation of his paranoic state of mind, proves on closer examination to be patterned not only on Maudsley's *Pathology of Mind* with its emphasis on the perils of isolation and on the pathological traits of genius, but also on Nietzsche's brilliant insights into the psychology of resentment as recorded in *The Genealogy of Morals*.

Even that infamous novel, *The Defense of a Fool*, though it purports to be the story of Strindberg's marriage to the actress Siri von Essen, is less a defense and an act of revenge than a study in psychopathology of unusual complexity. For, as in *The Father*, the marital tangle, the war of the sexes, has been transformed into a representation in symbolic form of the conflict between the ego and the unconscious. The novel reflects Strindberg's own ambivalence, but reflects even more his concept of the self, a concept of the self in conflict which we now primarily associate with the name of Freud. The very misogyny, which has made Strindberg so notorious, in effect proves to be a necessary adjunct of his psychology, because woman is robbed of her individual traits and transformed into a symbol of the irrational and the unconscious, while the male emerges as the representative of the principle of reason and of the ego.

Complexity of viewpoint, greater objectivity, and broader human significance are the most immediate effects of Strindberg's psychological interest on his novels.

Similar effects are engendered by his dialectic attitude to

the search for truth. Intensely dynamic and contradictory, Strindberg steadfastly refused to adopt a simple view either of the self or of truth. Throughout his life he argued the merits of the uncommitted life, insisting in the manner of André Gide on the virtue of inconstancy, on the writer's *disponibilité*, on his willingness to test new ideas, and on his opposition to all systems of thought.

Two words recur with exceptional frequency in his usage: *synpunkt* and *ståndpunkt*. The former means point of view, the latter standpoint or attitude. Thus he often spoke of his novels as "experiments with standpoints." By this he wanted to indicate that the particular commitment embodied in the novel, be it to an ideology, to a philosophy, or to a given mode of existence, was being tested as an avenue to truth.

That both the phrase "experiments with standpoints" and the method itself owe something to Søren Kierkegaard is obvious and has been admitted by Strindberg himself.[5] In his own curious but exceedingly interesting philosophical novels, Kierkegaard consciously experimented with various ways in which the individual might relate himself to the world.[6] In a similar manner, Strindberg's novels form an unbroken series of such experiments, tests of varied commitments, explorations of their consequences within the imitation of an action.

Nevertheless, Strindberg's fictional experiments with standpoints differ in two important respects from Kierke-

---

[5] Cf. also Gunnar Brandell's argument that "Kierkegaard indicated to Strindberg the dialectic possibilities in his own nature. . . . When he reverted to atheism, or returned to his belief in God during the Inferno period, it happened in part with the experimental view to live through an ideology and to realize its practical implications. This 'experimenting with standpoints' refers back to Kierkegaard and his 'stages' " (*Strindbergs Infernokris* [Stockholm: Bonniers, 1950], p. 24).

[6] On Kierkegaard's literary method, see F. J. Billeskov Jansen's edition of Søren Kierkegaard, *Vaerker i Udvalg* (Copenhagen, 1950), I, xvii.

gaard's: they are not so dispassionate and so objective as Kierkegaard's, and they do not project a series of stages leading the individual to the insight that the last stage is the only tenable one. Kierkegaard's stages are dialectic: the process leading from the aesthetic to the ethical and, finally, to the religious stage, though activated by acts of choice and not by necessity, is a logical one. Strindberg's experiments, on the contrary, constitute a series of brief forays into unexplored territory followed by subsequent returns to the starting point as the experiment proved unprofitable. While Kierkegaard's dialectic process ends in the security of the Christian faith, Strindberg's repeated tests of varied commitments end in the withdrawal to a nihilistic standpoint, affirming only the belief that no commitment is valid.

The impact of this experimental method on Strindberg's novels is varied. Besides contributing to the general complexity of viewpoint—a viewpoint often difficult to fix with any degree of certainty owing to his tendency to diffuse and to divide himself among the characters and to shift the angle of narration in midstream—it is, above all, responsible for the great intellectual vitality of his novels. Strindberg's novels represent, in fact, a lifelong dialogue with truth, in the process of which the entire spectrum of belief and unbelief of his age passes in review.[7] No new philosophy is embedded in

---

[7] Robert Brustein, in his brilliant chapter on Strindberg in *The Theatre of Revolt*, after calling Strindberg "the most restless and experimental" spirit in the modern theater, goes on to describe him as "a latter-day Faust with the unconscious as his laboratory—seeking the miracle of transmutation in the crucible of the tormented intellect. . . . His entire career, in fact, is a search for the philosopher's stone of ultimate truth through the testing of varied commitments. . . . In his religious and political attitudes, he covers the entire spectrum of belief and unbelief, skirting positivism, atheism, Socialism, Pietism, Catholicism, Hinduism, Buddhism, and Swedenborgian mysticism. In his scientific studies, he ranges from Darwin to the occult, from

his writings, for he was not an original thinker, nor a profound one, but to read his novels is to be in vital and intimate contact with the ideas of some of the greatest minds of the nineteenth century: Kierkegaard, Darwin, Schopenhauer, Nietzsche, Goethe. This is true of both his novels and his dramas. For instance, A *Dream Play* may be described as a dramatic representation of the philosophy of Schopenhauer and *Inferno* as a fictional representation of the visionary philosophy of Swedenborg. Strindberg's novels, if read in sequence, create a gigantic *Bildungsroman*, depicting the modern writer's Faustian quest for a set of values that will give order and meaning to his world. Despite this search for a lost absolute, there is, nevertheless, a remarkably open-ended quality in his novels, a sense of being on a journey which springs from the conviction that although an experiment has proved unprofitable, it is to be continued along new paths. This openness is often in stark contrast with the grim view of life reflected in the action. Much of the intellectual vitality of Strindberg's novels has its roots in a form of dramatic tension: a tension between the desire for order and meaning, on the one hand, and, on the other, the suspicion that chaos and meaninglessness are basic constituents of the very existence of man.

Many themes run through Strindberg's novels, but a single, integrated pattern may be said to compose the broad, general theme that gives unity and continuity to the works. This theme is the quest for identity, the ceaseless exploration of the self and the forces and things that condition its existence. Reflecting a problem of very broad scope, this theme has many facets: social, psychological, existential. Strindberg's novels probe all of them. In the process they also confirm the assumption that the quest for identity, though a major theme

Naturalism to Supernaturalism, from physics to metaphysics, from chemistry to alchemy" ([Boston: Little, Brown, 1966], p. 87).

in modern literature, has its roots in the Romantic movement.[8] For this reason it is hardly surprising that Strindberg in his pursuit of the theme should anticipate existentialism and psychoanalysis, as both are to a large extent offshoots of the Romantic movement.

One of the most characteristic traits of Strindberg's hero is self-consciousness, an excessive concern with selfhood. In its most intense and exaggerated form, the self-consciousness appears neurotic, and to a large degree it undoubtedly reflects Strindberg's own obsession with self. Excessively impressionable and contradictory, he possessed a precarious sense of identity which made him regard the ego in the framework of an economics of scarcity: each individual possesses only a given quantity of ego, and this portion others are always bent on appropriating in order to add to their own. Hence his fear of close personal contacts and of strong personalities. Hence also his ambivalent attitude to his friends, to women, to marriage.[9]

If Strindberg's novels reflect his own neurotic fears and obsessions, they also reflect his keen awareness of the very real threats posed by organized society against the individual's sense of identity. For his hero is invariably in revolt against any social or political pressures, any systems of thought which might rob him of his individuality, his sense of uniqueness.

[8] Cf. Wylie Sypher, *Loss of the Self in Modern Literature and Art* (New York: Vintage Books, 1965), and Robert Langbaum, "The Mysteries of Identity: A Theme in Modern Literature," *American Scholar,* 34 (Autumn, 1965).

[9] There is as yet, surprisingly, no really good biography of Strindberg. For reliable information about the man, it is therefore necessary to turn to his letters or to the well-edited collection of eyewitness accounts recently published (see Stellan Ahlström, ed., *August Strindberg: Ungdom och mannaår* [Stockholm: Wahlström och Widstrand, 1959)], and Stellan Ahlström and Torsten Eklund, eds., *August Strindberg: Mannaår och ålderdom* [Stockholm: Wahlström och Widstrand, 1961]).

Regarded from this point of view, Strindberg's grim and disenchanted view of personal relations as a form of psychological warfare is primarily a reflection of his unending concern with the problem of how to remain an authentic individual in modern society, a concern he shares with all existentialist writers, from Kierkegaard to Sartre.[10]

Strindberg's hero is, however, a most reluctant and uneasy rebel. In rejecting the traditional codes of morality and behavior imposed by authority, he is uncomfortable and suffers pangs of guilt, for although he refuses to conform or to belong, he secretly harbors the desire to do so. In rejecting society and seeking the life of solitude as a relief from pressure, he is tormented by loneliness and by feelings of being an outcast. In proudly rejecting the Christian faith as being a comfort to weak mortals who lack the strength to assume responsibility for their own fate and to be the creators of their own values, he is overcome by feelings of cosmic estrangement and homelessness and yearns for something beyond the self, an Archimedean point in an absurd universe.

A second basic trait in Strindberg's hero is, consequently, ambivalence. In addition to being excessively self-conscious, he is contradictory, split, disharmonious. While this trait, too, reflects Strindberg's own ambivalence, it also conveys his profound awareness of the problems of an age of transition, an age of rapid social change in which the old institutional values have broken down, leaving the individual without a firm sense of identity, without a firm sense of values, vacillating uneasily between extremes, between idealism and realism, between revolt and conformity, between the security of the old and the freedom of the new.[11]

---

[10] Cf. Søren Kierkegaard, *The Present Age*, trans. Alexander Dru (New York: Harper Torchbooks, 1962).

[11] For a penetrating analysis of the relationship between the problem of identity and rapid social change, see Allen Wheelis, *The Quest for Identity* (New York: Norton, 1958).

In general, Strindberg attributes the split and dishar-monious mind of his hero—and of himself—to his being the product of two eras, to his being a Romantic in a positivistic and materialistic age. Like the hero of J. P. Jacobsen's *Niels Lyhne*, he feels like a transitional figure, born either twenty years too soon or twenty years too late. This analysis appears quite valid, for, although our preoccupation with Strindberg's naturalistic dramas has tended to obscure the fact, he is at heart a Romantic writer. His Faustian search for the absolute, his restless and dynamic experimentation with both ideas and literary conventions, his revolt against bourgeois institutions and the systematic certainties and beliefs of the past, his progressive journey into the interior, into some form of in-wardness in his search for a firm vantage point in a shifting and insubstantial world: all these point to his Romantic an-cestry. Yet he was living in a naturalistic age and by no means immune to its new ideas: science, socialism, evolution. Hence the tension between the old and the new which is so char-acteristic a theme in his works.

Viewed with reference to the quest for identity, the emphasis on the ambiguities of the Romantic self takes on added significance, because it serves to place the problem in a new light.[12] It means, in effect, that the hero is doing battle not only against the social and political pressures that seek to rob him of his individuality and his integrity but also against still more formidable inner pressures that pose even greater threats to his selfhood. The pressures are of many different kinds—guilt, past dependencies, irrational and unconscious desires, injunctions of the superego—but they all contribute to the same end: to divide the self.

---

[12] In speaking of the Romantic self, I have particular reference to an illuminating article by George Boas, "The Romantic Self: An Historical Sketch," *Studies in Romanticism*, IV (Autumn, 1964), 1–16.

The key concept in Strindberg's psychology of the self is, consequently, ambivalence. Like Freud, he conceives of the self not as an abstract and coherent unity but as the focal point of a struggle among various forces that are always at war with one another.[13] Thus the desires of the individual clash with the desires of society, the demands of the instincts with the demands of culture, the needs of the ego with the needs of the unconscious. When I speak of the quest for identity as the major theme in Strindberg's novels, I am therefore referring to the hero's defense of his individuality against outside pressures, as well as to his struggle to integrate the self by extirpating or harmonizing the conflicts within the self. The concept of the self in conflict, this highly dramatic concept of the psychic life, is what gives Strindberg's pursuit of the theme its profundity, what represents the source of the vital tension of his novels.

In the development of the major theme, the quest for identity, we may distinguish among three stages, each characterized by the emphasis on one particular type of conflict. With due allowance for the fact that such a division is by necessity schematic, for the various forms of conflict overlap considerably, the development of the major theme may be outlined as follows.

In the early novels, that is, the novels written between 1879 and 1887, the artist-hero's conflict is primarily social and political. Searching for a vocation, for a meaningful social commitment of some kind, he is torn between his own desire for integrity and authenticity and the demands made upon him by a society that is cynical, materialistic, and opportunistic. While his revolt against the social order and its institutions, the family, the school, the church, is profound, it

---

[13] For a discussion of Freud's concept of the self in conflict, see Philip Rieff, *Freud: The Mind of the Moralist* (New York: Anchor Books, 1961), pp. 29 f.

remains ambivalent, for the hero is unable to endure the consequences of his revolt, the life of isolation. A rebellious outsider, he also feels he is an outcast, rejected rather than rejecting.

The broader existential and ontological problem, the problem of the meaningfulness of human existence as such, remains peripheral, though the short novel *Progress* anticipates the subsequent conflict between a faith in a meaningful order of the universe and the nihilism that denies the existence of such an order.

In the novels of the middle period, those written in the very productive years from 1888 to 1890, the picture of social life as a form of antagonism, as a ceaseless conflict between the self and the others, is intensified, but, in addition, a psychological perspective is added, a concept of the self as a stage where the conflicting inner forces of the psyche enact their dramatic conflict. The brilliant essay "Psychic Murder," which could serve as an introduction to these novels, envisions human relations as a barely disguised form of psychological warfare, as "a battle of the brains." [14] The world is posing constant threats against the individual's sense of identity, through suggestion, through the use of mass media and the pressures of public opinion. As a result the hero's efforts are bent toward the development of effective means of defense against such forms of psychic murder. But no form of defense proves effective, for both the withdrawal into solitude and dissimulation and the conscious wearing of a protective mask bring other conflicts in their wake, involving the hero in danger of what Strindberg calls "psychic suicide."

---

[14] The essay "Psychic Murder," the Swedish title of which is "Själamord," may be found in *Samlade skrifter*, vol. 22. "The battle of the brains" is a reference to a story in the same volume, entitled "Hjärnornas kamp." For a fuller treatment of the essay on psychic murder, see below, pp. 91–95.

This is because the hero is, above all, threatened by forces from within. The social and political pressures are very real, but still more difficult to cope with are the pressures from within, past emotional dependencies, the irrational instincts, the burdens of guilt. The scene of this "battle of the brains" has the self as its real battleground. Instead of being confronted with a conflict between the individual and society alone, we are confronted with a conflict between the head and the heart, the present and the past, reason and will, the conscious and the unconscious. From this conflict neither the withdrawal into solitariness nor the wearing of a mask provides any refuge. On the contrary, each tends to aggravate it. The central problem facing the hero is psychic integration, the establishment of a balance between the demands of the conflicting aspects of the self. His ultimate destiny is determined by his success or failure in overcoming his traumas, failure being madness or death.

In the last novels, that is, the novels written after the Inferno crisis of the 1890's, we note a further shift of emphasis, this time in the direction of the existential dichotomies of the human situation. Simultaneously, the inner split is intensified and the hero seeks to integrate the divided self. This entails an effort to integrate past experiences into a meaningful pattern as well as to come to terms with the contradictions of human existence.

The Inferno crisis is of profound importance from a psychological point of view; it is a dramatic and traumatic descent into the abysses of the mind, the result of which is that the knowledge of the unconscious is no longer repressed but integrated, and a balance is established between the conflicting aspects of the self. A cure for the divided self is also found in the paradox of self-abandonment, in the practice of self-denial, and in the self-forgetfulness accompanying artistic creation and identification.

Strindberg's concept of the self in conflict is, as we may well expect, closely reflected in the development of his narrative art and in his skepticism about the traditional concept of character in life and in literature. This skepticism is of an early date. Already in his earliest works of fiction, character is envisioned as synonymous with the role or roles that an individual enacts in social life. *The Son of a Servant* well illustrates his failure to reconcile the traditional concept of character as something fixed or static, as firmness of will, with his own inner conviction that human beings are contradictory, vacillating, inconsistent, subject to pressures from within and without. For this reason he terms his own characters "characterless."

A naturalistic world view is the foundation of this concept of characterlessness. The old concept of character, which tended to equate a person's identity with his social role or with a single trait or humor, is declared to be untrue to experience, a mere convention. It fails to do justice to the complexity of the individual, as evidenced by introspection, by psychology, or by the conflicting impressions recorded by others. Like his contemporaries, Strindberg was strongly influenced by the new biological and historical sciences, which were substituting the idea of growth and development for the more static concepts of an earlier era. The static concept of a fixed identity belongs to a static age, and it is irreconcilable with the image of a multifaceted, constantly growing and changing individual that emerges when a historical and biological viewpoint is adopted in chronicling his life.[15]

It is obvious that the concept of characterlessness is a positive value judgment. The characterless individual is su-

---

[15] In his essay "Character Change and the Drama," Harold Rosenberg has made a very successful attempt to unravel some of the complexities adhering to such concepts as character and identity when used in connection with literature (see *Tradition of the New* [(New York: Horizon Press, 1959]).

perior because he is open to new ideas, to experience: he has not stiffened in a mold like the "middle-class automaton," the individual "who has once and for all become fixed in his natural disposition, or has adopted himself to some definite role in life, who, in fact, has ceased to grow." [16]

Nevertheless, Strindberg's attitude was not destined to remain favorable. Being a dramatist, he had a keen sense of the art of dissimulation, and though he recognized the individual's need to protect his identity by role-playing, he also recognized the thin line separating this form of dissimulation from the hypocrisy and deceit of bourgeois society. Like the Romantics, he makes a distinction between the public life and the private life: between the persona and the buried or real self. The bourgeois is all persona; he has no self, no soul. The artist, the genius, the exceptional individual, is inwardness.

In Strindberg's late novels, we find this concept of character as a role becoming a metaphor for the counterfeit nature of social life, the nucleus of his vision of the illusory nature of life, the deception inherent in its existence.[17] A persistent theme in his last works is his feeling that reality is insubstantial, shifting, slippery, intangible. And character is the slipperiest substance of all. On closer examination, Strindberg laments, human beings seem utterly inconsistent and changeable, capable of innumerable transformations like experienced actors on the stage. Some wear masks in order to hide their evil motives, disguising themselves behind an improvised facade. Others are forced to wear a mask in order to protect themselves, having a role conferred upon them

---

[16] From the preface to Miss Julie (23, 103).
[17] Cf. the highly significant essay "Le Caractère un Rôle?" (1894), reprinted in Vivisektioner, trans. Tage Aurell (Stockholm: Bonniers, 1958), pp. 126–149.

against their will to disguise their vulnerability. Collect all available data about a man, says Strindberg, and "you will find a hodge-podge that does not deserve the label character. Everything appears to be random improvisations, and man himself the greatest liar in the world, continuously in conflict with himself."

No other aspect of his works conveys perhaps so clearly as his character psychology Strindberg's skepticism about man's sense of identity, for underlying it is a conviction that it is impossible to know human beings at all: that the idea of the continuous and stable self is the greatest illusion of all.

It is also this character psychology that makes his novels anticipate some of the developments in the modern psychological novel, particularly the fading sense of character which has become characteristic of modern fiction in the last sixty years.[18] As Jean-Paul Sartre has so accurately observed, we do not really find characters in Strindberg's works, only what he calls "personalities in a situation," personalities who are only what they make of others, or what others make of them.[19] Like the figures in the novels of D. H. Lawrence, they are dynamic rather than tangible, and like Lawrence in his often quoted letter to Edward Garnett, Strindberg might well have insisted that we should not expect the old stable ego in his characters. Conventional characters, that is, characters defined as types, or in terms of their milieu, are rarely found in his novels, The Red Room and The People of Hemsö being the two main exceptions to the rule. His major characters are complex, ambivalent, and contradictory figures. With the keen perception of the dramatist, Strindberg depicts his char-

---

[18] For an analysis of the fading sense of character in modern fiction, see Mary McCarthy, "Characters in Fiction," Partisan Review, XXVIII (March–April, 1961), 171–191.

[19] Jean Paul Sartre, "Strindberg, vår 'fordringsägare,'" Dagens Nyheter (Stockholm), Jan. 28, 1949.

acters as actors and actresses, carefully observing their histrionic talents, their gestures, their repartees, always accentuat-
ing their consciousness of acting a part.

It is to the credit of the Norwegian novelist Knut Hamsun that he was the first to perceive the significance of Strindberg's novels as contributions to a new kind of character
psychology and thus to a new kind of fiction.[20] Freely admitting the extent to which Strindberg had influenced his
own writing, Hamsun spoke as early as the 1890's of Strindberg as "the only writer in Scandinavia who has made a
serious attempt to produce modern psychology." Strindberg,
he continued, "realizes, realizes and recognizes, the inade-
quacies of the character psychology prevailing at present for
describing the split and disharmonic mind of modern man."
As we know, Knut Hamsun was soon to demonstrate that he
had learned the lesson of the master, in his own great psychological novels, *Hunger*, *Pan*, and *Mysteries*, novels that, like
Strindberg's own, explore the mysteries of human identity,
"the unconscious life of the soul" as well as the problems of
social interrelationships.

The most characteristic feature of Strindberg's exploration of the self is a progressive turning inward. This inward
turning is, as we might well expect, closely reflected in the
development of his narrative art, a development characterized
by a gradual shift from mimetic to illustrative plots, from
realism and naturalism to symbolism and myth.

The classic *Bildungsroman* with its episodic, open-ended,
autobiographical structure is the predominant pattern of the
early novels, in which the major theme is the hero's search
for integration into society. The minor characters represent

---

[20] Knut Hamsun, *Artikler* (Oslo: Gyldendal, 1939), pp. 15, 39,
44. Cf. also J. W. McFarlane, "The Whisper of the Blood: A Study
of Knut Hamsun's Early Novels," *PMLA*, LXXI (Sept., 1956), 570–
573.

social types or attitudes, or serve as mentors. The prevailing vision of life is naturalistic and receives its finest expression in Strindberg's most mimetic and most objective novel, *The People of Hemsö.*

A shift toward illustrative plot structures occurs in the novels of the following stage, the schemes of meaning of these novels of psychic murder being determined by psychological theories about the nature of the self. The characters no longer possess independent existence but perform roles illustrating these theories, representing, in fact, aspects of the self in conflict.

Owing, at least in part, to the influence of Edgar Allan Poe, there is a shift away from realism in the direction of a type of psychological romance. The novels of this period are by no means to be classified as "naïve" romance, for, like Jung, Strindberg seems to have realized that the older forms of narrative—romance, fairy tale, and myth—harboring as they do the archetypes of the collective unconscious, are depositories of human wisdom concerning the workings of the psyche. The characters in these novels possess distinct archetypal traits, representing the *anima* or the *shadow* in psychoanalytic fables of identity.

An increasing trend toward symbolism may also be observed in the novels of psychic murder. The world depicted in them is largely a projection of the hero's own mind. This trend toward symbolism culminates in *By the Open Sea,* in which the setting is not only the physical and tangible manifestation of the hero's isolation, but also the symbolic stage for the inner drama: the conflict between the ego and the all-enveloping, maternal unconscious.

In the late novels, symbolism has become a permanent feature, the outer world being reduced to an objective correlative for the hero's state of mind or vision. At times the world is grotesquely distorted in order to express Strindberg's vision of life as an inferno; at other times it is portrayed as a stage on which the tragicomedies of life are enacted, illustrating his Schopenhauerian view of the unreal spectacle of appearances. In these novels the minor characters perform symbolic or metaphorical functions.

An equally pronounced characteristic of the late novels is the trend toward myth, the word being understood in a general sense. Even in the early novels Strindberg reveals a tendency to project his heroes in great mythical roles. Johan in *The Son of a Servant* is conceived as an Ishmael, and Borg in *By the Open Sea* in the Titanic guise of both Hercules and Prometheus. But in *Inferno* and the following novels, this tendency becomes more pronounced, Job, Faust, Jacob, Orpheus, the scapegoat being added to the gallery of mythical heroes.

This form of mythical projection has been regarded by some in a negative light, as a manifestation of Strindberg's neurotic compulsion to display his own personality and to aggrandize himself by identification, as a vulgar form of Titanism, but it may also be regarded in a positive light. From the point of view of the critic of fiction, it appears analogous to Strindberg's dialectic attitude to the search for truth, and may thus be considered as a way of projecting his experiences onto a more objective plane where they become more meaningful in terms of general human significance.[21] Myth serves Strindberg the novelist, as it did Joyce, as a way of conferring order and meaning on the chaos of experience.

In most of the novels, it is of course only a question of the hero having certain mythical traits ascribed to him. We may, however, regard the plot structures in some novels, notably in *By the Open Sea*, in *Inferno*, and in *The Scapegoat*, as constructed on the pattern of mythical narratives, because

---

[21] Cf. Walter A. Berendsohn, *Strindbergsproblem* (Stockholm: KF:s Bokförlag, 1946), p. 97.

the hero's behavior is determined to a large extent by the mythical role he is reenacting. *Inferno*, for example, projects the hero's conflict in the form of a choice between two mythical roles, Faust and Job, the problem being how to determine which of the roles is the most applicable in the hero's situation.

The world of the later novels has, in addition, become mythicized in another way, that is, through language, through metaphor. The younger Strindberg had a negative attitude to imagery in general, an attitude reflecting his generally low opinion of fiction as such. He regarded the use of imagery as an irresponsible play with words, or worse, as a falsification of reality, and so favored precision of expression.

This attitude underwent a radical change in the 1890's, in part owing to the influence of the general European trend toward symbolism, in part as a result of his new vision.[22] Under the influence of Swedenborg, Strindberg began to regard likenesses as a means to penetrate the layer of appearances disguising reality, as a means to reveal the universal patterns of created life. This had two important consequences. First of all, it changed his attitude to fiction, to poetry. Having once considered these forms of literature useless and ineffective falsifications of reality, he now regarded them as avenues to truth, as instruments capable of revealing the divine order of creation. Second, it made the image a more significant structural element in his works. While the images are important in his earlier novels, particularly in the description of character, they now serve as elements of order, providing unity to the novels.

The increasing reliance on symbolism and myth is not the only reflection of the progressive inward turning in the

---

[22] This development has been excellently analyzed by Karl-Åke Kärnell in *Strindbergs bildspråk* (Stockholm: Almqvist och Wiksell, 1962).

development of Strindberg's narrative art. An equally significant feature of the late novels is the development of modes
of expression transcending the limitations of traditional narrative forms: the monologue, stream of consciousness, musical
leitmotivs, modes of expression we associate primarily with
the modern psychological novel. That it is Strindberg's new
vision of life, and, above all, his new concept of the self and
of character, which are responsible for this new development,
is quite obvious. His skepticism about the unity and continuity of the self, and about the tangible nature of reality,
has progressed to a point where the old narrative forms have
lost their efficacy.

Always an experimenter in the realm of ideas, Strindberg
finally becomes an experimenter in the art of fiction as well,
seeking, in the manner of the modern psychological novelist,
not only to record and to analyze, but also in some measure
to retain the very inwardness of mental experience. Noting
that his most modern, most advanced novel, the beautiful
and moving *The Roofing Feast*, was written at a time when
he was embarking on his most daring dramatic experiments,
the Chamber plays, we can only speculate on what the future
would have brought, had not the theater again occupied all
his attention.

Strindberg's novels are, then, the story of his search for
self-discovery and self-integration, the story of his personal
education. But they are also the story of a modern novelist's
use of his art to explore the self and the problems of human
identity. It is this story that we trace in the following chapters.

‿2. The Red Room

A CHARACTERISTIC FEATURE of Strindberg's novels is the introductory episode that in a symbolic form anticipates the action and the theme of the novel as a whole. His first novel, *Röda Rummet* (*The Red Room*), opens with such an episode.

It is a beautiful day in early spring. The young hero of the novel, Arvid Falk, stands on a hill called Mosebacke which overlooks Stockholm. Below him is the hustle and bustle of the large city. Around him the birds are busy building their nests. As he leans over the barrier and observes the city at his feet, his face, having to now mirrored anxiety and sorrow, suddenly takes on an expression of defiance and determination: "it was as if he were observing an enemy; his nostrils dilated, his eyes blazed, and he lifted his clenched fist, as if he had wanted to challenge or threaten the poor city." Presently, the church bells begin ringing and with the sound of the bells, Falk's face changes anew. This time the defiant rebel is transformed into an orphan child: "His expression softened, and his face registered the pain that a child experiences when it feels left alone. And he was alone, because his mother and father lay in Klara cemetery from where the bell was still to be heard, and he was a child, because he still believed in everything, in the truth as well as in fairy tales" (5, 7–8).

Falk's meditations are interrupted by the arrival of Struve, a newspaperman highly respected by him for his liberal views. As Falk begins to praise Struve as a man of progress, the latter, visibly embarrassed (he has actually that very day joined the staff of a conservative newspaper!), suggests that it is too beautiful a day to discuss matters of such serious nature. Falk proceeds to tell Struve of his momentous decision. He has decided to abandon his career in the civil service in order to become a writer. Now he is seeking Struve's advice. The latter warns him that the vocation of the writer is a thorny path; for a man with a wife and children the sheer necessity of earning a daily ration of bread takes precedence over everything else. He concludes: "You have to adjust yourself to things, you see. You have to adjust yourself! And you don't know what a writer's situation is like! The writer is outside society!" To this Falk replies that he detests society "because it does not rest on a free contract, it is a web of lies." He will gladly take leave of it. Struve's only remark is: "It is getting cold" (19).

While Struve leaves for his home to write an article based on Falk's satirical account of the absurdities and the inefficiencies of the civil service (this account is in itself a brilliant piece of comic writing), a closing vignette captures Falk's mood as he heads for his lonely attic room at the outskirts of the city:

He felt like a bird that had flown against a windowpane, believing that it was spreading its wings to fly straight out into the open air, and now lay maimed on the ground. He sat down on a bench by the edge of the water and listened to the lappings of the waves; a light breeze rustled through the flowering maple trees, and the half-moon shone with a pale light on the dark water. There lay twenty, thirty boats moored beside the quay, tugging at their chains and momentarily poking up their heads one above the other before ducking down again. The wind and the waves seemed to drive them forward, and they made their assaults upon the bridge like a pack of incited hounds, but the chain pulled them back, and so they champed and pawed as if wanting to tear themselves away. (20)

The major themes of the novel are neatly introduced in this opening scene. Innocence encounters experience, the idealistic quest for sincerity and authenticity is dampened by the spirit of compromise and bad faith. The writer who rebels against society is destined to become a lonely outsider, alienated from the world about him, that is, unless he compromises with the social order. The image of the bird beating its wings against the windowpane, and of the boats vainly tugging at their chains, is particularly apt, because it anticipates Falk's destiny: the futility of his rebellion against society and his final surrender after a frustrating struggle. When we recognize the fact that Arvid Falk is but the first in a series of heroes whose expectations come to nought, the image indeed develops into a symbol representing Strindberg's vision of the destiny of the good man in a world devoid of integrity of purpose.

Nevertheless, *The Red Room* is not so pessimistic in tone as these remarks would seem to imply. The humor, the good spirits, and the sheer vitality of the writing give the lie to the pessimism, which is as yet only a dark undercurrent.

In *The Red Room* Strindberg is in a rare generous mood, willing to portion out the blame for the evils of the world. Society is at fault, but so is Falk's naïve idealism, and so are those who have instilled this idealism in him. Which is another way of saying that Falk is not simply Strindberg's alter ego, that the point of view is much more complex.

Arvid Falk is a younger Strindberg, a Strindberg in his first *Sturm und Drang* years. When Strindberg wrote *The Red Room* in 1879 he was thirty years old. He felt he had left his stormy youth behind him and was getting ready to settle down. He was a respectable civil servant with a position in the Royal Library, and his need for recognition was satisfied by the rewards he had received for his accomplishments as a Sinologist. He was happily married to the beautiful actress Siri von Essen, and he was soon to become a father. Hence the tone of good-humored acceptance which persists in the novel despite the biting satire and the undercurrent of disillusionment.

Many novelists have left their imprint on *The Red Room*, but the decisive impulse for the writing of the novel came, according to Strindberg's own testimony, from his discovery of Dickens. Reading Dickens, Strindberg conceived the idea of using the form of the novel to launch an attack on a society whose values he was unable to accept. Simultaneously, he wanted to express the disillusionment of his generation, its frustrated expectations. But this was all to be done in the manner of good-natured satire, for the hero was to discover that the world is really not as bad as it appears to be (19, 160).

Originally, he seems to have contemplated writing a Swedish counterpart of *The Pickwick Papers*, but then he decided to make his protagonist into a reporter before whom society would pass in review (160–161). As a result, *The Red Room* has a structure that is a combination of the *Bildungsroman* and the picaresque novel. The novel spans the time of about a year and a half and ends with the hero's initiation into the world. Owing to its episodic structure and its large gallery of characters, it is difficult to sketch a brief outline of the action in the novel. While such a pattern is, admittedly, overly schematic, the simplest overview emerges from a division of the characters into two groups. One group is composed of Falk and the Bohemian artists, who live on the outskirts of the city and frequent the Red Room, the café from which the novel derives its title. To this group belong, among others, the sculptor Olle Montanus and the young medical student Borg. The other group is composed of a large congregation of businessmen, publishers, clergy, insurance brokers, newspapermen, members of Parliament, society women, all of whom taken together represent a broad spectrum of bourgeois society. The action in the novel consists of the dramatic confrontation between these two groups, between Bohemian and bourgeois and the values they represent.

Owing to his desire to paint a very broad canvas, Strindberg has not limited himself to a satirical account of those institutions with which Falk in his capacity as a reporter would be likely to come into contact, but has also introduced chapters in which Falk is not involved in the action. Five chapters compose a subplot chronicling the ill-fated venture into the world of the theater of a young aristocrat, whose name is Rehnhjelm. In this subplot an actor, Falander, plays a significant role as mentor. Four chapters focus on the life and opinions of Arvid's brother, Carl Nicolaus Falk, and his brother's wife. A final chapter is a review in the form of a letter reporting the state of affairs at the end of the novel.

All this makes for a novel of loose structure, in which some chapters at first glance seem to form independent units. On closer examination, however, even these bear a definite thematic relation to the work as a whole.

But *The Red Room* gains its essential unity not from

the plot structure or the theme but from a consistency of tone or sensibility. The unity is embodied in the language of the novel, in Strindberg's tone, and this tone is, in turn, the expression of a sensibility not to be identified with the subjective experience of any one character in the novel. Strindberg's consciousness is always present, interposing itself between the reader and the characters and the events. The author is omniscient, regarding even his hero from above. Such detachment from the persons and actions described is of course essential to the comic mode, and *The Red Room* is a comic novel.

The stylistic and structural features just described are very characteristic of some of the novels of Dickens and particularly of *The Pickwick Papers*. It is also my feeling that *The Red Room* owes more to Dickens and *The Pickwick Papers* than most scholars have been willing to concede. For there are other similarities between the two novels than these. The theme is the same in both: the encounter between innocence and experience. Both Falk and Pickwick discover the world by moving about a good deal, and by a series of experiences which bring a comic mode of recognition. It is also significant that both heroes after they have gained insight into the nature of the world withdraw from it in order to create a private domicile, their own safe corner. Having failed to find goodness in the world they will create their own world. While the recognition of the evil and the indifference of the world is obscured by the high spirits of *The Pickwick Papers* in the same manner as in *The Red Room*, Strindberg's novel does have its darker undertone of pessimism, as I have already suggested. *The Red Room* also raises and seeks to answer the question that Dickens does not as yet confront: What is the person to do who will not or cannot withdraw from the world? [1]

---

[1] For some of the major points in this discussion of *The Pickwick Papers* I am indebted to J. Hillis Miller's excellent study of

Thus both novels use a comic and picaresque mode of expression to serve the function of the *Bildungsroman*, the hero's initiation into the world.[2]

Arvid Falk is in many ways the typical hero of the *Bildungsroman*, less defined as a character than his mentors. He is a pale and passive hero, an "unheroic hero," as Giraud has called this type of young man, also so common in the nineteenth-century French novel.[3] The defiance and vitality and determination of Falk glimpsed in the opening scene is never demonstrated again.

The chief trait of the hero of the *Bildungsroman* has been said to be educability.[4] Falk is eminently educable, for he is young, naïve, sincere, and believes what he has been told. He is "a child who believes in fairy tales." He lacks identity, because he is as yet uncommitted to a set of values which will provide such a sense of identity. What he experiences is a disenchantment with the institutional values of the world in which he has grown up, values to which he has never been consciously committed. For this reason his eventual compromise with a corrupt society is hardly tragic, because his ideals are not held with great conviction. His idealism is mostly naïveté. He is hoping, above all, to find truthfulness and sincerity. We are told that he is somehow

---

Dickens (*Charles Dickens: The World of His Novels* [Cambridge: Harvard University Press, 1958]).

[2] In a highly illuminating recent essay Göran Printz-Påhlsson has analyzed the place of *The Red Room* in relation to the development of the traditional *Bildungsroman* ("Krukan och bitarna: Strindberg och 1800-talets romantradition," *Bonniers Litterära Magasin*, 33 [Dec., 1964], 740–754; 34 [Jan., 1965], 12–28).

[3] Raymond Giraud, *The Unheroic Hero in the Novels of Stendhal, Balzac, and Flaubert* (New Brunswick: Rutgers University Press, 1957).

[4] For a discussion of the general characteristics of the *Bildungsroman* in the tradition beginning with Goethe's *Wilhelm Meister*, see Roy Pascal, *The German Novel* (Manchester: Manchester University Press, 1956).

committed to ideas contrary to his own welfare, that he is for the workers, for the oppressed, and for social justice, but we see little of this commitment in action. His profession is that of the reporter, but he aspires to become a poet.

Arvid Falk also lacks identity in the sense that he has been unable to develop self-esteem or self-assurance. From childhood he has been "robbed" of this vital quality (5, 213). This has been done by teaching him that he is "bad" while others are "perfect," thereby instilling in him a "highly tender conscience" (26). He has been taught to demand much of himself. The result is that he feels very insecure and extremely sensitive to either blame or praise. He is very self-conscious and blushes easily. He never wants to hurt anyone. He is slow to think of a good answer. To Strindberg he is a sad product of "the old lie," that is, "the admonishments and advice of parents" (79). He is badly equipped to live in the society in which he finds himself.

Despite his rebellious attitude to the world about him his sense of identity is not really secure enough to sustain a lasting conflict. Like a number of Strindberg's heroes he suffers noticeably from his feeling of being isolated from the society of his fellowmen and particularly from his family. He is disturbed by the fact that his brother regards him with sorrow and contempt as a radical. In spite of his detestation of society and his stated inclination to take leave of it, he is unable to do so. Being held in contempt and disrespect by others is unbearable to him. He himself cannot respect the one whom all others disrespect, that is, himself (212). Not until the moment when his brother accepts him as a well-known poet does he regain his sense of security. Then he radiates warmth toward those who have again "admitted him to society without demanding any explanations or insisting on repentance" (295).

Not surprisingly, Falk is happiest among simple and unaffected people or in nature. He is most at home among the Bohemian artists who live uncommitted lives, without a thought for tomorrow. These Romantic Bohemians are of course also in revolt against middle-class society, but it is a revolt without moral or idealistic overtones. They are free, and they are poor, and they are without the duplicity and hypocrisy of the world about them. If Falk cannot find a permanent refuge among them it is because he has the liberal individualist's concern about the good of society. He is committed to the reform of society. The Bohemians have only one commitment, and that is to art.

In his capacity as a reporter Falk is quickly initiated into the ways of the world, an experience that almost destroys him. The principle of confrontation is simple and highly effective and a source of rich comedy. Falk's idealism is repeatedly jolted by his discovery that appearance and reality do not coincide. As he moves from one institution to the other the image of the world as a great deception slowly takes form before him. Passing through the offices of various government agencies, of clergymen, business leaders, and publishers, through the conference rooms of large insurance companies, through sessions of the Parliament, Falk discovers only fraud and deceit, the desire for private power and gain. Strindberg's gifts as a satirist celebrate their greatest triumphs in the scenes depicting the social institutions of his day. The disciple of Dickens and Mark Twain is already a master of the art of satire, but then Strindberg's nature was also once and for all such that he was at his cheerful best when he was able to rip the veil of illusion from the eyes of his heroes and unmask the fraud.[5] But in *The Red Room* this is done in

---

[5] Strindberg had a high regard for several American humorists and satirists from whose works he published two volumes of selected prose in 1878 and 1879. Among the selections were chapters from Mark Twain's *Roughing It*.

a fairly good-humored fashion, without bitterness or rancor.

Through his experiences with various aspects of society Falk thus discovers that everything is different from what he had believed. And from his many encounters with man as a "social animal" he concludes that man is a deceitful liar. Strindberg is quick to point out, however, that this view is one-sided. Falk, he says, has acquired his disenchanted view because of his profession as a reporter, for having had to visit a large number of public gatherings he has heard too many official lies, too much empty rhetoric. Strindberg agrees that in public man is a hypocrite and a liar, for in order to achieve a measure of civilization man must disguise his real motive, which is to crush and dominate his enemy, but he is willing to grant that behind the mask there is "another animal, which in private is rather lovable if not irritated, and willingly consents to exhibit its faults and weaknesses so long as no witnesses are present" (212).

This view of human relations as a barely disguised state of warfare and a constant struggle for power has had a distinct effect on the manner in which character is delineated in *The Red Room*. Character is regarded as a persona, a role or mask, and human beings perform in society like actors on the stage. Some are changeable like chameleons, playing the part that serves their immediate ends, others wear permanent masks designed to disguise their real motives.

In the second chapter, "Between Brothers," Arvid Falk pays a visit to his older brother Carl Nicolaus, a very successful businessman. Carl Nicolaus, who is well aware of the timidity of his younger brother, seeks to impress him with a well-rehearsed performance. As he listens to Arvid's request for money he paces the floor "impetuously with his head bent and hunched shoulders as if he were rehearsing a role. When he seemed to know it, he stopped in front of his brother and looked him straight in the eye with a long, sea-green, false gaze, which was meant to resemble confidence and pain, and with a voice designed to sound as if it came from the family grave at Klara cemetery, he said: 'You are not honest, Arvid! You are not hon-est!'" (26). When he goes to the safe to find a document he goes with "such a confident expression and such an assured gesture, as if he had rehearsed it for many years in order to be ready to appear as soon as the cue had been given" (27). Having made his point he is overwhelmed and needs an audience: "The scene had repaid him too well, and the triumph was too great to be enjoyed without an audience." He calls in his clerk, and with the repetition of the key line "Arvid, you are-not-honest!" he has a well-rounded final repartee, after which any additional remarks are superfluous. He jingles his key chain as if he were giving the signal for the curtain to fall (29).

Carl Nicolaus Falk's histrionic talents are again emphasized in the chapter "Audiences" in which the painter Lundell is doing his portrait. As Falk sits down he adopts a stately air and the statesman's pose, but Lundell tells him to speak: "Your face is of course interesting in itself, but the more shades of character it can express the better" (291). It is little wonder that the firmness of will and character advocated by Carl Nicolaus is nothing but fraud and deceit to his younger brother (296–297).

Throughout the book Strindberg seems to accentuate his belief that public life leads to the development of histrionic traits. The talent for this kind of acting seems in fact to be so widespread that it leads the actor Falander to say, when asked by Rehnhjelm whether he (Falander) considers him without talents as an actor: "No, of course not! I don't consider anyone unsuited for that! On the contrary! All human beings are more or less adept at acting parts" (187).

In depicting Carl Nicolaus Falk's performance Strindberg stresses conscious role-playing. Falk is deliberately putting on an act in order to impress his brother. In most of the other characters the gaze is veiled, for since these figures unlike Carl Nicolaus wish to disguise their real motives, their real selves, they wear a mask. Thus Struve in the opening scene wears glasses, "which seem rather to be designed as protection for the gaze than for the eyes" (8). Pastor Skåre, the minister turned businessman, *is* a mask: he has no face, "it has been lost somewhere" (106–110). The editor of Gråkappan has a long, billowing, full beard, "which hid all the weak features his face possessed, and where the soul otherwise would have peered through without hindrance" (135).

Before long Falk surrenders. By September he is beginning to feel "old, tired, and indifferent," disillusioned by the struggle (212). Not only has he lost all respect for man but he has lost his own self-respect, for he has continuously been treated with disrespect and condescension, which has been difficult for him to endure, seeing that he has from the beginning been "robbed" of his self-assurance. He is vacillating between "fanaticism and absolute indifferentism." He is beginning to veer toward the latter, because it promises a peace of mind that his constant concern about humanity has shattered. He is beginning to reconsider the original advice of Struve, repeated in somewhat different terms in one of the central chapters of the novel, chapter 18, significantly entitled "Nihilism." Struve here tells Falk:

May I give you some advice, some advice, for life, something experience has taught me? If you want to prevent the spontaneous combustion that you as a fanatic are heading for, adopt as soon as possible a new point of view on things; train yourself to regard the world from a bird's-eye view, and you will discover how petty and insignificant everything appears; assume that the whole thing is a rubbish heap, that human beings are refuse, eggshells, carrot stalks, cabbage leaves, rags, and you will never be caught unawares again; you will never again lose any illusions, but in return you will experience much joy every time you observe a beautiful trait, a good deed; to put it succinctly: adopt a calm and relaxed contempt for the world; you need not worry about becoming heartless on account of that. (235–236)

For the time being "fanaticism" carries the day, and Falk intensifies his efforts for the oppressed. When the inevitable disappointment occurs he is rescued by his friends who whisk him off to the seaside to restore his sense of reality and bring him back to reason. At the end of the summer (of the following year) the tough and cynical medical student Borg who has become Falk's mentor reports in a letter to Struve that Falk has recovered, that he has regained his self-esteem and that he is "returning to society, enrolling among the cattle, and about to grow respectable and gain social status" (345). Having failed to come to terms with the world on his own idealistic terms, Falk is now adjusting himself to the values of the society in which he lives. In a "Review" at the end of the novel we learn that he has become a teacher in a girls' school, that he holds several comfortable positions in the civil service, that he lives only for his work, that he is planning to get married, and that he collects coins as a hobby. He is said to be "so devoid of views that he has become the most charming person, consequently loved and respected by his superiors and his friends" (350–351).

Like the classic *Bildungsroman*, like Goethe's *Wilhelm Meister*, the prototype of the genre, *The Red Room* ends with the hero assuming his role in social life. Falk follows the advice of Struve and Borg, the realists who take the world on its own terms. But *The Red Room* is not only the story of Falk, and the realistic point of view advocated by Struve and Borg is only one of several points of view explored in the novel. In *The Red Room* Strindberg is experimenting with points of view in the manner he had already practiced in his early historical drama *Master Olof*. In that drama, Strindberg tells us, he manipulated his characters in such a way that in the three main figures he was able to balance three points of view. In Olaus Petri, the Protestant reformer who is the central figure in the play, Strindberg appeared in the guise of the idealist; in King Gustav Vasa, who uses the Reformation to advance his own search for power and to consolidate the kingdom, he appeared as the realist; in Gert, the fanatic revolutionary, he appeared as the rebel and the nihilist. Toward Master Olof, his hero, who renounces his ideals and chooses to compromise with the King, Strindberg remained, he insists, "impartial." The final word "Traitor" is directed at Olof and it rings in the ears of the audience as the curtain is lowered, but it is uttered by Gert and represents his point of view. In the end, says Strindberg, "all are proven right and are relatively right, because there is no absolute right." He adds that at one time he had thought of calling the drama "What Is Truth?" (19, chap. 2).

In *The Red Room* Strindberg's point of view is equally complex. Far from being a weakness as some critics in the past seem to have assumed, this is the strength of the novel. The lack of a consistent point of view and the lack of consistency in the portrayal of the characters are not the consequences of poor composition but of Strindberg's desire to express a number of views with respect to the problem. By his method he has avoided a narrow viewpoint, and the novel has gained in objective significance.[6]

Although *The Red Room* has a larger gallery of characters than *Master Olof* and dramatizes a wider spectrum of views, the constellation of three basic attitudes remains iden-

---

[6] This point has been made in an essay that still remains one of the very best studies of the novel (cf. Algot Werin, "Karaktärer i Röda rummet," in *Synpunkter på Strindberg*, ed. Gunnar Brandell [Stockholm: Aldus, 1964], pp. 78–93).

tical: idealism, realism, nihilism. While the characters in the
novel do not represent as well-defined points of view as those
in the drama, a number of them do appear as mentors consistent with the pattern of the *Bildungsroman*. In the end
Falk chooses to follow the advice of two such mentors, Borg
and Struve, the practical realists. He has, however, in the
course of the novel also been confronted with another radically different point of view, the nihilistic attitude to life
represented by the actor Falander and the sculptor Olle Montanus. While Falk at the end of the novel has to all appearances assumed a realistic view of life, there are indications
that the nihilistic viewpoint has not lost its appeal for him
and that it might, in fact, point to his possible future development. I might add that Falander and Olle Montanus
are the most interesting figures in the novel, figures who tend
to haunt the reader long after he has put the book down.
This contributes considerably to the feeling that the viewpoint they represent has by no means been rejected or tran-
scended.

The picture is complicated by the fact that there is no
personal contact between Falander and Falk, for the actor
appears in the five chapters that chronicle the events in the
theater of the small town of X-köping. Falander serves instead as a mentor for the young aristocrat Rehnhjelm. Rehnhjelm is, however, in many ways similar to Falk: they are
both naïve idealists, products of the "old lie." But most
important, there is an indirect contact between Falander and
Falk, in that Montanus is a disciple of Falander and thus
able to transmit the ideas of the latter to Falk.

Falander is a complex figure. Both in his appearance
and in his views he has many traits of the Romantic hero
of the Gothic variety.[7] His aspect is demoniac, his hair falling
in ringlets like snakes, the gaze of his eyes penetrating like

---

[7] Printz-Påhlsson, *op. cit.*, p. 23.

the muzzles of a gun. He is also demoniac in that he is a seducer, a seducer of the young. With his belief that all society is corrupt, that it is founded on nothing but lies, he has made it his role to tear down, and to remove the props and the foundations, so that the young with their only too great readiness to commit themselves to "the old lies" will not be deluded but able to face reality (5, 192). Falander is also a decadent figure. Like Byron's Cain he subscribes to the belief that knowledge is sorrow, that consciousness is a burden. He has become addicted to absinthe, because it "stifles all the noble feelings that entice man into committing follies" (193).

Although Falander is attacking the whole value structure of contemporary society, its ethics, its art, its form of education, he is not really a social revolutionary. He gives vent to his passionate indignation over the corruption of society, particularly as it affects the young, but his attacks on the evils of society are part of a campaign of much larger dimensions. Falander's rebellion is metaphysical: it is a rebellion against the very order of things. He is a Lucifer in rebellion against the gods (he is also nicknamed "the Devil") (184). He is a skeptic and pessimist whose masters are Schopenhauer and Kierkegaard. In his denial of the meaningfulness of existence, he is a thoroughgoing nihilist.

In the chapter "On the Altar" Falander expounds his views to Rehnhjelm. Against Rehnhjelm's willingness to see greatness and perfection all about him Falander injects a metaphysical dimension: "if you see perfection and excellence in everything here, how will you ever come to long for real perfection? Believe me, pessimism is the real idealism, and pessimism is a Christian philosophy, if that relaxes your conscience, because Christianity teaches the wretchedness of the world, from which we must seek to die" (265). And he adds that the greatest of all chimeras is the search for happiness and fortune.

It may sound absurd to call Falander a Christ figure. Yet his role—to open the eyes of the young to the wretchedness of existence when measured on the yardstick of an eternal perfection and to make them rise up in rebellion against the dogmas of their elders—is the role in which Strindberg at this time imagined Christ. In one of the long poems in "Sleepwalker Nights," published in 1884, Strindberg describes Christ in this light, as a skeptic and a pessimist, a nihilistic rebel not only against the old order but also against the order of things.

But Falander has another affinity with Christ. He is a scapegoat, assuming the sufferings of others. When he takes absinthe it is because he cannot bear the wretchedness of the world, and what is hardest for him to bear is the manner in which the young foolishly stumble into disaster. The chapters involving Rehnhjelm illustrate Falander's role as scapegoat. With the aid of Falander, Rehnhjelm, who has excessively idealistic notions about the life of the theater and a high regard for the purity of women, is taught a bitter lesson. He learns that even in this supposedly moral institution dedicated to what is great and admirable in art everything has its price: his "pure" Agnes with whom he has fallen in love succeeds in obtaining the role of Ophelia in *Hamlet* but only at the cost of spending the night with the director. Falander seeks to comfort the brokenhearted young man, and his compassion is vividly captured in a final image. As Falander sits down beside him Rehnhjelm suddenly feels "something hot like a spark of fire fall on his throat" (276).

Throughout *The Red Room* there is much discussion of "point of view." Struve has his "birds'-eye view" from which everything appears petty and insignificant. Borg has his par-

ticular angle of vision: he regards "human beings with the
look of absolute indifference; I take them as geological speci-
mens, as minerals" (337). Falk is finally able to attain "the
elevated point of view" from which he feels "reconciled to
the order of the world," observing that it might not matter
if things are black or white, since if they are black they are
probably supposed to be black (241). Falander's nihilistic
point of view is deceptively similar to these "elevated" views.
But there is a fundamental difference. Whereas Falk's view
has made him "old, tired, and indifferent" and led to resignation and acceptance, Falander's view makes him burn with
indignation and only too painfully conscious of the sufferings
of others.[8] The hot tear falling on Rehnhjelm's cheek is the
most eloquent testimony to his compassion, but there are
other indications mainly of a metaphorical nature that Falander is literally "burning up," with passionate indignation,
that is (183). Falk, on the other hand, feels a need to "put
out the fire under the boilers" (240).

As a scapegoat identifying himself with others through
compassion Falander is also "characterless," a fact that is
further accentuated by his being a member of the acting
profession. Though not without an identity of his own his
main function is to serve as an intercessor. Falander is the
man "who welcomes the sorrows and worries of everyone and
blows on them so that they vanish; how he dissolves everything: insults, humiliations, donkey kicks, misfortunes, need,
misery and lamentations, into nothing; how he teaches and
admonishes his friends not to overestimate anything, above
all not their sorrows" (197). As a characterless individual he

---

[8] The difference between the nihilistic "indifferentism" of Struve
and Borg and the compassionate, rebellious, nihilism of Falander, has
been ably demonstrated by Bo Bennich-Björkman in "Fåglar och
författarroller hos Strindberg," *Samlaren*, 83 (1962), 1–66.

is both outside and above society: as an actor he can transform himself at will.

In Strindberg's gallery of heroes Falander is a figure we shall soon encounter in different guises. He is the artist in the age-old role of the scapegoat, the artist who assumes the burden of human suffering and expresses man's burning indignation at the absurdity of the world in which he finds himself. The writer Falkenström in *Black Banners* and the lawyer Libotz in *The Scapegoat* are his kin.[9]

Olle Montanus, though never fully developed as a character, is a disciple of Falander and may be said to follow the latter's philosophy to its logical consequences in thought as well as in action. By vocation a sculptor he becomes increasingly disenchanted with art and condemns it in terms of Plato's aesthetics. Reality is only a poor reflection of the real world of ideas. Hence it is "low, of no consequence, secondary, accidental." Art is, in turn, merely a reflection of a reflection, hence of even less significance (358–359). When in the end Montanus commits suicide it is because he has finally come to an absolute impasse in his development as an artist (though it should be added that it is also because he has simply lost the desire to live). He has found it impossible to reconcile his idealistic conception of art with his own performance and his social conscience. His art has been unable

---

[9] Since he effectively combines the role of the scapegoat with that of the rebel Falander also has close affinities with the two central types of hero in the novels of Balzac. Like a Lucien de Rubempré or a Raphael de Valentin he is "the artist suffering at the hands of a vulgar and immoral society." Like Vautrin he has "the aspect of a fallen angel of light," for having once been "a sensitive and even radiant soul" he is now seeking to outwit the world of uninhibited selfishness at its own game through his intellectual superiority and will: he is the artist on the verge of the criminal life (cf. William Troy, "On Rereading Balzac: The Artist as Scapegoat," *Kenyon Review*, II [Summer, 1940], 333–344).

to express a single idea, he says, and thus it is worthless. In addition all art is useless, he insists, for according to (German!) aesthetics only the useless is beautiful. The artist who produces a work that reveals an intention or a thesis is creating something ugly (357).

Olle Montanus is a gentle, simple, sincere individual. He is clearly the victim of an utterly absurd idealistic aesthetics. Strindberg's reasons for allowing Montanus to express his views in the posthumous document "To Him Who Wants To Read" are obscure, but we may not be too far wrong if we speculate that he wants to call Falk's and our attention to the absurdity of this aesthetics and by implication point to the value of a different philosophy of art, one that would allow for the artist's active engagement and involvement in human affairs and would not shy away from the ugly and sordid side of life.

Whether Falk has understood the message we do not know. We know that he has read it, and we know his summary dismissal of the views expressed in it (363). But we also know that the figure of Montanus continues to haunt Falk after his compromise and withdrawal. In all likelihood he will haunt Falk even more after his death. His act of suicide might not have been in vain, if it has unsettled Falk and indicated a new stage in his future development as an artist. In this regard Borg's final remark about Falk in the concluding "Review" is of interest: "Falk is a political fanatic, who knows that if he allowed the flame some air he would burn up; that is why he extinguishes it with strict, prosaic studies. But I don't think he will succeed, because no matter how he restrains himself I fear an explosion someday" (386–387).

Thus Falk has been introduced to a radically different point of view. At the end of the novel he himself has failed both as a man and as an artist. Like Pickwick he has withdrawn to a safe and sheltered nook to cultivate his garden. As an artist he has been ineffectual, because he has not been ready to bear the scorn and pain of being an outsider: he has wanted to be a critic and yet be admired and loved. We do not know what will ultimately happen to Falk, but in Montanus and Falander he has encountered the artist in a different role: the artist who engages himself actively in human affairs, who rebels against society but also against the order of things, and who is ready to enact the role of the scapegoat by assuming the burden of human suffering.

When *The Red Room* appeared it had as a motto Voltaire's saying, "Rien n'est si désagréable que d'être pendu obscurément." On account of his failure to get *Master Olof* performed, Strindberg felt that this was an accurate description of his situation. But *The Red Room* changed all that, for it caused a stir of excitement, and Strindberg suddenly found himself the most debated writer in Scandinavia. The book was a success, financially as well as artistically. Despite some of its obvious shortcomings, its freshness and vitality of style, its concrete and impressionistic local color, its narrative verve, and its sure satirical touch, all combine to make it the first truly modern Swedish novel, and a book that it is still a pleasure to read. A beautifully balanced treatment of some of the major themes in modern literature, the conflict between the artist and society, the quest for authenticity, and the problem of identity, it deserves wider recognition as a minor masterpiece among nineteenth-century novels.

⤙ 3. *Progress*

AMONG STRINDBERG'S finest works of fiction are his historical tales. Of varying length, and written and published over a long period of time, between 1882 and 1904, they are collected in two volumes (11 and 12). In subsequent chapters I discuss two of the longer narratives from the late 1880's, *Tschandala* and *A Witch*; in this chapter the emphasis is on an earlier work entitled *Utreckling* (*Progress*) and first published in 1883.

A beautiful work of art, *Progress* is of major significance for the development of the general theme, for it projects the quest for identity in a new light. In *The Red Room* the problem of identity was seen as intimately connected with the question of finding a meaningful role in social life. In *Progress* the social problem is secondary to a more fundamental, existential question about the meaningfulness of life itself.

In *Progress*, as in *The Red Room*, art and the artist are in the foreground, for both the major figures in the novel are painters, but Strindberg now appears less concerned with the artist's situation than with art as a mode of expressing different attitudes toward human existence, in this case the two diametrically opposed attitudes of medieval asceticism and Renaissance sensualism. In *Progress* Strindberg dramatizes, as he himself has observed, his own spiritual conflict, the conflict between "the monk" and "the satyr," between the denial and the affirmation of life.[1] Expressed in other terms, this may also be regarded as a conflict between the old and the new, between the old Christian world view with its emphasis on the insignificance and the unworthiness of man's existence and the new naturalistic philosophy with its stress on man's life as an integral part of nature, and thus of an organic, meaningful pattern moving toward a higher degree of development.

The tale is set in Sweden in the early years of the sixteenth century, more precisely at the moment when Protestantism replaces Catholicism as the official religion, and simultaneously the pagan spirit of the Renaissance reaches the far north and acts like a life-giving tonic after a period of life-denying asceticism. Unlike the conventional historical tale, however, it is not a costume piece, for Strindberg's intention is to establish an analogy between the Renaissance and his own age, the common element here being the breakup of the old order, the revolt against authority. As in the nineteenth century this revolt against the old order contributes to a new sense of freedom, but the sense of freedom is purchased at a high price.

---

[1] In a letter to Jonas Lie in June, 1884, Strindberg writes: "You must read a Swedish destiny in vol. 2 called *Progress!* There you have me in two parts" (quoted in Martin Lamm, *August Strindberg* [2d ed.; Stockholm: Bonniers, 1948], p. 90n).

As Erich Fromm has shown in his psychological study, *Escape from Freedom*, "there is probably no period since the sixteenth century which resembles ours as closely in regard to the ambiguous meaning of freedom." [2] The Reformation was, Fromm observes, "one root idea of human freedom and autonomy as it is represented in modern democracy," but it also had another facet, an emphasis on "the insignificance and powerlessness of the individual." The individual lacked freedom in medieval society, for he was chained to his role in a structuralized whole, but the lack of freedom was compensated by a sense of meaning. There was no place for doubt. Man had a sense of security and of belonging. Suffering and pain and death were made tolerable by being interrelated meaningfully within the order of the Church. There was little awareness of one's individual self as a separate entity.

The Reformation and the Renaissance changed all that by giving birth to the individual. Man discovered himself as a separate entity when he discovered the world to be an object set apart from himself. This brought him a new sense of freedom, but also an increased sense of isolation, of doubt, and anxiety, and insecurity. For instance, by being freed from the bondage of economic ties, he lost the security he once possessed. But by having lost his fixed place in a closed universe man lost the answer to the meaning of his existence, his cosmic security. Hence his sense of being overwhelmed by a feeling of individual nothingness and impotence, particularly before suffering and death.

It is this ambiguous meaning of freedom that Strindberg has dramatized in *Progress* by interlinking the destinies of his two central figures, Botvid and Giacomo.

Botvid is not himself a monk, but a pious young painter who is brought to a Carthusian monastery near Stockholm.

---

[2] Erich Fromm, *Escape from Freedom* (New York: Rinehart, 1941), chaps. ii, iii.

Botvid is to paint the Annunciation for the chapel of this strict and ascetic order dedicated to the mortification of the flesh in the name of the spirit. This motif has brought him into a dilemma. He is uncertain as to how to represent this union of the natural and the supernatural, for he is under a strict injunction to erase all erotic or sensuous images from his canvas. The red rose of love is too pagan and has to become a virginal white lily from which even the golden stamens are removed. The archangel Gabriel has to be painted in a sexless manner. Despite fasts, nightly vigils, and prayers, Botvid fails in his efforts to grasp the image of the Holy Virgin. His only concrete vision is the gatekeeper's beautiful daughter, Maria.

Where Botvid fails, Giacomo succeeds. Having just arrived from Italy he is imbued with the new spirit of the Renaissance. He radiates vitality and joy. He literally brings sun, light, and air, and relishes the good things of life, strong ale, pretty girls, and beautiful songs. Giacomo believes in the evidence of his senses, and that the world is neither sinful nor evil. His gospel is that man should not deny the world, for the world is God's creation, and that God manifests himself in the beauty of the world, as Raphael incidentally affirmed by painting his mistresses and calling them madonnas. He is now ready to do the same himself: the beautiful Maria, the gatekeeper's daughter, is to become the model for the Virgin.

The educable Botvid is soon convinced by the persuasive Giacomo whose very being radiates the new pagan gospel. He is ready to embrace the new, heeding Giacomo's warning: "A new age with new winds is rushing in; come along, Botvid, or you will capsize; don't go against the current because you will be sucked under. The old gods are dead but nature is alive, because it is eternal!" (11, 225). Having broken the old bonds, Botvid soon begins to live in a frenzy of new pleasures. Like Giacomo he says yes to life, loves nature, and worships beauty.

The success of Giacomo's new aesthetics is vividly dramatized in the religious fervor with which the monks receive the painting. But the triumph is short-lived, for the new age soon manifests itself in a number of ways, not all of which are positive and progressive, and Giacomo's philosophy of life is soon put to the test and found wanting.

There is a feverish activity in the air, much hustle and bustle, an atmosphere of change and progress, but to the skeptical Botvid the new gradually appears less and less new and more a return to something old, to a previous age, and we realize that Strindberg's intention is to debunk the myth of progressive evolution by substituting the idea of a cyclical repetition. Thus the castle that has been almost in ruins rises again as the power of the Church declines, and Giacomo and Botvid find employment adorning the new building with works of art, painting pictures that are no longer based on religious motifs but, and this is Strindberg's ironic point, on motifs from the rediscovered world of classical mythology. And the monastery is torn down, but the chapel remains, destined to become the center of a new, still more severe form of asceticism of the Protestant variety. This we come to realize in the scene in which Giacomo, having entered the chapel to look at his painting, finds it erased by order of the new Lutheran priest, who not only denounces images in any form as idolatry but preaches the unworthiness of the individual, his inability to rely on himself, and his consequent need to subordinate himself to a greater power outside himself.

The validity of the priest's bitter message seems also to be borne out by the dramatic events that serve, above all, to test Giacomo's radically different new gospel. For Giacomo is a man who accommodates himself to what is. He is without the nostalgia for a lost security, without fear of the future. He believes in himself and in his abilities. Characteristic of his thinking is that he does not make the Christian distinction between body and soul, between flesh and spirit. His is an ideal of the whole man. His religion—he, too, is a religious man—is a worship of life, of the senses, and of beauty, which is God's gift to man, a gift not to be rejected.

It is this religion that is put to the test and found wanting in the most dramatic and powerful part of *Progress*, Strindberg's account of the sudden arrival of the plague, the first victim of which is the beautiful Maria. Giacomo is overcome with fear of death and overwhelmed by terror at the sight of Maria's monstrously disfigured face. Rushing to the chapel to find solace in the worship of her vanished beauty in art, in his own painting of her, a final blow is dealt his faith: the painting has been destroyed.

After the departure of Giacomo, Botvid sinks into a state of melancholy and grows increasingly indifferent to the world about him. The new age which he had greeted with such joy now satisfies him less and less. His peace of mind is gone, never to return. Like the Lutheran priest, he now feels that every step forward is in actuality but a step backward. What was declared good yesterday is bad tomorrow and good again the day after tomorrow. Life has no meaning: it is only a purposeless repetition. "To eat and to be eaten, to live in order to live, to die when the time comes. Nothing else!" is Botvid's despairing conclusion. "As the earth moves in its circular course about the sun without any but the repeatedly recurring changes of the seasons and the days, so the world was to move in its course; forever new, but forever beginning anew, and everything new was only a revival of the old" (258).

Botvid had welcomed the new age and helped tear down the old. Now that the old order has returned, he finds that it no longer satisfies him. The prayer, the incense, the old images: they have lost their power to instill any fervor in him. He is unable to feel either joy or sorrow. His despair is a sickness unto death, but he must live on though life is a burden to him, always torn between the old and the new:

His peace of mind was ended, because his soul was split in two perpetually feuding elements; he was the son of two periods, and this gave him two points of view on things, the monk's and the satyr's; he could still be carried away by something great or beautiful or good, but then there came at once the scornful smile of doubt and dissolved everything; his two eyes did not pull even, he used to say, one saw the face of the thing, the other the back, and that is why he was unable to keep a steady view of life capable of bringing him to a goal. (258–259)

To escape from his conflicts he joins, in the end, a Carthusian order in Germany, but not until after Giacomo's brief but dramatic return.

Botvid is the central figure in *Progress*, and it is on his nostalgic nihilism that Strindberg has placed the emphasis. Nevertheless, it is not Botvid's fate that leaves the strongest impression with the reader, for he remains a pale figure, a victim of a despairing form of nihilism. It is Giacomo who remains imprinted on our minds. He is one of Strindberg's most vivid portraits of the man in revolt, the existential rebel against a universe that is indifferent to man's desires and hopes.

Giacomo serves a double role in the novel, expressing Strindberg's complex and ambivalent point of view. On the one hand, he serves as a dubious mentor in relation to Botvid, for his worship of life and beauty is placed in an unfavorable light, seemingly incapable of dealing with the realities of man's existence, illness, and death. In this role his actions also serve indirectly to confirm the ascetic and life-denying

Christian world view as superior in its realism, because it awakens no false hopes.

But, on the other hand, Giacomo appears in the role of the nihilistic rebel whose destiny leaves us with an unanswered question: If beauty is God's gift to man, and if the worship of beauty is instilled in man by God, why does God so suddenly and so brutally rob him of it? The suspicion is near at hand that either the gods do make sport of us humans, or we are living in a universe that is totally indifferent to our hopes and dreams, a universe without gods in which everything that makes life worth living—beauty, love, and happiness—is fleeting and impermanent. It is this suspicion that Giacomo vehemently voices, as Strindberg makes him return to Gripsholm after a number of years have passed.

He is now a bit older and grayer, and his philosophy has changed: he now worships nothing, and lives because he happened to be born, and preferably the good and easy life. But he is still a rebel, and he has lost none of his vitality as a creative artist, while Botvid is unproductive. When the latter silently reproaches Giacomo for the fact that the name Maria hardly evokes a response from him, Giacomo shifts the burden of guilt onto the gods: "Can I help it that I am made in such a way that this grave concealing her is to me at this moment only a mound of dirt, a little grass and two wooden cross sticks? The feelings grow like the hair and the beard until they turn gray or grow thin and fall off. That is the way it is, and the devil only knows who is responsible! Ask him or those who made things that way!" (257).

But it is in meeting his death that Giacomo rises to Promethean heights of revolt. Hit by an arrow in his left eye, an arrow shot by Maria's father, he curses the gods, telling Botvid that he is going to steal "the secret of heaven" from the gods, be it from Zeus or from God, steal it as Pro-

metheus stole the fire, even if it means that he will be punished by being racked over ten acres and picked by vultures:
"Jealous gods," he cries, "who blindfold human beings and
let them out into the tumult! There you sit smiling at the
fools when they hit their heads one against the other. You
give human beings desires, strong as the flow of spring. You
close the dam locks and say to the river: Stop! What kind
of sport is that? You give us flesh quivering with the desire
to live, and you say to the flesh: Die! Do you see any sense
in that, Botvid?" (260).

After a violent struggle, Giacomo dies with a curse on
his lips, and Strindberg leaves us with a vivid image. Beside
the lifeless body of the man who only minutes before had
been so full of life, a pool of blood mirrors the sun in the
church window and the deep-blue autumn sky glimpsed
through the open window. Giacomo's warm blood and the
deep-blue autumn sky: how bold and vivid an image of the
defiant rebel facing the indifferent universe!

Like *The Red Room*, then, this beautiful short novel
may be considered as an experiment with standpoints. Two
conflicting world views have been dramatically confronted,
and both have been found wanting. The new naturalism,
with its worship of the life of the senses and of beauty, and
with its faith in an organic and meaningful process of natural evolution, has been proven incapable of dealing with
the realities of man's condition, and the concept of cyclical
repetition more tenable than the theory of progressive evolution. Similarly, the Christian world view, though more realistic, because more disenchanted, than naturalism, has inspired only a life-denying and unproductive form of existence.
In the end, we are left with the image most firmly imprinted
on our minds of the nihilistic rebel grappling with the dichotomies of human existence.

⤙ 4. The Son of a Servant

In his book *Modern Man in Search of a Soul* C. G. Jung has made a useful distinction between two kinds of psychological novels, a distinction based on the relative interest to the psychologist of each type.[1] "The novels which are most fruitful for the psychologist," Jung maintains, "are those in which the author has not already given a psychological interpretation of his characters, and which therefore leave room for analysis and explanation, or even invite it by their mode of presentation." Melville's *Moby Dick,* which Jung regards as the greatest American novel, belongs to this type. What interests the psychologist the most is a narrative in which the author is unconscious of the groundwork of psychological assumptions on which his work is constructed.

The other type of novel, by the layman often labeled

---

[1] C. G. Jung, *Modern Man in Search of a Soul* (New York: Harcourt, Brace, n.d.), p. 178.

"psychological," is not as rewarding for the psychologist for in this mode of fiction, Jung argues, "the author himself attempts to reshape his material so as to raise it from the level of crude contingency to that of psychological exposition and illumination—a procedure which all too often clouds the psychological significance of the work or hides it from view." Such a novel, Jung observes, has done its own work of psychological interpretation.

Strindberg's *Tjänstekvinnans son* (*The Son of a Servant*), a novel in four volumes, written in 1886–87, belongs to the latter category of psychological novels. It is nothing less than a uniquely autopsychoanalytic work before the advent of psychoanalysis.

In *The Red Room* the problem of identity was approached from a sociological point of view, as a problem of social integration. By finding his role in society and by adjusting his expectations within the social framework of values, the hero regained a measure of identity. Although these actions implied a degree of conformity and a loss of independence, the loss was regarded not as tragic, but as a necessary evil in the process of maturation.

In *The Son of a Servant*, some seven years later, the problem of identity has become much more complex and formidable. Although the problem of overcoming isolation is still the central concern Strindberg is now bent on a psychological analysis of the factors that have determined the course of his life, and particularly those factors that have destined him to become an outsider alternately praising or cursing his condition.

For this reason the tetralogy also marks a turning point in Strindberg's development as a novelist. After the trial following the publication of *Married* in 1884, after several years of enforced exile and artistic unproductivity, beset by feelings of bankruptcy both as a writer and as a human being, having sought, as he put it, to deal with realities but having found none, Strindberg shifts his attention from social and political problems to psychological. Isolated, profoundly disturbed by marital problems, fearful of losing his mind, Strindberg begins to study the writings of contemporary psychologists, the works of Jean Martin Charcot and Maudsley and Ribot among others, and inspired by them he begins to examine his own past.

The immediate result of this self-analysis is *The Son of a Servant*. Subtitled *The Story of the Development of a Mind*, it is a record of his quest for self-knowledge, a record covering all his thirty-seven years (and some additional months, it should be noted, for Strindberg was ahead of his time in taking cognizance of prenatal influence on the child). In this novel Strindberg searches for the motives behind his actions and analyzes the reasons for his perpetual vacillations, his inability to commit himself to anything or to believe in anything or anyone for any length of time, and for the excessive sensitivity that makes it so difficult for him to be with others.

The Son of a Servant also introduces a period of rich productivity in the novel with the development of new themes and new forms of expression. For although Strindberg thought of the autobiographical novel as an emancipation of literature from art, as a contribution to the new science of psychology, it marks a gradual change in his attitude to literature. Having consistently taken a very cursory view of fiction, his main objection being that it was too constructed, too arranged, and too bound by conventions to be a truthful account of reality, he now discovers new possibilities for literary expression in the new areas of human experience explored by the new science of psychology. The psychological novel offers him an opportunity to concentrate on his own experience without having to invent characters and affords him the

pleasure of accomplishing two cherished objectives simultaneously: making a contribution to science and setting the
record straight about his own life and opinions. Yet *The Son
of a Servant* is not a confession or a defense. It bears little or
no resemblance to the confessional genre of autobiography
begun by Rousseau, nor to the stylized and formalized self-
portraits of the eighteenth century by a Gibbon or a Holberg,
nor to the anecdotal autobiographies of our own time. Inspired by an ambition to produce a very scientific kind of
naturalism, Strindberg has as his goal an objective psychological analysis of the factors that have determined his development. And yet it is fiction, for although Strindberg has
sought to weed out everything that has the stamp of literary
convention, everything that is constructed or invented, plot,
character, and atmosphere, and has virtually succeeded in
this respect, he has, as he himself had to admit, arranged his
experiences in a fictional manner.[2] *The Son of a Servant* is,
in the final analysis, therefore not different from most fictional autobiographies; it belongs to a genre that, as Northrop
Frye has well observed, is "inspired by a creative, and therefore fictional impulse to select only those events and experiences in the writer's life that go to build up an integrated
pattern." [3]

What Strindberg has chiefly eliminated are, in fact, the
qualities that create a feeling of immediacy and intimacy.
He has not sought to bare his soul, to make himself interesting. He has not included any episodes because of their
piquancy or curiosity value. He has not exploited his stylistic

---

[2] Cf. the significant little parenthesis in his letter to Edvard
Brandes on June 9, 1886: "(because they are not *confessions* or
mémoires, a good deal is arranged)" (Georg Brandes and Edvard
Brandes, *Brevväxling med svenska och finska författare och vetenskapsmän* [Stockholm: Bonniers, 1939–1942], I, 83).

[3] Northrop Frye, *Anatomy of Criticism* (New York: Atheneum,
1966), p. 307.

abilities to produce a witty account of his experiences.[4] The material included is there because it is relevant to the thesis. Even the experiences of early childhood on which most auto-biographers tend to dwell with such loving care are here re-duced to the realm of documentary evidence for some psycho-logical observation. In the process of the hero's development the search for self-knowledge becomes progressively public, the actions of the hero being increasingly motivated by well-defined ideological motives, a fact that gives the reader the feeling that he is reading chapters in the intellectual history of the nineteenth century.

How are we to evaluate such a novel? It is clearly too intellectualized, too analytical, too discursive to be evaluated in the same terms as, say, a novel by Henry James. The novel fails to move us, for we find it difficult to empathize in any way with the hero, seeing that he has few spontaneous feel-ings or sentiments. I think it has to be evaluated on its own terms, as a fictional autobiography, that is, in terms of its objectivity, its candor, and its depth of insight. We must seek "the integrated pattern" that Strindberg has built up. This pattern may, to quote Northrop Frye again, "be some-thing larger than himself with which he has come to identify himself, or simply the coherence of his character and atti-tudes." It is, after all, "his success in integrating his mind" on some theoretical and intellectual questions "that makes the author of confessions feel his life is worth writing about." [5]

On this score, *The Son of a Servant* has received much praise. The book illustrates, in the words of Alrik Gustafson, "how clear-headed and eminently rational he [Strindberg]

---

[4] "I believe there is scarcely a single figure of speech in the whole book, or what you might call 'style'; not a single witticism, no satire, no landscapes, and no women" (Brandes and Brandes, *op. cit.*, p. 83).

[5] Frye, *op. cit.*, pp. 307–308.

could on occasion be in dealing with himself and his time." Labeling the novel "an autobiographical work which seeks to place its central figure in the total social and intellectual contexts of the day," Gustafson maintains further, that "it does so with an astonishing objectivity considering the frequency with which Strindberg had earlier come into conflict with the world around him. Though it has sharp things to say about parental tyranny and the backwardness of school and university education, and deals out caustic observations on social conditions, politics, and religion, it does so with little rancor and less bitterness; and in dealing with himself in this work Strindberg maintains a frankness and candor quite unusual in autobiographical literature." [6]

On the whole, the novel well deserves this generous evaluation. In its self-analysis it is candid, revealing a keen awareness of the real motives buried under the apparent ones, observing the hero's contradictions and rationalizations, balancing his weaknesses and his virtues. And despite some only too obvious contradictions, outbursts of indignations, and blatant exaggerations, Strindberg retains a good measure of objectivity.

In my own judgment, the weaknesses of the novel are most apparent in the intellectual context. As I have already suggested above, a characteristic pattern in the book is that the hero's search for self-knowledge becomes progressively public, and that since his actions are seen as motivated in terms of current ideologies, we get the feeling that we are reading chapters in the intellectual history of the nineteenth century. This is the customary pattern of the *Bildungsroman*, in which the hero in his search for his place in the world also seeks to orient himself among the ideas of his time. But although Strindberg lets his hero run the gamut of the ideol-

---

[6] Alrik Gustafson, A *History of Swedish Literature* (Minneapolis: University of Minnesota Press, 1961), p. 263.

ogies and the philosophies of the day, a number of the discussions, notably those of Kierkegaard and Marx, appear to be based on a very superficial acquaintance with the works of these thinkers, and the writing is careless and hurried. On the whole, Strindberg's weakness in this context is his superficiality. He is vitally interested in all the new currents of thought, but he seldom appears willing to examine them in depth.

But this weakness of the novel is more than offset by its strength in the psychological context, an area in which Strindberg celebrates great triumphs as a penetrating analyst of the self and its maladies. This anatomical investigation is of course based on self-analysis, but its implications are wide, for although Strindberg was, first and foremost, trying to make sense of his own life, he was also using his own life as the basis for a scientific investigation of character formation. As if to confirm his thesis—in which he moves beyond the documentary naturalism of Zola—that the only real avenue to knowledge about human beings is through self-analysis, the novel also offers some remarkable insights into the nature of the self and the forces and things that condition it. That these insights should anticipate the discoveries of psychoanalysis is hardly surprising in view of the fact that Strindberg had already read Eduard von Hartmann in the 1870's. In addition, the novel constitutes a brilliant analysis of the antinomies of Romantic individualism, its cult of the unique and autonomous self, of the lonely outsider, and its equally strong yearning for something beyond the individual self, be it religion, sex, or work. In this respect, *The Son of a Servant*, too, is an analysis of the self in conflict, a psychological portrait of the man who, as a product of his heredity, his milieu, and his time, has to contend with the problems of living in an age of transition. Its most persistent note is also the disbelief in the stability and coherence of the self.

Despite the dissimilarity between the two novels in other respects, *The Son of a Servant* thus has an integrated pattern of development not unlike that of Kierkegaard's *Either/Or*. This is undoubtedly no coincidence, for Kierkegaard was one of the chief exponents of the type of Romantic individualism that Strindberg had embraced in the 1870's, and in *The Son of a Servant* a considerable amount of space is given to an early essay on Scandinavian literature based on the dialectic pattern of *Either/Or*. The structure of Kierkegaard's novel is based on the movement from one stage of life to another; from the aesthetic stage, considered as synonymous with a Romantic attitude to life, to the ethical stage, the life of social responsibility. Similarly, *The Son of a Servant* exhibits a shift away from Romantic individualism in the direction of social involvement.

The first volume, entitled *The Son of a Servant*, takes the hero through childhood and adolescence, from 1849, the year of Strindberg's birth, to the year 1867, when he leaves for Uppsala to begin his studies at the university. Like the second volume, *The Age of Ferment*, covering the years 1867–1872, it portrays the central figure, who has been given the name of Johan, as a rebel against the established order, family, school, university. *The Age of Ferment* also treats of some of the writers who influenced Johan during this period, among them Kierkegaard, Ibsen, and Georg Brandes. The third volume, *In the Red Room*, covering the years 1872–1875, marks a gradual change away from Romantic individualism, signaled in the drama *Master Olof* (1872), in a romantic love affair, and in the search for a professional career. The fourth volume, *The Writer*, spans a period of ten years, from 1877 to the moment of writing, and marks the hero's integration into society, as evinced by his marriage, his work, and his faith in life and in human beings, in socialism and democracy.

At the end of *The Writer*, there is, however, a significant departure from this pattern, for Johan appears anew destined to embrace a still more radical form of individualism. Again, we may note an interesting parallel in *Either/Or*, for at the end of the second volume of the latter, a question is suddenly raised concerning what Kierkegaard calls "the teleological suspension of the ethical," which is essentially the question of what the man is to do who has honestly sought to reconcile himself to the demands of the ethical, that is, by marrying and becoming a good citizen, but has been unable to do so. A third stage, a third way, is anticipated, the religious life, which, in Kierkegaard's definition, is outside the ethical categories of society and thus another form of individualism. Strindberg's problem in 1887 was, in a way, not unlike Kierkegaard's. Kierkegaard was unable to marry, hence his problem. Strindberg's marriage was falling apart, and, along with it, the chief source of his reconciliation with society, hence his problem. For the time being, their paths were to move in different directions; in the end, they were, as we shall soon see, to converge.

Of the four volumes the first is usually regarded as the best because it is less discursive and less didactic than the others. Through a vivid account of the hero's childhood Strindberg depicts the horrors of a nineteenth-century education (whether this account is true or not need not concern us here). Despite some occasional lapses into vehement outbursts against the family as an institution Strindberg performs exceedingly well in his newfound role as a sober, dispassionate child psychologist, proceeding with care in offering hypotheses as a scientist should. At times he falls out of this role so unsuited to his temperament and lectures the reader in a highly didactic manner on a number of topics: child-rearing, housekeeping, education, masturbation, psychosomatic disturbances. These remarks have the distinct tone of the introductory textbook and the lecture hall. In some cases he tells us in no uncertain terms how much he knows which his poor hero does not know: "He [Johan] also noticed that the poorly dressed children received more punishment than those who were well dressed, in fact, the nice boys escaped altogether. If he had studied psychology or aesthetics then he would have understood this phenomenon, but at the time he did not!" (18, 39).

Strindberg's readings in psychology are also reflected in another tendency, one that lends the book an added measure of apparent objectivity. He is careful to list a number of motives for Johan's actions. Illustrations of this tendency may be found in the list of reasons given for Johan's becoming a pietist (129–130), or for his falling in love with a woman twice his age (135).

Strindberg's main intent is also naturalistic and scientific in its ambition: to analyze the formation of his hero's character in terms of the factors that have molded it—heredity, milieu, and education. Here Strindberg's language is unequivocal. Johan's lack of a sense of identity springs from the emotional insecurity fostered by a combination of unfortunate socioeconomic circumstances and a mistaken upbringing. The child grew up in an atmosphere of fear and insecurity, both emotional and economic. The family was in straightened financial circumstances when Johan was born. He was an unwanted child, and throughout his childhood he was starved for love and affection. His mother died when he was very young. His will was broken by the prevalent authoritarian methods of child-rearing, designed primarily to inculcate obedience. In the school he was worried about his class status: his father was an aristocrat, his mother a servant woman. Did he belong among the upper classes or among the workers? His sympathies vacillated between them. His re-

ligious education instilled in him a fear of sex, a sense of
guilt, and the Lutheran inclination toward excessive introspection and self-analysis, stifling spontaneity.

The detailed consequences of this education are vividly
illustrated. Johan is a self-righteous prig, anxiously watching
to make sure that everyone else gets his punishment. He
enjoys being hurt and overlooked (53, 81). He often behaves
capriciously and is given to inexplicable tantrums. He suffers
from aphasia (64). We are told that he feels the loss of his
mother with such emotional intensity that it is bound to be
with him all his life (49). He already knows now that for
this reason he will "never be himself, never liberated, never
a full-blown individual." He is bound to be "a mistletoe,
which could not grow without being supported by a tree;
he was a clinging vine, that had to seek a support" (46–47).
He is a lonely outsider, unable to be with others on account
of his abnormal sensitivity, but he suffers from his loneliness
(56). He is vacillating and indecisive, unable to make even
the prosaic choice between two brands of tobacco (216).

That this young man is poorly equipped for life seems
a foregone conclusion, and Strindberg affirms this toward
the end of the volume: "Religion had ruined him, because
it had educated him for heaven and not for the earth, the
family had ruined him because it had molded him for the
family and not for society, and the school had prepared him
for the university and not for life" (215).

In view of this analysis our skepticism is bound to be
aroused when it suddenly becomes apparent that Strindberg,
contrary to our legitimate expectations, makes a rapid turn-
about and seems bent on convincing us that the child who
has been submitted to this treatment is destined to become
a remarkable, if not to say superior, young man.

This surprising conclusion emerges on the last pages of

the novel in the final assessment of Johan's character. Johan has been disturbed by his lack of a stable self as reflected in his lack of confidence in himself, in his constant vacillations, and in his tendency to find a multiplicity of motives for his actions. He has been chided for his lack of willpower, for his insincerity, for his lack of character. He has suffered from these criticisms. Now the teenager suddenly realizes that this suffering has been unwarranted. In measuring himself against others he has used the wrong yardstick. He has used an antiquated definition of character or the self. He has conceived of the self as something fixed and firm. Lacking this stable self he has been unable to be true to himself, constantly presenting a different image to the world.

Now he realizes that the self is neither here nor there, not an entity of some kind, but "a multiplicity of reflexes, a compendium of drives, desires, some repressed at times, others released now and then!" Those who present a definite image, firmness of character, are those who have assumed a role, who have learned the art of dissimulation in social life. Such individuals are insincere. Johan having not yet found his role is totally sincere.

The lack of character, "characterlessness," as Strindberg calls it, is thus actually a virtue, and a distinct mark of superiority. To be a character, or to possess a firm character, is to be a conformist, "a middle class automaton." Strindberg says,

A so-called character has only one point of view in regard to the extremely complex conditions of life; he has decided once and for all to have one and the same opinion in a certain matter; and in order not to make himself guilty of characterlessness he never changes his opinion, no matter how simpleminded or unreasonable it is. A character must consequently be a rather ordinary person and what you might term a little stupid. Character and automaton seem roughly to coincide. (212)

Johan, on the other hand, is characterless, skeptical, intelligent, and critical, unwilling to adopt a role or have a ready-made role conferred on him, unlikely to become an obedient little cog in the social machinery.

It should be added that had Strindberg written the book some years earlier he might not have been able to assess Johan's characterlessness in such a positive light. But in the meantime he had studied the psychology of Ribot, and in Ribot he had found a concept of character which fitted his own, for Ribot, although he was writing about the maladies of personality, saw nothing abnormal in the type of instability Strindberg had discovered in Johan's character. Writes Ribot,

Common observation shows us that the normal ego is but slightly endowed with cohesion and unity. Irrespective of characters that are perfectly concordant (which in the strict sense of the word do not exist) there are in every one of us all sorts of tendencies, all possible antitheses, and among these contradictions, all kinds of intermediate shades, and among those tendencies every possible combination. This is because the ego is not only a memory, a storehouse of recollections connected with the present, but an aggregate of instincts, tendencies, desires, which are merely its innate and acquired constitution coming into play.[7]

The concept of a static ego-identity is to Ribot a prejudice that has been fostered by education and by the supposed evidence of consciousness. It has also to some extent been fostered by philosophers and artists, though they often speak of the conflict of two selves: "Two souls," said Goethe, "dwell within my breast." Ribot comments: "Only two! If moralists, poets, novelists, dramatists, have shown us to satiety these two egos in a state of conflict within the same ego, common

---

[7] Théodule Ribot, *The Diseases of Personality* (Chicago: Open Court, 1891), p. 72.

experience is still richer: it shows us several, each one excluding the other, as soon as it advances to the front. This may be less dramatic, but it is very true." [8]

The suspicion is near at hand that Strindberg in depicting and evaluating the young Johan's character has attempted to realize two contradictory aims: to vent his indignation and to play on the reader's sympathy by portraying his hero as an Ishmael, as an outcast and a victim, unfit for a normal existence; and to depict his hero as a budding genius, superior to the common run of men because of his difference. To some extent this is of course true, and such cross-purposes are quite typical for Strindberg, but at the same time we must admit that the account also reveals Strindberg's keen insight into Johan's character and his profound awareness of the warring traits that will determine his destiny.

He has seen that Johan is bound to remain emotionally immature, and that he will always lack true autonomy, bound to feel insecure and lacking in confidence among others, excessively self-conscious and lacking in spontaneity. He has also seen that these weaknesses may be turned into virtues. For the qualities that have made Johan an outsider will also make him an individual, a skeptical rebel who will think for himself and not like the common run of men. Hence Johan's lack of self-confidence may become the cornerstone of a healthy skepticism: "Doubt! He did not receive thoughts completely uncritically, but developed them, combined them. For this reason he could not become an automaton and enroll in organized society." And an excessive sensitivity to outside pressure might foster a debunking spirit: "Sensitivity to pressure! Therefore he sought in part to decrease it by elevating himself, in part by directing criticism at the superior in order to discover that it was not so superior and thus not so desirable" (219).

The very qualities that make for Johan's lack of a sense

---

[8] *Ibid.*, p. 74.

of identity are here construed as a source of potential strength for the writer to be. It is evident that Strindberg is adopting in some measure the language of Romantic individualism. The Romantic emphasis on authenticity and the belief that this authenticity may only be retained by being an outsider, by being different from others, underlie Strindberg's analysis of Johan's predominant character patterns. But there is also a deeper insight emerging, here partly fostered by the reading of Ribot and partly by self-analysis, that the stable ego is a myth, that human beings play many roles, and that the writer, in particular, is a man with many faces.

But Johan is also predestined, as Strindberg well realizes, to be forever confronted with the dilemma of Romantic individualism: the ambivalent attitude to the solitary life, and the persistent but paradoxical search for something greater than the self. On the one hand there is the pride in being the lonely outsider, the rebel, on the other, the feeling of being rejected and unwanted. To Johan, Strindberg says,

solitariness was bound to be a desert walk, because he did not possess a sufficiently strong individuality to be able to be by himself; his sympathy for other human beings was to remain without response, because their thoughts could not keep pace with his; and then he was to go about and offer his heart to the firstcomer, but no one would receive it, because it was foreign to them, and so he was to withdraw into himself, hurt, humiliated, overlooked, bypassed. (56)

Similarly, Johan's unsatisfied religious need to believe in something greater than the self is obviously bound to conflict with an equally strong need to assert his own uniqueness and worth by debunking all faiths, all systems of thought.

The major theme of *The Son of a Servant* is also isolation and its overcoming.[9] In this sense, too, the novel belongs

---

[9] This theme has been traced by Thure Stenström in his brilliant comparative study *Den ensamme: En motivstudie i det moderna*

within the classic genre of the *Bildungsroman*. We might also recall that Strindberg when he began writing the novel was suffering from his enforced isolation and warning others of the dangers of the isolated life, insisting that a life outside the circle of the family or the community is a life deprived of its fullness and meaning. It is only consistent that the account of Johan's further development should be colored by this point of view. The three subsequent volumes consequently depict Johan's quest for identity, for a profession or a vocation that will allow him to express his unique talents and perform an authentic role in society, and for a faith or a set of values that will silence his doubts and give a meaning to his existence. In view of what has already been said above about the dilemma of Romantic individualism we might expect that this quest is bound to fail. The picture is also further complicated by the fact that when Strindberg was writing the last volume in which he brings Johan's development up to the very moment of writing, that is, to 1886, he was again moving toward a more affirmative view of the solitary life.

A recurrent theme in Johan's search for a meaningful role in society is his insistence on the fact that it must not restrict his freedom. His initial contact with the teaching profession having left him dissatisfied because of its confining nature (he had to teach history by the textbook), Johan realizes that he does not "want to be registered in the corps of society, become a member, a cogwheel, a nut." "He was not to be tamed. He wanted to stand on the outside and to observe, to learn and to preach" (288). For a little while he sees the possibility of realizing his aims in the medical profession, as a doctor, and begins to study medicine.

But he feels even more at home among the Bohemian

---

genombrottets litteratur (Stockholm: Natur och Kultur, 1961), pp. 246–253.

artists whose company he frequents, like Falk in *The Red Room*. For the artists have "a free society within society." It is a world full of joy and freedom, a world in which Johan feels he might be at home, because it is "without all conventional social restrictions, without responsibilities to society, and, above all, without contact with dull reality" (303–304). Nevertheless, he does not feel that he would be able to express himself as a painter, and turns instead to the acting profession, "this privileged estate, outside of and above the laws of society" (309). In the role of the actor Johan as the Romantic also enjoys the pleasure of magnifying himself, identifying with other, more important imaginary figures (310). But with the great roles denied him (Johan wanted only to perform these), the acting profession becomes a boring routine, from which the career as a playwright affords an escape and the additional pleasure of being able to use the theater as a forum from which to launch attacks on society. This, he believes, is his destiny, his role in life, but its path is strewn with thorns, because in spite of some initial success, it fails to bring him financial security (343).

In the best Romantic tradition Johan worships the rebel. Having read Schiller's *Die Räuber* he identifies with Karl Moor in his revolt against the law, society, customs, religion (276). In Byron's Manfred he discovers a kindred spirit, a rebel against heaven and the divine order (285). In Ibsen's *Brand* he feels akin to its hero who "dared believe that he was in the right against the whole world" and who insisted that "all ties, of concern, of love, were to be broken for the sake of the 'cause'" (355). In the novels of Victor Hugo Johan relishes the revolt against society, the solitary poet's worship of nature, the ridicule of the general stupidity, the frenzy against the religion of the priests (378).

But underneath this Romantic swagger and pose, which Strindberg accentuates with a combination of detachment and admiration, Johan feels a lack of meaning in his life because of his being an outsider. At the university he feels lost when left to his own devices, deprived of the collective endeavor in the classroom (238). Casual sexual affairs leave him dissatisfied despite their freedom from obligations and responsibilities. Though he feels at home among the Bohemians and among the Jews whom he envies as "homeless" and "liberated" (289), it is still in his return to his home and family that he feels protected, sleeps with peace, and feels a firm foothold in the world as he watches "quiet, patient people come and go, working and sleeping at regular hours, exactly as before, without being disturbed by dreams or ambitious plans" (397).

When he fails as an actor and in his studies at the university he also feels disturbed at the thought that friends and relatives will consider him excessively changeable (19, 57). And after repeated returns to his home he feels unwelcome, like the prodigal son, met by contempt, and he wonders if there is to be no place for him in a society so rich in careers (58). After a failure in a new profession, as a newspaperman, he again experiences the pleasure of being with people who are happy in their menial tasks (101–102).

Gradually Johan finds his role in society, at least for the time being, and with that his Romantic revolt also begins to wane. He begins to dissociate himself from the idealism of Kierkegaard and Ibsen, and under the influence of the English historian Henry Thomas Buckle he cultivates a spirit of skepticism. The rebel becomes a skeptic, a nihilist, and a pessimist (42). He excoriates the monk, the fanatic, and the masochist in himself, learns to improvise, to live without views, living as most people do (46–47). In his drama *Master Olof* he shows that it is possible to combine the role of reformer with the roles of father, citizen, and husband (34).

Of particular significance in this context is also his discovery of Eduard von Hartmann's book *The Philosophy of the Unconscious*, a pioneer work in European psychology, anticipating the discoveries of Freud in regard to the role of the unconscious. It is not clear from Johan's random references to von Hartmann's work to what extent he had really grasped its significance, for he seems in essence to regard him as a nihilist and iconoclastic debunker of myths and illusions about human happiness. He couples von Hartmann's philosophy with what he labels "the essential teachings" of Christianity and Buddhism: that all is vanity, that conscious life is pain, and that only "savages, children, and ordinary people can be happy, because they are unconscious of the deceit, the deceit of the unconscious will that moves them to action" (60). The main impact on Johan's development seems clear. The philosophy of von Hartmann serves to counterbalance his Romantic revolt with a strong skepticism.

A similar skepticism is also fostered by the American writers whose acquaintance he makes. In these humorists he finds an iconoclastic spirit that boldly proclaims that all idealism is bunk, and a point of view "purified of all hallucinations, all ideals and all romanticism," facing "life's relative and heaven's absolute nothingness" without flinching (109).

And so Johan settles down in the respected position as a librarian and a civil servant in the Royal Library. He enjoys the esteem of his colleagues, and buries himself in scientific work. He has done what he had vowed not to do: he has "obeyed the law of society and integrated himself into society" (155). Like many a young man he has found the meaning of life in his work and in marriage. In his own home, Johan experiences the pleasure "never to be alone, but constantly to be in the presence of a loved woman" and for him this is "like having all his old dreams about his home and

mother realized" (157). With the realization that he is going
to become a father he even experiences a sense of immortality (170).

But Johan soon resumes his old role as the rebel against
society, for the truce is built on a precarious foundation. The
"happy erotic stage" in the midst of the family is bound to
be transitional (218). As Johan's revolt begins anew it assumes a new form, for Johan is now consciously bent on re-
forming society. He is giving close scrutiny to some of the
new ideologies that offer a practical program of social change.
While this sounds like a realistic point of view, it soon becomes apparent that Strindberg considers even this desire for
social reform as a reflection of Romantic idealism. Strindberg
seems in fact determined to bring Johan to a nihilistic point
of view, to the realization that any other point of view is
Romantic and to be discarded. Johan's future development
is, as a result, depicted in terms of conflicting philosophical
ideas, his conflict situations reflecting those typical of the
age in which he is living.

Two of Johan's traits in particular are now singled out
as the reflections of a Romantic world view: his self-consciousness and his idealism.

Self-consciousness, which is also labeled egocentricity or
egoism, is, according to Strindberg, the consequence of Christian individualism, "with its eternal burrowing into the self
and its vices" (18, 239). "The egoistic self-criticism of Christianity," says Strindberg, "had accustomed him to busy himself with his self, to fondle it, to fuss over it, as over a beloved
person" (271). "This was the sickness of the age, formulated
into a system by Fichte, who considered everything to be in
the self and through the self, without which reality did not
exist. It was the formula of Romanticism and subjective
idealism" (272). The excessive self-consciousness fostered by
this Romantic idealism has, however, also fostered a com-

pensatory desire to return to the unconscious, to a state of undivided bliss. "Every man who has developed to the point of seeing clearly," says Strindberg, "must, though he feels that consciousness is progress, miss the unconscious life of feeling as a lost pleasure, and consciousness is pain for the man who has begun with hallucinations" (19, 139–140). Johan, who is a Romantic of the purest water, is such a man, for he feels the loss of "the blissful intoxication of unawareness in which he had grown up" (140). Thus he often seeks to become like a child again, to believe, to hope, to play, to romp and frolic.

Like other Romantics Johan seeks to heal through woman the split within himself occasioned by this excessive self-consciousness. Woman is salvation, she is the angel, for, since she represents the mother, she also represents the origin of things, the bliss of childhood to be experienced anew. Through woman man can reestablish the tie with the mother and with nature, and thus regain his strength. By combining her life of the feelings with his intellectual life, Johan believes, "a perfect type of human being might be formed" (130).

And, to go one step further, since woman as the mother represents the origin of things, she may also be a substitute for the lost God. As the young atheist answers when asked by Johan how he could manage without God: "We have woman instead" (235). Hence the modern cult of the madonna, the woman as mother.

But the desire to escape self-consciousness may take other forms, as Johan realizes when he reads Kierkegaard, who preaches the paradox, which is one way to silence reflection. Kierkegaard preached madness, says Strindberg; and he asks: "Was that the despair of the self-conscious man—of being always conscious? Was it the penetrating intellect's longing for the intoxication of insensibility?" (18, 387).

This observation, put in the form of a question, is an accurate analysis of the manner in which Kierkegaard resolved his dilemma, for faith by virtue of the absurd was undoubtedly his way of silencing his own overly reflective mind. By reasoning, he argued, man involves himself in contradictions, until one way seems as good as another, and the result is nonaction. Faith is the solution, for faith cuts through this state of indecision in rejecting reason as the guide to action, faith to Kierkegaard being defined as faith only in that which is contrary to the understanding, in that which is paradoxical.

But Johan's way is not Kierkegaard's stage of religious faith. It is the ethical stage, in which marriage and a job serve at least temporarily to silence the gnawing doubts of reflection (19, 218). In this context it is interesting to note the pronounced similarity between Johan's reflections on the role of woman in the life of the man and those of the Judge in the second volume of Kierkegaard's *Either/Or*. The Judge, we recall, is admonishing the overly reflective young poet, whose life has been described in the first volume, to marry and become a good citizen and thus save himself from a life of despair. It is the manner in which the Judge describes his own wife and her role which is so strikingly similar to Johan's.

The Judge insists that "woman has an innate talent, a primitive gift and an absolute virtuosity for explaining finiteness." [10] By this Hegelian language he means that woman is "in harmony with existence (as no man is or should be)." Man is self-absorbed, he is separated from the world about him, because he is or ought to be "in chase of infinitude," constantly seeking to transcend himself and the world. Thus woman is man's "deepest life," she makes man happy, by providing him with what he lacks, the contact with the world. That is woman's function: to be a comfort to man, to make

---

[10] Søren Kierkegaard, *Either/Or*, trans. Walter Lowrie, rev. Howard Johnson (New York: Anchor Books, 1959), II, 313–323.

up for his lacks. Woman is "man's refuge" from his tortured battles with the life of the mind.

This role I believe, is the one Strindberg wished to confer on his women; it explains why he, like Kierkegaard's Judge, abhorred the idea of the emancipation of women, and it explains perhaps why his marriages were such troubled affairs. In the end Strindberg too, like Kierkegaard, very logically moved on to the religious stage.

At the end of the novel Johan is left with his self-consciousness. No cure has been found, and the temporary escape into the erotic is a stage that is coming to an end. But while this deep-rooted psychological problem remains unresolved, the ideological conflict has a happier outcome in a very positive affirmation of a nihilistic point of view. The conflict between Romanticism, which here stands for the faith in the old Christian order based on the belief in God, and naturalism, which here represents the conception of the universe as operated by mechanical and immutable laws, the conflict that Johan sees as the central conflict of his age, is resolved. It is resolved in a nihilism that rejects faith—both in God and in a meaningful universe operated by laws in conformity with reason—as a Romantic and rationalistic illusion inspired by man's wishful thinking and desire to impose an order on chaos.

Gradually Johan's faith in a Divine Providence guiding all for the best is undermined as he finds it increasingly difficult to reconcile his vision of the world with the existence of a loving and personal God (238–239). Unlike his contemporaries Johan fails to find any meaningful pattern in the evolution of the universe or of man, any progress toward greater happiness or rationality. Contrary to the teaching of Christianity or the theories of Darwin he feels there is no order in nature, no progressive evolution. All is helter-skelter: all is caprice and hazard, nothing is planned (185–186).

There is change but not necessarily a change for the better. Progress is made, but it is often irreconcilable with individual happiness. Johan's conclusion is that the quest for connecting links, for the origin, for meaning, is only idealism. What then is the meaning of life? The answer is simple: Life itself! The meaning of life is to live until you die (238–248).

With this realization Johan's education is completed for he has now divested himself of much of his Romanticism. He has been thrown back on himself, he stands alone, no longer looking for his destiny outside of himself (277). Without God he is responsible for his own life. With the rejection of a built-in meaningful order in the world he is free to create his own.

Johan's nihilism also resolves his dilemma as the rebel against society, for socialism, the ideology that had progressively attracted him as a program for reform, is now also rejected as but another form of Romantic idealism, as an "expression of the subjective spirit's desire to order the world" (274). It is only a philosophical system, a fiction bearing no resemblance to the chaos of a reality that is indifferent to man's desire for order. Marxism is a system born in a philosopher's brain, subject to the limitations of Karl Marx's limited vision. Socialism, too, is Romanticism and Christianity in a new guise (280).

With the rejection of socialism Johan also seems about to reject his democratic sympathies and to embrace a new kind of aristocratic individualism, the aim of which is the development of a new nobility, but one that, unlike the old nobility based on inherited privileges, constitutes a nobility of mind and sensibility (283). Along with this new shift of attitude the old insistence on the importance of the solitary life receives new emphasis (202–205).[11]

---

[11] An amusing illustration of this rapid shift of point of view is Strindberg's request to Albert Bonnier that the publication of the

It is at this point in the story that Johan, thrown back on himself and ready to forge his destiny, wonders about the nature of the self, about his identity, and finds "a motley confusion, lacking substance, changing form according to the observer's point of view and with perhaps no more reality than the rainbow, which can be seen but does not exist." So he decides to write a book investigating the history of the origin and development of his mind. This book is of course *The Son of a Servant*. Did he discover his identity during this "sad walk in the shadowy world of memories?" No, not really, but he made unexpected discoveries. Nevertheless, "the result, the summing up" is missing. "Where lies the truth?" Johan asks. It lies, he maintains, in the thousand printed pages of the book, because one must recognize, he continues, "that the truth is not to be found, because like everything else it is in a state of continuous evolution." There are contradictions in his account, he admits, but the writer is "an experimenter," who observes life from shifting points of view, and there are errors, of course, but who knows, says Johan, if they really are errors. "One wants a faith," Johan observes, "a definite view, because it is so convenient. But faith means standing still; the point of view has to be altered in a few years, when new discoveries have refuted it. And in our age of quest not to believe anything is an advantage, since the quest itself is the main thing" (277–279).[12]

Thus Johan's quest for identity ends in an affirmation

---

fourth volume not be delayed, seeing that the last three chapters already indicate where he *now* stands (*Brev*, VI, 132).

[12] In a preface to a later edition (1909) of *The Son of a Servant* Strindberg adds this interesting observation, reflecting his religious vision of life in later years: "If the writer in reality, as he has sometimes believed, has experimented with points of view or incarnated himself in different personalities, polymerized himself, or if a merciful providence has experimented with the author will be evident to the enlightened reader from the texts" (19, 459).

of the quest, in an affirmation of the uncommitted life, of the nonidentity of the writer who experiments with points of view, forever adjusting his angle of vision. That this condition of nonidentity is a positive state, in fact the only truly authentic state, is here made quite clear. In his younger years Johan had evidently believed that the life of the poet was "a shadowy existence," the poet being without a self, living only in other selves. This belief is now questioned:

Is it so certain that the poet lacks a self, because he does not have only one? Perhaps he is richer who possesses more than the others? And why is it better to have only one, when the single self in any case is no more one's own than several selves, since a self is a résumé composed by parents, educators, company, books? Perhaps because society like a piece of machinery demands that its units, the selves, must become integral parts as wheels, nuts, machine parts, and work in a limited, automatic manner. But is not then the poet more than the machine part, since he himself is a whole machine? (18, 436)

The most striking feature of this conclusion is the radical manner in which Strindberg has liquidated the Romantic idea of the self. For just as socialism has been rejected as a futile endeavor to impose a rational order on the chaos of existence, so the idea has been rejected that the self has an identity that can be fixed through reason. The self is not to be identified with the social role or function performed by an individual, nor is it to be identified with the unconditioned and creative will as the Romantics believed. To think of the self as having a single clear identity, a fixed contour of some kind, is to impose a logical reconstruction on our existence.

In *The Son of a Servant* we are left with a self that has dissolved into what Wylie Sypher in his discussion of Bergson's idea of the self has described as "the mobility of consciousness—a consciousness almost unconscious, having only a direction or a submerged duration, not an heroic or evident identity." [13] That this description should be so applicable in the case of Strindberg is perhaps less surprising if we recall that Bergson as well as Strindberg was profoundly influenced by biological and evolutionary theories. Having noted this affinity between Bergson and Strindberg the strikingly Proustian ending of *The Son of a Servant,* the insistence that the truth is not to be captured by some logical summing up but that it is embedded in the thousand printed pages, seems fitting indeed. For if the self has been dissolved into the infinitely "mobile consciousness" then this fluidity can only be captured within the fluid medium of time, that is, in a literary work of art.

The Son of a Servant, nevertheless, bears little resemblance to Proust's great novel, for it is a book about a split and divided modern mind and how it evolved. Strindberg has made a giant effort to heal the split by rejecting all traces of Romantic idealism, and in so doing he has touched the rock bottom of nihilism. There is only one thing he has proudly affirmed and that is the creative ordering of the artist. Having found nothing else to cling to, he clings as he will again and again, to the one meaningful activity, his vocation as a writer. That affirmation *The Son of a Servant* shares with *The Remembrance of Things Past.*

---

[13] Wylie Sypher, *Loss of the Self in Modern Literature and Art* (New York: Vintage Books, 1965), pp. 58–60.

ᴥ 5. *The People of Hemsö*

BEFORE EMBARKING on our discussion of the novels of psychic murder written during the years 1887–1890 we must briefly consider a novel that does not fit into the general pattern of the period. This is *Hemsöborna* (*The People of Hemsö*), begun in August, 1887, and rapidly completed. Strindberg's most popular novel, it illustrates the variety of his art of fiction as well as the breadth of his vision. On our thematic journey we may regard it, as he himself did, as "an intermezzo scherzando" (21, 366).

Unlike *The Son of a Servant*, that bold experiment in "the literature of the future," *The People of Hemsö* is a conventional novel, perhaps Strindberg's most conventional work of fiction. Gone is the modern psychology, the anatomical probings into the nature of the self, the lengthy discussion of social and political problems. Instead we have "pure" fiction, "L'art pour L'art," to quote Strindberg again (19,

148). A good story well and briskly told; colorful comic characters with the added charm of being uncomplicated; burlesque and ribald, almost folksy episodes; concrete and vivid impressions of life in the archipelago, to Strindberg as well as to many Stockholmers associated with fond memories of summer vacations—these are the ingredients of *The People of Hemsö* and the secrets of its lasting appeal.

To this we might add that *The People of Hemsö* is Strindberg's most "objective" work of fiction. It is true that he wrote about an island in the archipelago where he had spent happy summers as a child, and that the characters are patterned on live models, but from his memories of the island of Kymmendö he has fashioned an independent, self-contained world, that special precinct of comedy. In the novel he makes his presence felt only as the impersonal and omniscient narrator telling the story. He has no ax to grind, no theories to defend, no moral to propound, no indignation to vent. The result is a work of epic tranquillity and plastic clarity, as finished and as perfect in its own right as *Madame Bovary*, that masterpiece of the objective novel. When we add the fact that the novel is bathed in the warm light of a sense of good humor and acceptance of life as it is and as it shapes itself, there is little reason to wonder why *The People of Hemsö* is Strindberg's most widely read novel and a genuine Swedish classic. He himself also labeled it his "sanest" book.[1]

The simple plot of the novel is based on a pattern characteristic of much of Strindberg's fiction: the pattern of rise and fall. The novel begins with the arrival at Hemsö of the hero, Carlsson, an enterprising fellow from the province of Värmland. On the island he is to assist the middle-aged widow Flod put her farm in order. Seeing the opportunity of becoming his own master, Carlsson proposes to the widow, and

---

[1] *Brev*, VIII, 273.

the two are wed. In the process he gains a formidable enemy in the widow's son, Gusten, who attempts to place various obstacles in his way. Carlsson's final downfall results from his weakness for the fairer sex, for when the widow, after having discovered Carlsson and a serving maid in a compromising situation, catches pneumonia and dies, Carlsson finds that the farm has been left to Gusten. In the end, as the coffin with the body of his wife is brought across the frozen sea to the church, Carlsson accidentally drowns, leaving Gusten as the undisputed master of Hemsö.

Several features immediately strike the reader of *The People of Hemsö*: the brisk narrative pace, the zest and vitality of the language, the immediacy and concreteness of the sensuous surface.

The mode of storytelling is picaresque in the manner of Fielding or Smollett or Captain Marryat.[2] The captions of the chapters set the brisk pace and the unsentimental, comic tone. The caption of chapter five may serve as an illustration: "In which there is squabbling on the third Sunday of the banns. The couple go to Communion and celebrate their wedding, but, even so, do not get to the bridal bed." And how void of sentimentality the caption of the last chapter: "In which Carlsson's dreams come true; the bureau is guarded, but the administrator comes and makes final settlement."

Illustrations of the general zest and vitality of the language may be found almost anywhere in the novel, as this random sample, the opening paragraph of the third chapter, well shows: "Bream spawned, juniper shed its smoky pollen, bird cherry blossomed, and Carlsson sowed spring rye above the frozen autumn grain, sent six cows to the slaughterer, and bought dry stable hay for the others so that they got on to

---

[2] I mention Captain Marryat here because Strindberg had a great fondness for this now almost forgotten writer of such delightful books as *Masterman Ready*, *Peter Simple*, and *Jacob Faithful*.

their feet and could be let out into the woods. Constantly on the go, he saw to everything, did the work of two himself, and had a knack of making the hands set to which defied all resistance" (EHS, 60).

Despite the rapid narrative pace, Strindberg allows himself to linger lovingly on things, on the sensuous surface of reality. Admittedly, this keen attention to things at times tends to degenerate into a mere catalogue of words, particularly for the reader who is not familiar with the names of shorebirds, fish, or various forms of fishing gear, but at its best, as in the following interior, it becomes a form of delicate impressionism. This is how the inquisitive and highly perceptive Carlsson takes in the widow's parlor:

A fire was burning in the cottage parlour, and the white deal table was covered by a clean cloth. On the cloth stood a bottle of schnapps, waisted in the middle like an hourglass, and around it a coffee service of Gustavsberg china, in a pattern of roses and forget-me-nots. A newly baked loaf, crisp rusks, a butter dish, sugar basin and cream jug completed the table arrangements which, to Carlsson, had a look of prosperity about it that he had not expected, here at the back of the beyond. There was nothing amiss with the cottage either, as he appraised it in the flaming glow from the fire that mingled with the light of the candle in its brass holder, shone on the hazy polish of the mahogany bureau, was reflected in the varnished case and brass pendulum of the clock on the wall, sparkled on the inlaid silver on the long damascened barrels of the guns, and outlined the gilt lettering of the backs of sermon- and hymnbooks, almanacs, and Farmers' Calendars. (27)

The hero of this comic novel is, as we may expect, a bit of a rogue, a man schooled in the life of hard knocks, a man looking for his main chance, a "room at the top." Among Strindberg's heroes, he is unique. He is without self-consciousness and inner conflicts, and although he is an outsider and thus not rooted in a definite milieu as are the other characters in the novel, he is not meant to typify our modern rootlessness. Carlsson's last and least worry is the question of who he really is or where he belongs. Though born "of somewhat uncertain parentage" he is no Ishmael, lamenting his homelessness. On the contrary, his lack of roots has provided him a rich fund of experience and many skills. As a result he has, as Strindberg puts it, "acquired a certain flexibility of temper and the gift of adapting himself to different conditions and to all kinds of people, of understanding their intentions, reading their thoughts and guessing their secret wishes" (60–61). To Strindberg, tormented by the problem of identity and living in exile in Switzerland, the good Carlsson may, in fact, have loomed as something of an ideal, the intellectual's nostalgic image of the simple and uncomplicated life.

Two letters illustrate the author's conception of Carlsson. In October of 1887 Strindberg writes to Axel Lundegård:

Sad and tired, harassed, hunted like a wild animal, last August I sat down at my writing desk to amuse myself. Wrote: the story of a farmhand, my summer memories of unforgettable days in the Stockholm archipelago (since I have had a lot of fun in my life, too). Banished the woman question, outlawed socialism, politics, all drivel, and decided to make a Swedish and an amusing and a broad, droll book, showing how a farmhand with sound nerves and a good temper, without gall, moves through life, taking what was offered, letting go without tears what he was unable to keep.[3]

In another letter, to August Lindberg in April of 1889, Strindberg has this to say about Carlsson: "Carlsson is, after all, an enterprising fellow. He came to Hemsö like a snowsquall on an April evening, his coat on all sorts of shoulders, ready to turn, unreliable, but exceedingly spirited, never unnerved, always knows his part, active, never passive." [4] In

---

[3] *Brev*, VI, 293.
[4] *Brev*, VII, 307.

Strindberg's characteristic shorthand, this is generous praise indeed, and we can only conclude that he harbored a great deal of admiration for Carlsson, who is here described as "characterless" in the best sense of the term.

The chief obstacle in Carlsson's path is the widow's son Gusten, and as soon as Carlsson has realized the possibilities of the situation in which a kind fate has placed him, he has to summon all his cleverness in order to come out on top in the inevitable conflict. Attempts have been made to view this struggle for the farm at Hemsö as a struggle for power of the kind Strindberg had outlined in his essay, "Psychic Murder," as a battle of the brains. There seems to be little or no basis for such a viewpoint. The conflict between Carlsson and Gusten is on a much more basic, less intellectual and psychological plane, and missing in it is the most characteristic feature of this type of mental warfare: the vibrating atmosphere that is due to a heightened awareness, in which every glance, every gesture, every nuance of speech is immediately registered in the consciousness.

One aspect of the problem discussed in the essay is suggested in *The People of Hemsö*: the dangers of isolation. Realizing the importance of his remaining aloof from the other servants at Hemsö, Carlsson quickly concentrates his efforts on obtaining his own room. Once installed in his attic room, he feels disturbed by the oppressive silence, grows suspicious of "the others," has difficulties in sleeping, and indulges himself in delusions of grandeur. His first evening in his own room is described in the following manner:

That evening, however, when he had come up to the attic, pulled down the blind, and lighted his candle, he began to feel a trifle depressed at being alone. A sort of fear of those from whom he had cut himself off came over him. Up to now he had always been accustomed to being a member of a flock, always prepared to hear himself spoken to, always sure of a listener when he wanted to chat. Now everything around him was oppressively silent, so silent indeed that, from sheer force of habit, he expected to be spoken to and imagined that he heard voices where there were none; and his head, which up to now had rid itself of ideas by means of the spoken word, began to fill with a surplus of unused seeds of thought, which germinated and swelled and tried to escape, in any form whatsoever, making him restless and irritable, and denying him the relaxation of sleep. (58)

Nevertheless, Carlsson's ultimate defeat is not to be attributed to his succumbing to the effects of isolation. His sanity is never threatened. He was simply a man who tried to rise in the world and failed. He used his wits as best he could, and he almost succeeded. He had two weaknesses which brought about his downfall: he was a landlubber awkward at sea, and he had an all too human weakness for the fair sex.

The most unique feature of *The People of Hemsö*, when viewed in relation to Strindberg's other novels, is therefore also the fact that the hero's defeat is without larger, tragic implications. The hero's downfall does not imply a larger defeat, the male's defeat in the battle against the female, the ego's defeat in the battle against the id, or man's defeat in his battle against the gods. The hero's downfall is simply an episode in the everlasting struggle for life, as inevitable as events in nature, for a man is sooner or later bound to commit acts of folly, as he is sooner or later bound to cede his place to a younger man.

What this means is that Strindberg, at least for the time being, has adopted a viewpoint that is both comic and naturalistic. In most varieties of the comic mode, the author, as Northrop Frye has observed, normally adopts the viewpoint of society against the hero, who appears as a rogue or a fool.[5] In Strindberg's novels the opposite is almost always

---

[5] Northrop Frye, *Anatomy of Criticism* (New York: Atheneum, 1966), pp. 43 f.

the case: he adopts the viewpoint of his hero against society. The hero's sufferings are customarily inflicted on him by an unjust and immoral society. In some novels, notably in *The Scapegoat* and in *Progress*, the hero's sufferings are not the result of what he has done, but simply of what he is.

But in *The People of Hemsö* Strindberg, in a rare mood of acceptance, sides with society against the hero. This does not mean that the author condemns him from a moral point of view. On the contrary, at the end of the novel he has the Pastor defend Carlsson when Gusten seems eager to judge him too harshly. What it does mean is that Strindberg has adopted a point of view from which the individual self is less important. Carlsson was a man who tried and failed, that is all there is to it. From a naturalistic point of view, his story is only an insignificant episode in the struggle of life, for life goes on. This naturalistic perspective is also strengthened by the seasonal pattern on which the plot structure is built. For although the novel covers a time span of about three years, the central episodes are focused on the seasons, each of which assumes a particular significance. Thus Carlsson arrives in spring, the time of new hopes and ambitions; the summer brings success, outwardly symbolized in the wedding; the fall brings crisis and disappointment; the winter spells death and defeat.

Carlsson's death is, consequently, not a tragic incident, nor is it an illustration of the moral lesson embedded in Gusten's "He got no more than he deserved" (214). It is only an incident in the chain of life; the old making room for the young. How unsentimental is the caption (already quoted; see p. 84) of the last chapter! And how free from any pathos the last lines of the novel, describing how the new master of Hemsö sails home to the farm that is now his: "And at the helm of his boat, the new master of Hemsö was rowed home by his men, to pilot his own craft across life's windy bays, and through its green and sheltered narrows" (220). The uniqueness of *The People of Hemsö* among Strindberg's novels is the result of this rare combination of a point of view that is at once broadly comic and naturalistic with a tone that is totally free of pathos and indignation.[6]

---

[6] In his remarkable study of Strindberg's imagery Karl-Åke Kärnell has also demonstrated the extent to which Strindberg has invariably linked the images to the setting. This harmony of milieu and metaphor is not only "unrivaled in Swedish literature," according to Kärnell, but also the best proof of the radical effort that Strindberg has made to adopt the islanders' own point of view, their own way of seeing (*Strindbergs bildspråk* [Stockholm: Almqvist och Wiksell, 1962], pp. 211–224).

⟶ 6. The Defense of a Fool

In *The People of Hemsö* the major theme, the quest for identity, temporarily recedes into the background, only to return in a more intensified form in the novels immediately following it. In the earlier novels we have observed the hero's efforts to relate himself to a meaningful order, either of a social or a philosophical nature. In the novels with which we are now confronted, the hero's sense of identity is threatened by forces both from without and from within, in a world in which the relationship between the self and the other is envisioned as a form of psychological warfare, a battle of the brains.

The best introduction to these novels is also, without doubt, the brilliant and provocative essay, "Psychic Murder," written in 1887 (22, 188–201). In this essay Strindberg argues that our age has seen the age-old struggle for power among human beings develop into a psychological conflict. In the

old days, he says, men destroyed each other by physical violence. In the modern age they achieve their aim by the development of other, infinitely more sophisticated means: by
robbing their fellowmen of all feelings of self-assurance and
self-esteem, by robbing them of their sense of integrity and
identity. They do this by means of what Strindberg calls
"psychic murder," that is, by means of hypnotism and suggestion, by the use of mass media and the pressures of public
opinion. "In the old days," says Strindberg, "you killed your
opponent in an argument without having convinced him,
nowadays you create a majority against him, 'convince him
that he is wrong,' unmask his intentions, attribute other intentions to him than he has, rob him of his means of sub-
sistence, deny him social prestige, make him ridiculous, in
one word, torture and lie him to death or drive him mad
instead of killing him." Such an innocent phrase as "to kill
by silence" hides a crime of enormous proportions.

Since public opinion nowadays has the monopoly on
truth the norm is the average. "Any man who is above or
below average, is considered 'not quite right in the head.' "
Galileo was mad when he insisted, contrary to the generally
accepted view of his day, that the earth revolved around the
sun. To remain sane is to refrain from thinking along independent lines, for then one runs the danger of being considered mad. Those who have the strongest faith in themselves are also those who do not think. According to the
English psychologist Maudsley, says Strindberg, individual
happiness requires either an adjustment to the ways of the
world or a rare combination of strength and power. Failing
either of these, the individual will "lose his sanity, commit
suicide, become a criminal, or end in poverty." Isolation,
withdrawal from the group, will not solve the problem, for
it too leads to the loss of sanity. "To stand alone with one's
view is as dangerous as to have enemies everywhere, as to

be subjugated, imprisoned." Isolation produces fear, suspiciousness, and persecution mania, and

from the lack of a yardstick, from the inability to appraise the relative magnitude of one's own ego, there soon easily arises overestimation—megalomania or underestimation—micromania. . . . Finally the cerebrum or self-consciousness loses all its power, all its ability, to meet and to judge the dangers, all control over the impulses; and now the motor and sensory nerves react to the first impressions. False causal connections, erroneous ideas, conclusions without sufficient foundation, optical and auditory hallucinations, and in the end rage or a perpetual defensive mania, expressed in aggression, soon manifest themselves.

In his essay Strindberg gives a number of illustrations of psychic murders: the actor who foolishly signs a ten-year contract and is "murdered" by not being given any roles that suit his talents; the writer who engages himself in a political campaign, is paid for his article, but finds it stuffed away in the editor's desk until the election is over; the novelist whose manuscript is made to disappear, thus bringing confusion and disorder in his mind.

But Strindberg's essay was written "apropos of *Rosmersholm*," and it is Ibsen's drama that supplies him with the best illustration of this modern form of murder. Labeling Rebecka "an unconscious cannibal who devoured the former wife's soul," Strindberg argues that Mrs. Rosmer suspected (with justice!) that Rebecka had plans to usurp her place in the home, and that Rebecka turned the table on Mrs. Rosmer by making the latter believe that she was suffering from "suspiciousness," a suspiciousness that was then aggravated by the wife's failure to find proof of Rebecka's intentions. Rebecka used the power of suggestion to make the weaker mind believe it was sick and then convinced Mrs. Rosmer or made her believe that death was "bliss."

Shakespeare's *Othello*, in which Iago murders Othello without having to use either a sword or a dagger but simply by means of awakening his suspiciousness, offers a close parallel to *Rosmersholm*, as Strindberg observes.

There are two kinds of defense against this type of psychic murder. One is isolation, withdrawal from society. The other is dissimulation, the conscious wearing of a mask. As we have observed, isolation is fraught with hazards and affords no safe avenue of escape. To don a mask is safer, but the danger is there. In modern life, says Strindberg, it has become necessary to hide one's intentions; dissimulation has become an instinct for survival. The smartest, the most successful man, is the man who is best able to mask his real intentions. This does not mean that human beings are conscious and deliberate villains: the instinct to lie and to pretend is mostly unconscious and automatic, fostered by necessity. To be truthful, to appear as one really is, to say what one thinks, is dangerous to life, like handling over one's weapon to the enemy. The oldest civilizations, says Strindberg, are also the most sophisticated when it comes to the mastery of deliberate dissimulation. Europeans, by comparison, are still naïve, and Americans have, according to Strindberg, regressed to the primitive violence of the revolver!

Even the man who is sincere must therefore play a role, don a mask. In the gallery of masks there is a wide assortment at his disposal, but Strindberg mentions only a few, and those few are all masks of the madman. The fool of the Middle Ages was such a seeming madman, granted freedom from responsibility and thus able to speak the truth in a very blunt manner. In reality towering far above his surroundings in intelligence, he pretended to be an idiot.

The humorist is another mask, for by laughing at his own weaknesses he prevents others from criticizing him, making others, in fact, into accessories to his own crime.

The dangers of this kind of dissimulation are broached in the concluding analysis of Hamlet's mask as a madman. Hamlet pretends to be mad in order to be able to express his thoughts and at the same time carry on his investigations. But in so doing, says Strindberg, "Hamlet committed psychic suicide, because in the end he lost his power of judgment and his will." By always dissimulating, by always wearing a mask, the individual runs the risk of losing his sense of identity by getting the roles confused. As a defense against psychic murder, "Hamletism" is, consequently, fraught with the danger of what Strindberg calls "psychic suicide."

The significance of this remarkable essay may not be immediately apparent. Nevertheless, besides anticipating the themes of the novels to follow, it lays the psychological foundation on which they are structured. The emphasis on the dangers of isolation, and of "Hamletism" in particular, suggests what the novels themselves so clearly reveal, that the real conflict is within, between conflicting aspects of the self, and that the hero's problem is, consequently, a problem of psychic integration. For whether these extraordinary psychological novels explore the effects of isolation (as in *Tschandala* and *By the Open Sea*), or an almost clinical case of hysteria (as in *A Witch*), or "Hamletism" (as in *The Defense of a Fool* and *The Romantic Organist*), they all demonstrate Strindberg's concept of the self in conflict.

In *The Son of a Servant* there is a strikingly noticeable gap covering the momentous years 1875 and 1876 when Strindberg met and fell passionately in love with the actress Siri von Essen. In line with his "scientific" approach to autobiography, Strindberg wrote to his publisher and suggested that he simply issue an additional volume consisting of the correspondence exchanged between himself and Siri during those years.[1] Nothing came of this project, for Albert Bonnier

---

[1] *Brev*, V, 357.

was reluctant, and the passionate love letters were not printed until 1919.[2]

The stormy marriage was rapidly approaching its dissolution, and by the fall of 1887 Strindberg decided that he had better write a different type of book about his marriage, a book in which he would tell the truth to the world. With his belief in an international conspiracy among European womanhood, he felt it necessary to tell his story before he would be silenced by some devious scheme. In particular he felt that there was a plot under way to make the world at large believe that he was insane. The result of his efforts to plead his case was *En dåres försvarstal* (*The Defense of a Fool*), a novel that has had a strange publishing history.

Strindberg wrote the novel in French, and entitled it *Le plaidoyer d'un fou.* The novel was completed in the spring of 1888, but the French edition was not published until 1895. The first edition in print was the German translation by Emil Schering in 1893. A Swedish edition of the novel did not appear until 1914 in a translation by John Landquist.[3] The most readable and most easily obtainable Swedish version of the novel today is the new translation from the French by Tage Aurell, published in 1962.[4]

There is also an old English edition of the novel, a poor translation from Schering's German version which gives a totally misleading impression of the nature of the book.[5] Schering entitled his German version *Die Beichte eines Toren,* and the English translator obediently rendered *The*

---

[2] Published under the title *Han och hon* (*He and She*), they are included in *Samlade skrifter,* vol. 55.

[3] *Ibid.,* vol. 26.

[4] *En dåres försvarstal,* trans. Tage Aurell (Stockholm: Bonniers, 1962).

[5] *Confession of a Fool,* trans. Ellie Schleussner (London: Stephen Swift, 1912).

Confession of a Fool. Somehow the word *confession* has stuck to the novel, which is absurd, for it is certainly not a confession; it is an impassioned *defense.*

Sven Rinman has called *The Defense of a Fool* "one of the most remarkable novels in modern European literature," adding the important reservation "provided one reads it as a novel about fictitious persons." [6] This should no longer be difficult. But that it was difficult for Strindberg's contemporaries to do so is understandable. They were too close to the sordid reality, and they could not help but feel that Strindberg in publishing this account of his marriage was simply washing his dirty laundry in public, disgracing his wife, and making a fool of himself. Much discussion of the book has consequently tended to focus on the question of whether Strindberg's allegations against his wife were true or not. Even the late Martin Lamm read the novel as a work of nonfiction, completely ignoring the elements of aesthetic distance, simply referring to the hero as Strindberg and to the heroine as Siri. Naturally he found the book exaggerated, confused, and contradictory.[7]

In his book *Strindberg og hans første hustru* Harry Jacobsen has shown how unreasonable it would be to consider *The Defense of a Fool* as a true account of Strindberg's marriage.[8] In 1886 Strindberg himself also argued, we recall, that if he were to write a novel based on the letters mentioned above it would be untrue, because it would be seen entirely from his present point of view. But five years later he insists that the novel is about his marriage and that "it is a frightful

[6] *Ny illustrerad svensk litteraturhistoria,* ed. E. N. Tigerstedt (Stockholm: Natur och Kultur, 1957), IV, 70.

[7] Martin Lamm, *August Strindberg* (2d ed.; Stockholm: Bonniers, 1948), pp. 146–150.

[8] Harry Jacobsen, *Strindberg og hans første hustru* (Copenhagen: Gyldendal, 1946).

book; but it is true." By "true" he means, as a following parenthesis indicates, true to the actual situation.[9] At a somewhat later date he wonders if the novel does not perhaps lack general significance, since it was written in self-defense, but goes on to argue that after all it deals with some vital problems of wide general interest: the problems of paternity, the battle of the sexes, sexual perversion, among others.[10]

What these remarks clearly reveal is Strindberg's confusion about the nature of truth in the arts, a confusion that seems to persist also in the minds of some of his critics. What matters in a work of art is truth to the human heart, not fidelity to an actual situation. And Strindberg should have no worries on that score. He somehow instinctively made great literature out of his personal experiences. *The Defense of a Fool* is no exception. It has high merit if read as a work of fiction. One function of criticism is, as D. H. Lawrence put it, to save the tale from its author, to read it without being prejudiced by the author's conscious intentions. This approach seems a proper one in this case and it pays large dividends.

We might remark at this point that Strindberg has made some attempts to achieve a degree of aesthetic distance. He wrote the novel in French, gave fictional names to his protagonists, and added a few odd prefaces. But these are ineffective devices, barely disguising the fact that it is his own marriage he is writing about.

Much more important for our purpose is the fact that the novel has a single and consistent point of view, that of the first-person narrator, for it is the use of this point of view which contributes the element of irony that is at the heart and center of this strange novel. *The Defense of a Fool*, as it turns out, belongs to the genre of the psychological novel

---

[9] *Brev*, VIII, 188.
[10] *Ibid.*, p. 266.

which Henry James was introducing in these years and Ford
Madox Ford and others were later to perfect. I refer to such
novels as *The Turn of the Screw* and *The Good Soldier*. Psychological novels of this type, in which a single point of view
is rigidly observed, bear, as Leon Edel has shown, a considerable similarity to the detective novel, a literary form that
was soon to engage Strindberg's interest, that is, after he had
discovered Edgar Allan Poe in the fall of 1888. As the detective sets about his investigations and presents his evidence to
the reader, so the first-person narrator of these novels invites
the reader to fathom the truth with him, and the reader is
encouraged to accept him in good faith. The intellectual excitement of the detective novel and the attentive interest with
which we follow the account of the narrator in the novel with
a single point of view are attributable to the same motivation:
we want to discover whether the narrator, or the detective,
is a reliable witness, a question to be answered only by in-
trinsic evidence. Such novels must be read with a good deal
of attention, for behind the story that is told is another story,
the story to be deduced. As readers we have to become amateur detectives, or we might well miss the central irony of
the novel.[11]

The narrator of Strindberg's novel is a Swedish writer
living in exile in central Europe. We know only his first name,
Axel. He suspects that his wife, having succeeded in isolating
him from the world, is trying slowly to kill him, with the
result that he feels he is losing his mind. In self-defense he
begins an investigation, a criminal investigation, in the pursuit of which he says he is going to use the most advanced
and scientific methods of detection as well as all his knowledge of psychology. By this investigation he hopes to prove
his innocence, to demonstrate his sanity, and to unmask the

---

[11] Leon Edel, *The Psychological Novel*, 1900–1950 (New York:
Lippincott, 1955), pp. 72 f.

real criminal, his wife, who is trying to kill him by the method we now know as psychic murder.

The irony of the narrator's tale is that it demonstrates the opposite of what he had intended. The detective discloses his own crime. In the introduction to the book Axel appeals to the reader to judge "this honest book," to determine whether it could possibly be considered the fruit of a lunatic's monomania (TA, 24). The verdict goes against him, for it is, alas, a madman's story. In the introduction he promises that the reader in following his story may discover "some elements of the physiology of love, some contributions to psychopathology, and, in the bargain, a curious fragment from the philosophy of crime" (24). This promise is fulfilled, but the pathological case bared by the narrator is his own. His exposé has become an unintentional self-revelation. An investigation of a supposed attempt at psychic murder has turned into an act of psychic suicide.

To what extent Strindberg himself was aware of the narrator's deception is of course difficult to know. In view of the fact that he wrote the novel in self-defense we might suspect that he was unaware of the fact. But then we must recognize that Strindberg often demonstrates an uncanny ability to regard himself from two points of view, from within and from without, both subjectively and with a remarkable degree of detatchment. *The Defense of a Fool* exhibits this blend of the two points of view, which contributes to its compelling power, its grotesque albeit unconscious comedy.

In this context the use of the word "fool" in the title of the novel is of particular interest, for it serves to emphasize the ambiguity of Strindberg's point of view. The word has two meanings in Strindberg's usage: it is synonymous with "idealist" and it is synonymous with "clown" or "jester." In its first meaning, it points to a man who has been tricked or duped, cruelly deceived. In its second meaning, it points to a man who is consciously acting the part of the fool. Now it is clear that Axel fits both categories, for, on the one hand, he is trying to portray himself as a man who in his innocence has been duped by a wicked and scheming woman, and, on the other hand, he is trying to depict himself as the man who is consciously playing the part of the fool in order to unmask his enemy and take revenge on her. In the former role, Strindberg is busy pleading his side of the case, that is, he is passionately involved in a matter of vital concern to himself; in the latter role he is performing the role of the dispassionate psychologist analyzing a case of "Hamletism." For his fool is like Hamlet pretending to be mad in order to be able to carry on the investigations that will make it possible for him to apprehend the criminal and to take his revenge. And like Hamlet he falls prey to the hazards of this kind of dissimulation, that is, he loses his power of judgment and his will. The fool who pretends to be a madman is ironically transformed into one.

Since it is the psychological analysis of a case of psychic suicide which makes *The Defense of a Fool* so interesting a novel, let us concentrate our attention on this aspect by following the steps whereby the fool is transformed into a madman.

In the preface the author speaks of his favorable impression of Axel, the narrator of the novel. The narrator left him, says Strindberg, with an impression of "absolute trustworthiness" (11). As critical readers we must ask ourselves whether this impression is justified by Axel's performance. Is he a reliable witness? The answer is a definite no. While Axel's account of the first year of his and his future wife's relationship is dramatic and sweeps us along with a steadily increasing tempo, the testimony is not convincing. Unwittingly Axel begins to paint his own portrait, becoming much more fascinating than the suspected criminal, his wife. Axel

is too contradictory, too vacillating, too impressionable, too
influenced by his feelings of the moment to be able to give
a trustworthy account of the past.

His testimony is conflicting indeed. One moment he
wants us to believe that Maria is exceedingly beautiful, the
next he tries to convince us that she is ugly. One minute
she is angelic, the next she is a vulgar coquette flirting las-
civiously with all men. One day she is a suffering martyr, a
saint, the next she is a witch trapping unsuspecting men in
her snares.

Though Axel accuses Maria of constant dissimulation it
is actually he who is always playing different roles (40). One
minute he portrays himself in the throes of passion, unable
to control his actions, the next he is the deliberate and artful
seducer carefully setting the stage for his conquest. One moment he is the innocent Joseph defending his virginity, the
next he is the wolf ready to swallow Little Red Riding Hood.
One day he presides at Saturnalian revelries dedicated to
Bacchus and Venus, the next he is a prude whose hair rises
because a young lady has made an immodest proposal to him
(she merely suggested that they go for a walk in the woods!)
(50).

Even more disturbing is a pathological trait in his character: his conscious awareness of a perverse need to make
Maria into a madonna, into a mother image that he can
then defile. He wants, in other words, to commit incest, but
in addition, he wants to commit an act of sacrilege, for his
madonna is, in fact, also a substitute for the God he has lost.

The young Axel, age twenty-eight, and by profession a
librarian, is a pessimistic and nihilistic young man, who has
become utterly disillusioned as a result of his failure as a
playwright. Having lost his illusions, including his religious
faith, he lives a hedonistic life, taking his pleasures where
he can find them, mostly in casual affairs, or with prosti-

tutes. But from his first meeting with Maria he begins to worship her as a "virgin-mother" (35). She quickly becomes an object of his compelling need to worship something or someone:

The vacuum left by a banished religiosity was filled: the need to worship was resurrected in a new form. God was expelled, Woman took his place, but woman as both virgin and mother; for when I regarded the little daughter by her side I could not believe that this birth had been possible. The thought of the intimacy between man and wife never produced the image of any sensual contact, to that degree their intercourse seemed incorporeal to me. From this moment this woman appeared as the incarnation of a soul, pure, unattainable, dressed in the virtuous body in which the Holy Writ is pleased to shroud deceased souls. In short, I idolized her against my will.[12] (41)

The worship of this woman assumes the same form as the worship of the God he had banished: "I wanted to worship, to sacrifice myself, to suffer without the hope ever to attain anything but the pleasure of adoration, sacrifice, suffering" (42). From now on his person is "consecrated" to her (48). Those who do not know his love are "heretics" (48), and again and again Maria appears as the madonna. In his apartment he arranges a portrait of her and her child surrounded by flowers, flowers that he carefully cultivates for the purpose of his "secret worship of the Madonna and the child" (58). His apartment is a "consecrated temple" (82). He also enjoys playing the role of being her little boy, as she seemingly enjoys playing the role of mother, taking care of him when he is sick (100).

Not surprisingly Maria cannot live up to this admittedly unattainable ideal, and after she proves willing to commit adultery Axel begins to see her as vulgar and coquettish, and is gripped by the need to defile the fallen madonna by re-

---

[12] Cf. also *The Son of a Servant* (19, 235–236).

ducing the nature of their relationship to a purely sexual affair between two human beings in the throes of desire. Thus as the statue of the madonna begins "to totter" (58, 62), he begins increasingly to speak of being "in heat," this expression being his particular favorite (100, 111, 114). He is no longer the master of himself and his actions: he is like an "elk in heat" (95). He is like a "masked male," and she is a "female in heat" (100).

The consummation of this strange relationship occurs, finally, not in the open air as the heated language would almost make one expect, but in Axel's apartment, the "consecrated temple," because the madonna has to be properly defiled. On the table is a basket of flowers and two lit candles, "all arranged like an altar," and under her feet is a book of poems with an image of Luther (!) on the cover of the leather binding. With a rose in her hair, Maria overcomes him with her beauty: "She appears to me like an overwhelming church painting." She is "chaste like an angel." But with pleasure he notes: "The idol is tottering, she shall fall" (132–133).

Afterward he thinks of her as a witch who has put him under a spell: "the hypnosis of the reproductive instinct" (151–153). Yet he loves her, and his account ends with this strange question: "Are my feelings perverse because I find pleasure in making love to my mother? Is it the unconscious incest of the heart?" (154).

Clearly this man is not a trustworthy narrator. He has the frightful lucidity of a madman, and the pathological case he is analyzing is his own, not his wife's. Without knowing it he is also busy pronouncing a verdict on his own actions.

As Axel's account of the marriage progresses, the lucidity with which he has hitherto revealed his own motives disappears, and he seems at times totally unaware of the motives that guide his actions. The attempted cool and scientific investigation deteriorates as his fear and hatred mount. The pace increases rapidly, years being covered in a few pages. The imagery grows increasingly grotesque. And finally Axel reaches the stage described in the essay "Psychic Murder" as he begins to indulge in "false causal connections, erroneous ideas, conclusions without sufficient foundation, optical and auditory hallucinations" (22, 190).

His "cool and lascivious Madonna" has now become a born slut and a whore, a vulgar and coquettish actress, and, as it turns out, a Lesbian in the bargain (TA, 157, 178). She has grown fat and ugly drinking five hundred bottles of beer a month, while Axel gets nothing to eat, the best cuts going to a giant mastiff dog, a veritable Cerberus who also blocks the door to her bedroom leaving poor Axel out in the cold. Without Axel being aware of the fact his exaggerations, grotesque as they are, begin at this point to produce a decidedly ludicrous effect.

In the meantime Maria is also supposedly at work undermining Axel's reputation, yes, his very sanity. She spreads rumors about him to the effect that he is mad, impotent, and ought to be locked up. She is pictured as a vampire drawing all his strength, as a female spider ready to swallow the male after she has been fertilized by him.

The climax is grotesque in its absurdity. Axel's suspicions about Maria's adultery mount, and he finally must have proof. His search for a chain of circumstantial evidence is farcical. In an album at the hotel he finds a series of caricatures of well-known Scandinavian artists. Among them is his own portrait, and on his forehead is a horn cleverly arranged by one of his curly locks (242). From this he draws the conclusion that all the world knows his wife has been unfaithful to him. A drama by a famous Norwegian bluestocking affords another piece of evidence. The portrait of the photographer Hjalmar Ekdahl in *The Wild Duck* is of course a portrait of Axel, for, as a writer of *romans à clef,* has he not been labeled a photographer? (244). Comical despite its grotesqueness is also the scene in which Axel after one of his attempts to use hypnotism in order to obtain some sort of confession from Maria sits down in front of the mirror while she gently massages his scalp. As he looks into the mirror he sees her face, "a deathly pale ghost studying my features in terror and with wildly staring eyes." Axel thinks this proves her guilt. But all indications point rather to the fact that she has discovered that her husband is a madman (263).

Ready to murder Maria, Axel finally decides to do so in a "psychic" manner, by going away in order to write a novel about her. In the process he turns into a veritable demon, for unable to endure the life of isolation he returns to Maria and the children to live with them while collecting the material for the book. He has become a literary vampire (274). The closing lines of the book complete his unmasking, for he suddenly reveals that his motive for writing the book is revenge: "The story is ended, my Love. I have had my revenge; we are even."

Ironically, the scientific and dispassionate investigator of the truth has unmasked his real motive, the passionate search for revenge, and, having sought to defend his sanity, he has, in fact, demonstrated his madness. For in seeking to unmask his antagonist, he has instead revealed his own inner contradictions and conflicts, his own unconscious motives.

Like *The Father,* which it resembles in so many respects, *The Defense of a Fool* demonstrates that the battle of the brains, here manifested as the war of sexes, is, in effect, a representation in symbolic form of the conflict between warring aspects of the psyche. For Maria, Axel's antagonist, is not at all individualized. She is depicted in the twin symbolic roles of woman so recurrent in the literature of the nineteenth century: as mother, and as seductress. In the role of the mother, she is the source of unqualified affection and the object of religious worship, a substitute for the lost God. In the role of seductress, she is the femme fatale, seeking to trap or to weaken the male.

In either role, woman is regarded as a symbol of a more primitive state of development than that represented by the male. As the mother she represents the origin of things, the return to a state of dependency, the unconscious. As a seductress she is more in harmony with nature, more sensuous, more irrational, more capricious. In either role, she poses a threat to the male whose function it is to carry the burden of rational thought.

Regarded in the light of this symbolism, which we might recognize as both Romantic and Freudian, the war of the sexes depicted in *The Defense of a Fool* is transformed into a conflict between the conscious and the unconscious.[13] As in *The Father*, the struggle between the male and the female is, in reality, a conflict between reason and the irrational will, between the head and the heart, between the ego and the id. In *The Father* the Captain's final collapse and death in the arms of the Nurse represents the total victory of the irrational; in *The Defense of a Fool* Axel's psychic suicide suggests a widening split within the self.

Profound ambiguity, ironic tension, and deep psychological insight are the main virtues of this passionate and extraordinary love story. With the appearance in recent years, not only of a new French edition of the novel, but also of a new and excellent English translation, it should, it is hoped, at last achieve the recognition it so justly deserves.[14] Judging

---

[13] Philip Rieff, *Freud: The Mind of the Moralist* (New York: Anchor Books, 1961), pp. 196–198, 202.

[14] Evert Sprinchorn's new translation into English, A *Madman's Defense* (New York: Anchor Books, 1967), also contains a brilliant critical introduction.

from the following excerpts from the enthusiastic reviews of two influential French critics, this day should not be far off:

A book that prefigures Freud and existentialism. Schizophrenia, the disease of our century, is here. Here, too, is the modern game of ambiguity: who is lying? who is mad? who is wrong? which one the executioner and which one the victim?

.   .   .   .

One of the masterpieces of world literature. . . . A prophetic book that contains in embryonic form the power of all the present-day conflicts of love and of alienation. You must read Strindberg: he is still our contemporary, and, sad to say, more *present* among us than a great number of our "living" writers.[15]

---

[15] *Ibid.*, p. xxvi. The excerpts are cited in the original French in Sven Rinman's article, "En dåres försvarstal," *Svensk litteratur-tidskrift*, 2 (1965), 75.

⤙ 7. The Romantic Organist

THE SHORT NOVEL *Den romantiske klockaren
på Rånö* (*The Romantic Organist*) which Strindberg submitted to his publisher on July 2, 1888, is one of his most
interesting works of fiction. It might have been a masterpiece, but unfortunately there is a distinct falling off in the
last three of the nine chapters. Nevertheless, even the weak
final chapters cannot obscure the power of the earlier ones,
nor can the sudden shift of the attitude to the hero, the
unexpected unmasking of his real motives, erase the wonderful portrait so lovingly drawn in the first chapters. Alrik Lundstedt, the romantic organist, is perhaps Strindberg's most delightful character creation.

It is evident that the novel in the process of writing
turned out differently than Strindberg had planned. In a
letter to Bonnier the author notes that the novel had been
intended as "a trivial portrait of an uninteresting organist

fellow, but has grown into something far more." [1] Bonnier
had raised some critical objections in regard to the last chapters, arguing that the story of the murder and the organist's
feelings of guilt had been introduced so suddenly and so unexpectedly that the total effect was one of contrivance. As he
did so often Strindberg refuses to discuss Bonnier's well-
founded criticism, insisting that there is nothing wrong with
the novel, and that he is not going to change a word. In the
same letter he also makes a candid statement about his artistic credo: "And I believe that the writer in the feverish
excitement is guided right, even if he afterward in a sober
state feels that things could be different. That is why I hardly
ever dare to make changes, and when I have made changes
I have ruined things. Summa summarum: what I have written, I have written!"

Alrik Lundstedt is a poet and a dreamer, a man who
is happy because he possesses the ability to transform reality
into a world of fairy tale and myth more pleasing to his
fancy. Strindberg suddenly reveals that Alrik's fantasies are
motivated by a need to repress his memories of an experience
in the past, an experience that has left him with feelings of
guilt. His fantasies are a flight from reality. While Bonnier
had objected that the nature of the ugly experience is never
made clear to the reader, Strindberg rightly argues that there
is no need to be specific on this point: "The end contains
the motivation, and it seems to me a virtue that the crime
is not more precisely indicated; the main thing is that there
was a corpse buried somewhere, no matter which."

It is in chapter six that Alrik Lundstedt's playful imagination is confronted for the first time with an aspect of
reality which it is unable to transform at will. Thus the precarious foundation on which Alrik's world is built is exposed.
Having obtained a position as an organist on a small island
in the outer skerries, Alrik meets a woman whose appearance

[1] *Brev*, VII, 103.

suddenly reactivates in his memory an experience that he thought he had buried deep in his mind. An expression in her eyes, a fleeting gesture, these have reminded Alrik of his mother. He returns home feeling that his whole existence is suddenly threatened.

It is at this point in the story that Strindberg suddenly becomes a psychological analyst, revealing the motives underlying Alrik's need to transform reality in his imagination. We learn that Alrik was born on a little island in the outer skerries, the youngest child in a family seemingly devoted to a life on the borderline of crime. When Alrik was still a child his mother died, and public opinion would have it that she was in fact murdered.

All the other children having left home, Alrik lived with his taciturn father, and it was during these years that he learned "to play." This was a result partly of his loneliness, combined with the barren, uninspiring natural surroundings, but mainly of a need to bury as deeply as possible everything connected with his mother's death:

What had happened during the difficult winter when the mother died seemed to require a burial in the young man's mind, a thick layer of earth and stone, a whole barrow of other memories to prevent it from arising again, and when the insignificant events of his drab and tedious life could not provide material quickly enough, he imagined events, lots of impressions, and heaped up fancies, visual and auditory delusions, into a thick layer that could cover the dark stain. And as soon as an impression had become a memory it had gained reality and was placed like a new rock on the barrow over the buried past, which was not to arise, and thus whatever was buried became as unreal or as real as that which had never happened, dissolved, evaporated, and was gone for long periods. (21, 245–246)

The tone of the novel changes here, for Strindberg suddenly ceases his earlier identification with Alrik, who is turned into a case history, his "playfulness" now suddenly labeled a form of self-deception born of anxiety and a sense of guilt. As a consequence of his need to bury the unpleasant memories of the past, says Strindberg, "a kind of instinct had originated with Alrik, an instinct to confuse the real and the unreal, a desire to deceive himself had been fostered, a need had been born not to run into any tangible reality that would recall the fatal reality that had one certain night appeared in his life, and the appearance of which in his memory was accompanied by a harrowing and piercing feeling of guilt." Alrik's behavior to other people is also attributed to his sense of fear. For fear of wounding anyone who might then turn into an enemy and unmask his guilt, Alrik has practically ceased to speak: he has become a listener whose facial gestures always give the speaker a feeling of being in the company of a very sympathetic person. Alrik's need to express his feelings and perceptions is instead satisfied by music, "in which he could tell his story without anyone being able to understand what he was saying or suspecting that he harbored a secret."

The incident at the manor, insignificant to all appearances, has now somehow recalled the buried past: "The whole stone mound of impressions he had thrown over the corpse caved in and the skeleton lay there, the cranium lay there, cracked by the icepick, and it was of no avail to try to imagine it gone; to confuse it with dreams, to play or read it away. He had been awakened and could not fall asleep again" (245–247).

Strindberg's contemporaries were not familiar with this type of unmasking and debunking. We who live in an age of psychoanalysis recognize the language. *The Romantic Organist* is a psychoanalytic fable. The hero is put on the couch, his fantasies turn out to be motivated by a need to repress guilt feelings, and so the hero is no more. While this approach has undoubtedly added a new dimension to Strindberg's novel, it has not improved it as a work of art. Bonnier's criticism is valid: Strindberg rips the mask off his hero's face too quickly, giving the unmasking the same sudden and brutal impact as in the much later Chamber plays. That Strindberg should suddenly reverse the hero's good fortune, and make the dreamer and idealist face reality, we are of course prepared for at this point, for that is a persistent theme in his novels, but what is unusual in *The Romantic Organist* is that the reversal comes so late and in so unexpected a manner.[2]

The problems inherent in the story are perhaps best explained by Strindberg's already quoted remark to the effect that the story grew into something more than he had originally intended.[3] His original intention was undoubtedly to write a psychological study of what he in the essay "Psychic Murder" had labeled "Hamletism." His study of the organist in the outer skerries was meant as a study of the "fabricated character," of the individual who has learned to play many roles, so as to prevent his "secret" from being discovered. In the process of such dissembling the individual may, as Strindberg observed, lose not only his power of judgment and will but also all sense of reality. The effects of such dissembling would in this case be aggravated by isolation. Strindberg also evidently had in mind portraying the happy but deluded fool whose happiness is based on a lie. In this sense he might have wished to depict another Hjalmar Ekdahl, which would not be surprising in view of the fact that he had just let the hero of *The Defense of a Fool* harbor

---

[2] A more conventional reversal of fortune has occurred earlier in the novel, at the moment when the arrival of Alrik's destitute father puts an end to Alrik's dream of remaining at the Academy of Music (21, 230).

[3] Originally intended as a short story to be included in a companion volume to *The People of Hemsö*, it grew into a short novel of almost seventy pages, divided into nine chapters.

the grotesque suspicion that Ibsen had caricatured him as the cuckolded husband in *The Wild Duck*.

What happened? My guess is that Strindberg, as the story progressed, found himself involved in the central problem for many writers, perhaps most of all for the Romantic writer: the problem of illusion and reality. For the Romantic organist, Alrik Lundstedt, is first a poet, and it is through language, through images, that he seeks to re-create the world to please his fancy. Alrik's fantasies do in fact center on an attempt to transform and to order the world, and by so doing to possess it, to master it, through likenesses. Let us make an attempt to follow Alrik's flights of fancy in some detail in order to illustrate the problem involved.

The opening pages of the novel give us a vignette of the young dreamer Alrik in a conventional Romantic pose. While the harvest moon shines on the idyllic little town of Trosa the young man, his chin resting on his hand, sits in his attic room watching the fantastic shapes assumed by the chimney covers as the wind moves them. In his mind they become a veritable witches sabbath, "the witches whirling in a dance with the dragons around the square pipe from which the smoke billowed forth as from an Easter bonfire" (193–194). The moon seems to smile good-naturedly at him, as if blessing his dreams and his new venture: his imminent departure for Stockholm where he is to study at the Academy of Music.

That his fancies are inspired not only by the moon we discover as the young man sets off for the capital in a carriage. Rocked by the rhythm of the carriage Alrik's "dreaming and playful disposition" is projected in vivid images:

And then he dreamed he was sitting on the Pleiades, riding toward the canopy of heaven where he heard a violin playing which had strings as long as the highway, sound posts as high as the mast trees and the bridges were of white china, and the north wind was the bow, resined by ice barks; and the violin played strains in new keys with three-quarter tones instead of halftones, and there was both E sharp and B sharp—he had always wondered what had happened to them, when God let man create the piano. (201–202)

As the carriage picks up speed going down a hill the musical metaphors are replaced by military ones. The sheaves of rye parade like troops on the battlefields, the mist in the hollows recalling the powder smoke after the battles of the day. To amuse himself Alrik plays that he is Napoleon speeding from the burning Moscow on a sled, the burning Moscow being the slowly setting moon behind a bell tower in the distance. With a somber glance he nods to his brave troops standing at attention along the highway (202–203).

Having played a Bach fugue on the organ and won the favor of his professor, Lundstedt is in seventh heaven. As he walks down the street he feels seven suns are shining in the sky, as if fire and light are radiating from his forehead, and as if the hearts of the people are warmed at the sight of the genius who is going to make them better and happier with his music. Everything in the city is an event staged in his honor. The prostitutes turn into beautiful damsels and the city is transformed into Venice as he travels across the water in a "gondola" (211–213).

Thus Alrik continuously transforms the world, letting his imagination paint it anew. He is the master of the world. But soon he encounters an object he is unable to transform: the great organ in Jacob's church. As the professor takes him into the interior of the great organ Lundstedt's imagination reels, and he has difficulties finding the similes that will put it within his grasp. But he tries. Thus the walk begins with the bellows which make him think of the lungs of a giant. As they rise higher they can see into the very framework or carcass, "spacious like the chest of a whale," the pipes and other parts turning into ribs and tendons and blood vessels and nerves. The organ is like a gigantic organism that seemingly

has needed a thousand years to develop; it represents a human work without an inventor like the cathedral, without
an architect like the pyramid, an enormous anonymous co-
operative effort of all Christianity. As it rises steeply it makes
him think of a mountain of stalactites. Alrik is gripped by
dizziness as he looks down at the tiny people in the pews,
but the professor smiles "like the tempter on the mountain
when he showed his beautiful world to the son of man." As
they descend Alrik feels as if he had been up in heaven
among the angels and seen Christ transfigured and light pre-
vail over darkness. Nevertheless, what disturbs him about the
great organ is that it "did not resemble any other thing in
nature or in art," and therefore he continues "to investigate
what he had seen, to relate its forms to other known ones
and thereby get closer to it, to bring it down to his level
and find peace." He is clear about the church: that is "the
primeval forest in which the heathens sacrificed people, the
pillars and the arches being trees and branches," but the
organ remained the organ. "It was not a plant, not an animal
—unless a coral—not a building—unless a mass of hanging
towers from medieval castles." He is unable to find the similes
that will satisfy his imagination. He remains overwhelmed by
the organ, but nevertheless as he sits beside the professor as
the latter plays it he gets the feeling that somehow "the
majesty of the organ elevated him, magnified him, added a
joint to his soul, as it were" (217–220).

In his imagination Alrik also envisions a romantic relationship with a young lady he observes in church on Sundays. He names her Angelika de la Gardie, for she must be
a countess. Gradually he realizes that she is unattainable for
a man of his low status in society, and transfers his longing
and desire to the organ that then assumes all the perfections
of his beloved (231).

In an encyclopedia Alrik then finds the simile that he

has been looking for. In the book he has seen a picture of the basalt grotto at Staffa, and from that day the organ becomes a great basalt grotto with the bellows blower as Aeolus, the god of the winds. But deep down in the bottom of the grotto is a troll, who will appear if you press a certain button, but then the grotto will also cave in. The idea of the troll has been fostered by the Professor who has told Alrik that there is a certain button that is not to be pulled along with the others at the risk of destroying the organ. Sometimes Alrik sits fingering this button and in moments of depression he wishes to pull it: "to hear the thunder and the crash that would ensue when the organ with its heavy, basalt pillars would crash over him and he would be permitted to die a glorious, famous death in his youth, before the eyes of Angelica and in God's own house" (232–233).

After his examination Alrik has to forsake his dreams to continue his studies and he becomes organist in the parish of Rånö, where he was born. In a barren, isolated parish of few inhabitants, Alrik has greater need than ever for his "incredible playfulness" (234). Thus he names the schoolchildren after the characters in Cooper's novels. By the open sea he finds many things to look at and "play" with: a cork from Russia, a broken oar, an empty bottle. Sometimes he repaints the clouds and the waves, or renames bays and inlets. He has difficulties with the organ, for it is a decrepit instrument. But his imagination finally succeeds even here, for with the aid of a "magic mirror" he is able to visualize the interior of Jacob's church behind him, and thus the organ too is transformed (236).

Seemingly evident in this brief account is Lundstedt's persistent habit to daydream and to let the life of fantasy compensate for the insignificance and emptiness of real life, and also the manner in which his imagination operates in transforming reality. Lundstedt masters the world by finding analogies for it, in metaphors or similes, that is by the technique of poetry. When he has difficulty in finding an analogy for an object or an experience, as in the case of the great organ, he is troubled until he succeeds. Poetry serves him as a way to master the unknown and unfamiliar. A chaotic disorder is brought down to a level where it is robbed of its multifariousness.

Karl-Åke Kärnell has observed that Strindberg in this novel anticipates his later conception of the poet as the man who reveals the inherent unity of creation through his ability to discover analogies and correspondences, but that Strindberg's attitude to the writer's ability to transform reality still remains ambivalent, for when Lundstedt encounters the woman at the manor he also encounters too strong a reality.[4] When he sees himself as the object of her desire he is gripped by a feeling of insecurity and uncertainty. He has to flee, or he will, he feels, be captured.

After the unmasking that then takes place we can only ask ourselves: Does Strindberg defend the life of daydreaming and illusion, the life of fantasy, or does he condemn it in the name of reality? The novel is too ambiguous to provide a simple answer, but one thing is certain: seldom has Strindberg manifested such joy in his writing as in depicting Alrik's playful imagination. Perhaps that may be taken as the clearest indication of his true sentiment. Yet the unmasking is cold and clinical, and the effect of it lingers in our mind, despite the fact that Strindberg seemingly lets Alrik recover his poetic gifts after the priest absolves him of his guilt.

In the final analysis it is probably Strindberg's unusual psychological insight that accounts for the ambivalence, for Strindberg has recognized that the poet in his play with as-

---

[4] Karl-Åke Kärnell, *Strindberg's bildspråk* (Stockholm: Almqvist och Wiksell, 1962), pp. 242–248.

sociations and analogies is not as free as he might believe he is; his imagination is tied by invisible links with the unconscious mind. Ibsen's drama *Peer Gynt* affords us an interesting parallel, because it has considerable affinities with Strindberg's novel.

Peer Gynt too is a dreamer, who decks himself out in his imagination as an emperor ruling the world. He too seeks to escape from a sordid reality. He too is a "liar" and a poet, and despite the irresistible charm and vitality with which he has been equipped it is evident that Ibsen in this drama was also sitting in judgment on himself as a poet.

An aspect of *Peer Gynt* which has proved of the greatest interest to the psychologist is Peer's close ties with his mother, ties that in fact prevent him from having sexual relations with Solveig, in whom he sees his mother, whereas at the end of the play she sees Peer as her child. In this play Ibsen has very consciously dramatized the ties that bind a man to the mother, and in particular, the ties that bind the artist to the mother figure, for what Peer and his mother share more than anything else are stories.[5] We might say then that in *Peer Gynt* Ibsen has not only revealed the source of creative inspiration but also the chief obstacle to self-realization, that is, the repression of unconscious feelings of guilt. For the rest of his life Peer is also without identity, a faceless individual, until rescued at the end by Solveig, who in the role of the mother has been the guardian of his soul, his true self.

The Romantic Organist lacks the richness and complexity of Ibsen's drama, but it raises similar problems, problems to which Strindberg was to return again and again, notably in some of his very last works. With his characteristic ambivalence to poetry he seems, at least for the time being,

---

[5] See George Groddeck's psychoanalytic interpretation of *Peer Gynt* in his book *Exploring the Unconscious* trans. V. M. E. Collins (New York: Funk and Wagnalls, 1940), pp. 153–178.

to have expressed a point of view that, mistakenly or not, is considered representative of Freud's aesthetics, the point of view that stresses the affinities between artistic creation and psychic disturbances, bringing the work of art into proximity with the neurosis as something that can be analyzed in terms of the poet's repression.[6]

---

[6] While this point of view underlies Freud's famous essay on Leonardo da Vinci, it should be noted that it is unfair to reduce Freud's aesthetics to this basic theory. For a study that shows the potentialities for a broader theory of artistic creativity based on Freud's psychoanalysis, see Herbert Fingarette, *The Self in Transformation* (New York: Harper Torchbooks, 1965).

⤙ 8. *Tschandala*

Tschandala has never found much favor with the critics. It is, nevertheless, as Hjalmar Söderberg maintained in a review of 1897, "a strange book, as engrossing in its bizarrerie as in its profound and pronounced originality." Though he called the fable "the strangest and most improbable story," he nevertheless felt that the novel possessed "a life and an intensity which confer on it precisely the inner truth which is and remains the significant fact." [1]

Martin Lamm considers the novel an interesting psychological document but questions its merit as a work of art, insisting that Strindberg did not give himself sufficient time to transform the actual events at Skovlyst.[2] The latter criti-

---

[1] Hjalmar Söderberg, *Samlade verk* (Stockholm: Bonniers, 1943), X, 5–7.
[2] Martin Lamm, *August Strindberg* (2d ed.; Stockholm: Bonniers, 1948), p. 198.

cism seems quite without foundation, for while it is true that Strindberg has based the novel on an actual episode, and that very short time passed between these events and the writing of the novel, he has certainly transformed these events into a highly complex and significant work of art.

Let us sketch the background.[3] On May 1, 1888, Strindberg and his family moved to a run-down château at Skovlyst north of Copenhagen. The château was owned by a somewhat degenerate lady of the nobility, Miss Louise de Frankenau. On the premises was also a caretaker, Ludvig Hansen. The rumor had it that Hansen was Miss Frankenau's lover. Strindberg was in economic difficulties, and he often thought of suicide, but he seems to have found the place very pleasant, at least to begin with.[4]

Soon a number of strange events occurred, and Strindberg somehow got the notion that Hansen was a thief (and a Gypsy!) and accused him publicly.[5] Hansen traded the countercharge that Strindberg had had an affair with his half sister. Soon Strindberg felt threatened by Hansen, and the family moved to a nearby hotel on September 2.

A letter to Edvard Brandes, written on September 4, is of interest because it reveals that Strindberg's imagination was already transforming events and shaping them into a novel: "Since and after May 1 I have resided at an extremely peculiar summer place, from which I was driven out by revolver shots, burglaries, Gypsy dances and eight dogs, after having paid the rent in advance for September. Now I am staying at Hotel Nyholte and grieving over my lost money,

---

[3] For an excellent study of the background of *Tschandala* see Harry Jacobsen, *Digteren og Fantasten: Strindberg paa "Skovlyst"* (Copenhagen: Gyldendal, 1945).

[4] *Brev*, VII, 99.

[5] *Ibid.*, p. 112.

my honor and my books which the villain has taken as lien for counterfeit bills. It will be a novel later!"

In the same letter he comments on his state of mind in the following terms: "Frightfully nervous, and mild persecution mania after stormy days and sleepless nights! I go about with revolver and man-killer in order to protect my blond boy against the Gypsy's robbery attempts." [6]

On September 15 Hansen was arrested after Strindberg had informed the police. In a letter to Siri, his wife, Strindberg admits that he had had sexual relations with Hansen's half sister, but only once, he insists (in an interview the seventeen-year-old girl said *twice*, for she liked Strindberg!).[7] Before the court hearing Strindberg fled in panic to Berlin, and sent a telegram to the court: "Auf Reise nach Paris bereit alles schriftlich mitzuteilen." On September 24 he returned to Copenhagen. No charges were made against Strindberg in court, but the press had a field day. Thus *Aftenbladet* featured this headline: "The Woman Hater Raped Her." [8] What is of greater significance is that seemingly all along Strindberg was planning his novel. In a letter of September 27 he speaks of "the crime novel," and on October 4 he writes to Edvard Brandes: "now I am starting the criminal psychology novel." In a letter to Pehr Staaff on the same day he says he is wondering what is behind the whole affair, and concludes: "I don't know, but I shall try to find out in a novel." [9]

The novel in which he tries to "find out" is *Tschandala,* a crime novel in the Gothic manner of Edgar Allan Poe. The most significant aspect of this novel is the aura of mystery with which Strindberg has enshrouded the characters and

[6] *Ibid.,* pp. 112–113.
[7] *Ibid.,* pp. 118–119.
[8] *Ibid.,* p. 123.
[9] *Ibid.,* pp. 121, 130, 131.

events of the fable. But this aura of mystery is not a cheap trick, it is not an end in itself. As in the early novels of Hamsun the mysteries harbor a psychological significance. The secrets to be bared are in the human psyche. And as in *The Defense of a Fool* the criminal investigator in pursuit of the supposed criminal again unconsciously reveals himself, his own inner conflicts. The battle of the minds that the novel depicts is in reality a battle within a single mind, a battle within the self.

For the sake of aesthetic distance Strindberg has set the novel in the past, in the seventeenth century. The hero is a middle-aged professor at the University of Lund. In search of a summer place he is approached by a strange pair, a baroness accompanied by an insolent Gypsy who is either her servant or her lover. The professor, whose name is Törner, hesitates to rent the château they are offering him, but finally accepts the arrangement. The château turns out to be as strange as the people who own it, and there are a number of mysterious goings-on about the place. Törner begins to suspect that the Gypsy is a thief, and starts an investigation. A strange battle of minds ensues, in which Törner attempts to trap the Gypsy while the Gypsy fights back with every means available to him. The professor is hampered in this conflict by his inability to use the crude tactics of his lower-class opponent. Törner's position is weakened for he has succumbed to his desire for the Gypsy's daughter owing to a long period of enforced celibacy (his wife is ill). Unable to expose the Gypsy for lack of evidence, Törner finally persuades himself that such scum must be removed from the face of the earth and he summons up all his knowledge and intelligence in order to destroy him. Realizing that the Gypsy's most vulnerable spot is his primitive and superstitious mind, Törner finally resorts to magic. With the aid of a lanterna magica he projects images into the night frightening the Gypsy who is then bitten to death by dogs. This leaves Törner on the battle-field triumphant over his victory, a victory of intelligence over the primitive mind.

The story has more than a generous sprinkling of features we associate with the Gothic tale. There is the mysterious setting with its exotic inhabitants and strange events. There are elements of moral depravity: adultery and incest. There are strange transformations: nothing is what it appears to be. Gestures are exaggerated and violent. There are mysterious signs and symbols, ciphers and secret writing. And there is mesmerism and magic. It is little wonder that Strindberg after his discovery of Edgar Allan Poe a few months later could write about *Tschandala*: "It is Poe before Poe! Completely!" [10] He also adds that the novel is not as good as it might have been, "partly because I had not read Edgar Poe yet." [11]

There are several aspects of this Gothic fable which require closer scrutiny if the full meaning is to emerge.

Nearest at hand is the suspicion that Strindberg's chief motive in writing the novel was to take revenge for the indignities he had suffered at Skovlyst, but that would be to ignore the complexity of the fable and the extent to which Strindberg has transformed the actual incidents at Skovlyst. The theme is revenge, I would grant, but a revenge of a much higher order.

It is to the works of Nietzsche and particularly to *The Genealogy of Morals* that we must turn if we are to get a clear conception of the kind of revenge involved. Strindberg had of course become acquainted with the writings of Nietzsche in the spring of 1888, roughly when he moved to Skovlyst. His enthusiasm about Nietzsche knew no bounds as his letters amply reveal. In all likelihood he did not read

---

[10] *Ibid.*, p. 248.
[11] *Ibid.*, p. 273.

a great deal by Nietzsche, though the latter personally sent Strindberg some of his books.[12] Be that as it may *Tschandala* seems strongly influenced by Nietzsche, for it develops in fictional form Nietzsche's analysis of the two moralities known as the master and the slave moralities.

Now Strindberg did not receive his copy of *The Genealogy of Morals* until the middle of December, 1888, that is, after *Tschandala* was completed, which is important in view of the fact that it is in this work that Nietzsche's discussion of the master and the slave morality was, as Danto has observed, "deepened and sharpened . . . and complemented with a more refined psychological analysis of the mentalities of the two *human* types whose moralities these were." [13] This would suggest that Strindberg in focusing just precisely on the *psychological* aspects of the master and the slave morality has in fact anticipated Nietzsche's conclusions.

The two psychological concepts that Nietzsche added in *The Genealogy of Morals* were *resentment* and *bad consciousness*. In analyzing the slave morality Nietzsche shows how the slave resents his own impotency but fears his master's strength. Being unable to express his resentment openly, the slave must therefore use guile, take his revenge in an oblique manner. His method of revenge is also subtle indeed: he gradually makes the master accept the slave's code of values and evaluate himself from the point of view of the slave. The result is that the master acquires a sense of guilt, a bad conscience, and gradually channels his strength, normally expressed in aggression against others, into self-aggression, inward, against himself. By this psychological analysis Nietzsche

---

[12] Like most Scandinavians of this time Strindberg was introduced to the philosophy of Nietzsche through Georg Brandes, and his actual knowledge of Nietzsche's work probably did not extend much beyond what he learned from Brandes.

[13] *Brev*, VII, 210; Arthur C. Danto, *Nietzsche as Philosopher* (New York: Macmillan, 1965), pp. 155–161.

sought to buttress his charge that religion, and the Christian religion in particular, was the villain in this transvaluation of values, which was in his opinion likely to undermine the strength of the race.

It is this psychological conflict between the master and the slave that Strindberg has dramatized in *Tschandala*, with Magister Törner as the "Aryan" aristocrat and the Gypsy bailiff as the "pariah." The irony of the story is based on the fact that Törner who suspects that the Gypsy is guilty of a crime gradually begins to feel that he himself is the guilty suspect. For as his investigation continues he gradually begins to regard himself from the Gypsy's point of view, to think the Gypsy's thoughts, yes, in fact to resemble the Gypsy. The Gypsy resents Törner, primarily because the latter with his superior intellect is able to see through him. His revenge is to nestle himself into Törner's waking and sleeping thoughts and stubbornly remain there as a thorn in the flesh (12, 266). In this manner Törner's mind progressively grows preoccupied with the Gypsy to the extent that his mind is no longer his own. Before the officer of the law he feels "like a convicted criminal with bad conscience and terrified of the eventual discovery" (349). This hampers him in his pursuit of the criminal, as does also the fact that he is unable to use the devious means of the Gypsy, since this would be to demean himself (331). He feels like the Greek fighting against the barbarian, a battle that he fears will be won by the barbarian with his cruder tactics. Significantly it is only after he, Törner, has actually behaved in an immoral manner, and can actually feel a specific guilt, that he decides that the only way to defeat the Gypsy is by killing him (329). In killing the Gypsy he is of course committing a crime, as he knows, but it is only by means of the criminal act that he can reassert the superior strength of the Aryan. Had he not had the ability to commit the crime he might have lost and the pariah would

have had his revenge (375). In committing the crime he has
also, he recognizes, been able to overcome those "foolish old
doctrines" in which his fear and reluctance to act have their
source, doctrines about the forgiveness of our enemies, about
compassion and pity, as well as the equally insidious notions
about the goodness of the people and the evil ways of the
rulers (362).

This should I believe suffice to show that Strindberg in
Tschandala has explored the psychology of resentment and
guilt which we have observed as the central aspect of Nietzsche's analysis of the master and the slave moralities. In
Tschandala, however, Strindberg, by shifting the focus of the
conflict somewhat, has succeeded in deepening the psychological analysis of the problem involved. By making Törner
an intellectual instead of a man of power, and the Gypsy a
man with a very primitive frame of mind, Strindberg has
dramatized a still different form of revenge. In order to consider this aspect of the novel we must begin with a review
of the hero's motives.

It has been argued that Strindberg has failed to motivate
the actions of his hero. Martin Lamm cannot understand how
a refined and learned man like Törner should have become
involved with an inferior individual like the Gypsy.[14] Aside
from the very obvious answer, which brings us to the very
heart and center of the novel—the answer that Strindberg
may precisely wish to illuminate the fact that a man of re-
finement and learning may have all sorts of unconscious desires—Strindberg has, I think, given a number of plausible
reasons for Törner's decision to rent the place and to stay
there. Törner's reasons are practical (there was no other place
available, the rent was low), scientific (there are rare plants
in the area), and above all, psychological (Törner is said to

---

[14] Lamm, *op. cit.*, p. 197.

be of a curious and inquisitive nature, he is eager "to unlock the secret workshops of the soul") (238, 265).

In his fine study of the background of *Tschandala* Harry Jacobsen has argued that the book is unsatisfactory as a crime novel because at the end it offers no satisfactory explanation of the nature of the Gypsy's crime.[15] Törner's destruction of the Gypsy is not acceptable in terms of the detective story, for he has not succeeded in proving that the Gypsy has in fact committed a crime. There is, I think, an answer to this criticism. *Tschandala* is a psychological crime novel, and the most important thing about it is that there is no crime: the criminal and his crime are fictions of the hero's imagination. The destruction of the Gypsy is acceptable only in psychological and symbolic terms, as Törner's final success in repressing his own irrational fears and anxieties by a great effort of his will and intellect. The Gypsy is his double, a repressed aspect of his unconscious self.

Of particular significance in this context are the changes that Törner undergoes during his stay. He suddenly finds that he is beginning to resemble the Gypsy, mimicking his speech and gestures. As he perceives these changes in himself his sense of identity begins to falter, and this is followed by feelings of weakness, cowardice, and fear (266). His obsession with the Gypsy has become an obsession with himself (297–298).

If *Tschandala* is interpreted in symbolic and mythical terms, as I think it ought to be, it emerges as a novel based on the archetypal theme of the double or the *shadow*. The archetypal image of the shadow in the psychology of Jung represents our "other side," our "dark brother," an invisible but inseparable part of our psychic totality. It has been defined as follows: "the shadow is the inferior part of the

---

[15] Jacobsen, *op. cit.*

personality; sum of all personal and psychic elements, which, because of their incompatibility with the chosen conscious attitude, are denied expression in life and therefore coalesce into a relatively autonomous 'splinter personality' with contrary tendencies in the unconscious." [16] It is a split-off portion of our being and yet firmly attached to us. It appears as a frequent motif in art and literature: Shakespeare's Caliban, Stevenson's Mr. Hyde, Chamisso's Peter Schlemihl, Hesse's Steppenwolf, and Goethe's Mephisto are examples. The shadow figure is usually of the same sex. It may be manifested either in an inward, symbolic figure as in a dream, or in a concrete figure from the outside world. In the second case, which seems more applicable here, one or more latent unconscious traits are projected upon someone in our environment who is suited to perform the role. The shadow has both an individual and a collective or mythical aspect. In its individual aspect the shadow stands for those contents of the psyche which have been repressed or rejected by the conscious mind: "in its collective aspect it stands for the universally human dark side within us, for the tendency toward the dark, and inferior that is inherent in every man." [17]

The Gypsy in *Tschandala* may well represent the darker side of Törner's self understood in this sense. He represents those aspects of the self which Törner has repressed and rejected, but which suddenly force their way to consciousness, almost to the point of threatening the autonomy of the ego. As to what specific aspects of Törner's self the Gypsy represents we can only speculate, but a clue might be found in Törner's profession. He is a scientist, an intellectual who quotes Descartes, who has cultivated the rational faculties, perhaps and in all likelihood to a disproportionate degree

---

[16] Jolande Jacobi, *The Psychology of C. G. Jung*, trans. Ralph Manheim (New Haven: Yale University Press, 1962), pp. 106 f.

[17] *Ibid.*, p. 108.

(306). The life of the feelings and the instincts may have suffered in the process. His wife has been ill, and he has been leading a life of celibacy. When removed from his customary environment the repressed elements force their way to consciousness.

Of particular significance is also the manner in which Törner succeeds in finally overcoming the Gypsy. He defeats and destroys the Gypsy by means of his superior intellect. Translated into psychological terms this means that the shadow and what it represents has merely been *repressed*. It has not been integrated into the total psyche. This would be no problem whatever were the repressed tendencies that the shadow represents obviously evil. But, as Jung has observed "the shadow is merely somewhat inferior, primitive, unadapted, and awkward; not wholly bad. It even contains childish or primitive qualities which would in a way vitalize and embellish human existence." [18] Now the Gypsy in *Tschandala* is certainly not wholly bad. He might, in fact, only represent the other fellow, the scapegoat, on whom Törner and most of us lay the blame for our troubles. Törner's victory is an uneasy one and only apparent, for the shadow is likely to reappear in a new guise and in a more threatening form. By merely repressing the shadow Törner has failed to obtain a greater self-knowledge.

We ought not to leave *Tschandala* without some speculation about Strindberg's tendency to idealize the power of the man of the intellect in these years. We recall that the hero of *The Defense of a Fool* was also an amateur detective in pursuit of a suspect, summoning up all his intellectual powers to apprehend the criminal. We shall soon make the acquaintance of Axel Borg, Strindberg's intellectual *Übermensch* doing battle with the ignorant rabble.

Tschandala belongs very distinctly to the genre of fiction

---

[18] *Ibid.*, p. 109

we call romance, and the romance is, as Northrop Frye has observed, "nearest of all literary forms to the wish-fulfilment dream." [19] The central form is "dialectical," that is, it involves a conflict between two main characters, a protagonist and his enemy, the antagonist, a conflict in which all the reader's values are bound up with the hero, while the antagonist assumes demonic qualities. Though the hero of the romance is human, the conflict assumes mythical forms, and may, consequently, easily be translated into archetypal and thus psychological terms. The figures are less "real people" than stylized characters who easily expand into psychological archetypes, which explains why it is in the romance "that we find Jung's libido, anima, and shadow reflected in the hero, heroine, and villain respectively." [20]

If then the quest romance, translated into dream terms, is "the search of the libido or desiring self for a fulfilment that will deliver it from the anxieties of reality but will still contain that reality," *Tschandala* may well be interpreted as a reflection of Strindberg's desire to repress his fears of going insane.[21] His idea of personal relations as a battle of the brains then appears in a different light, for the battle is within the hero's own mind. In this context Strindberg's suddenly awakened interest in Edgar Allan Poe is of interest, for having discovered Poe shortly after *Tschandala* was finished, Strindberg writes: "The Battle of the Brains is all Poe." [22] He was probably thinking of such romances as *The Gold Bug*, in which a man uses all his powers of logical reasoning and scientific knowledge to solve a mystery. Or he might have been thinking of such a story as *The Murders in the Rue*

---

[19] Northrop Frye, *Anatomy of Criticism* (New York: Atheneum, 1966), pp. 186 f.

[20] *Ibid.*, p. 304.

[21] *Ibid.*, p. 193.

[22] *Brev*, VII, 218.

Morgue in which the detective hero Arsène Lupin exhibits superhuman capacities for deduction. Strindberg clearly felt that these stories were the products of a mind with close affinities to his own. He probably did not know that Poe was fighting to preserve his sanity when he wrote his first detective story, that Poe, as Joseph Wood Krutch has suggested, may well have invented the detective story so that he would not go mad.[23]

---

[23] *The Portable Edgar Allan Poe,* ed. Philip van Doren Stern (New York: Viking Press, 1951), p. 330.

✍ 9. A Witch

In his dramas Strindberg has drawn some unforgettable portraits of women, a Miss Julie, a Queen Christina, but in the novels he confers only minor roles on women. An exception is the short novel *En häxa* (*A Witch*) published in the third volume of the historical tales in 1890. A psychological study of a woman of the seventeenth century, it creates a memorable portrait in depth and is drawn with the utmost artistry.[1]

The seventeenth-century setting as a backdrop for a psychological study of a woman naturally brings J. P. Jacobsen's masterpiece *Marie Grubbe* (1876) to mind, a novel that Strindberg had attempted unsuccessfully to adapt for the

---

[1] *A Witch* is actually a completely rewritten version of an earlier less successful story, entitled *Genvägar* (*Shortcuts*). The latter was first published in German in 1887 and later was included in *Samlade skrifter*, vol. 54. *A Witch* appears in vol. 12.

stage. There are also a number of similarities between the two novels. Both novels focus on a conflict between fantasy and reality, both stress the problem of class differences, and both exhibit keen interest in abnormal psychology. But the differences between the two novels are significant. Jacobsen draws a portrait of a woman of the upper classes who is able to find happiness only when she marries a farmhand who beats her, for hers is the modern dream of sexual fulfillment through "the right man." Strindberg draws a portrait of a woman of the lower classes who dreams of sharing the pleasures of wealth and status. Sex is her only means to realize her dreams.

But there is a still more important difference between the two novels. Jacobsen was a Romantic naturalist. He believed that happiness springs from the satisfaction of natural needs and desires, and that false ideals often frustrate the satisfaction of these desires and cause disaster. Marie Grubbe's abnormal behavior, her sadism, her masochism, her religious fanaticism, her thoughts of suicide, her attempt to kill her husband, are all the results of her sexual frustration, perverted expressions of her healthy natural inclinations. When Strindberg wrote such stories as "The Reward of Virtue" in *Married* he too, I think, shared this philosophy, but by 1890 his pessimism had reasserted itself after the brief naturalistic interlude. In *A Witch* his heroine, Tekla Degener, is a neurotic woman, but her neurotic behavior is not to be explained in terms of the frustrations of natural desires, nor is she to be cured by a social readjustment. The causes of her neurosis are deeply embedded in heredity and environment, and she goes to her eventual downfall with the same kind of inevitability as Miss Julie.

A Witch may aptly be called a study in hysteria. No other work reflects as clearly Strindberg's deep interest in psychology at this time of his life. He had evidently followed the experiments of Charcot closely as the essay "Psychic Murder" with its pronounced stress on the power of suggestion indicates. But it is again Maudsley's *Pathology of Mind* that seems to have afforded him the insights into the nature of hysteria on which he based his novel.

Maudsley stresses two basic traits of hysteria: "simulation of disease" and "an enervation of will." Hysterical women, says Maudsley, "exhibit a desire for and a love of imposture which approaches moral insanity." Mostly they simulate symptoms of illness in order to gain attention or sympathy. Owing to their lack of willpower such women lack the power to coordinate ideas and feelings, and "having no well-formed will of their own, they become the easy victims of ideas forcibly impressed upon them by others." Such women are also, says Maudsley, "favourite subjects of mesmeric experiments and of religious revivals," falling easily into convulsive seizures, paralysis, or states of somnambulism.[2]

Not only has Strindberg stressed the same traits as Maudsley in his portrait of Tekla Degener, but, more significantly, he has also adopted Maudsley's moral point of view. Although Maudsley is willing to grant that there are cases in which simulation is not voluntary or even conscious, he mostly condemns it in strongly worded moral terms, as manifestation of "a strangely perverted or defective moral nature." The cure is moral discipline and the strengthening of the will. At the same time however, he looks upon these women as "easy victims of ideas forcibly impressed upon them by others." Strindberg's point of view is identical. He could not bear dissimulation, and when Tekla is putting on an act he lets us know how he feels about it. Yet the stress is on Tekla as the victim of a mistaken upbringing, an unfortunate milieu, and the ideas of the age. A *Witch* escapes

---

[2] Henry Maudsley, *The Pathology of Mind* (New York: Appleton, 1880), pp. 323–324.

being a mere case history by the inevitability, the logic, with which she moves like a sleepwalker to her tragic end.

Tekla Degener grows up in the Old Town of Stockholm. Her father is a city guard, her mother a concierge. The mother leads a life of unbearable monotony and boredom: her life literally centered on a string that has to be pulled every ten minutes, night and day. Characteristic of the mother is also a lack of will and initiative; she receives all impulses from the outside and can only respond (12, 119). These are qualities that Tekla inherits. She was born with a hatred of the bell and what it represents, an involuntary response to outside stimulus. As a child she is sensitive and nervous. In school she discovers that she belongs to the lower classes, but her religious instruction imbues her with the delusion that all men are equal before God, and with the aspiration to emulate the ways of the upper classes. Simultaneously she becomes sexually aroused by a young man, a member of the upper class. The result is that she begins to spend her days dreaming of a better life. Ashamed of appearing as one of the working class, she develops a fear of open places, seeking out the dark lanes, and finally begins to simulate headaches and fever every morning. But in the afternoon she puts on her best gown and visits the parks and areas of the city studying the manner of her peers. Seeking by all means to attract the attention of a handsome young man, she finally makes the acquaintance of a young man of the middle class, whom she selects as the man who will liberate her from her monotonous life, but also, as she puts it, from the effort of thinking, speaking, and acting: "Oh, how lovely not to have to live oneself and yet live" (154).

Her life of bliss soon leads to boredom, but a dramatic experience rescues her from her monotonous life. It also spells her doom. One day she happens to stray to the waterfront where a witch is ready to undergo the water test (if a woman

charged with witchcraft were to stay afloat after being cast
into the river with her hands tied, it was accepted as proof
of her innocence). There Tekla meets Ebba, the daughter
of a count and a member of Tekla's confirmation class. Together they watch the witch undergo the trial. Tekla who has
always been starved for attention envies the witch her beauty
and pride but above all the fact that she is the center of everybody's attention. In the excitement Ebba falls into the water
and is rescued by Tekla who acts without thinking. As her
reward she is invited to stay at the count's residence, where
her life is like a prolonged holiday. But one day she sees Ebba
visiting a strange hut in the woods. Tekla decides that Ebba
must be a witch. Visiting the count's library she discovers a
book of black magic, which leads her to conclude that she
herself has secret powers (186). In a state of excitement she
goes to the beach with Ebba, and has a hysterical attack
when Ebba floats on the water in a manner that recalls the
episode of the water test. Having forgotten about her husband, and eager to test her "magic" powers, Tekla then
tries to attract the attention of a Baron Magnus, Ebba's
fiancé. She succeeds, but she and her new lover are surprised
by Ebba.

Driven out of paradise Tekla now curses God and
abandons herself to the devil. On her way through the woods
she comes to a clearing where a stage has been erected. Climb-
ing onto the stage she envies in her mind the actor's ability
to gain the attention of others and set their feelings into
vibration, until discovering traces of blood she realizes that
it is not a stage but a place of execution (199). Suddenly
she recalls the fate of the witch, and the idea is born: How
wonderful to end in such a way! She quickly decides to go
to the city and turn herself in so that the whole world shall
know who she really is, and that she is in alliance with a
spirit who is greater than the Lord and his servants. But she

is robbed of her triumph. She is deprived of her official execution, because she dies of a hysterical attack caused by fright while passing the torture chamber on her way to a hearing before the judge.

A mere plot summary conveys little of the strange and compelling power of A Witch. The logic and inevitability of Tekla's actions are suggested by other means, particularly by a very conscious and skillful use of color imagery.

Strindberg often shows fondness for color in his works. In his own paintings he preferred a stark black and white, but in some of his novels, in The Red Room, for instance, he "paints" in the manner of an impressionist. There a character's face is often depicted as a daub of white, or red, or green, without any definite features. Some of the interiors are described by a man who takes a great delight in colorful texture. Strindberg's use of color becomes gradually more deliberate, and the colors begin to represent something; they become part of the structure of meaning, as leitmotivs, or as symbols of spiritual and moral qualities. We may also note Strindberg's fondness for naming his books by a color: The Red Room, Black Banners, A Blue Book. In the last novels Strindberg's use of color has also become so codified in a definite pattern that an exact meaning can be ascribed to a color.

In A Witch Strindberg uses color images for two purposes: for dramatic effect, using stark contrasts between black and white, and red and black; and as leitmotivs, lending a sense of inevitability to the events in the novel. Thus each color means something, and when we can sense what it means we also know what is going to happen next.

Blackness is associated with Tekla's childhood and home environment. The house in which she lives is on the Street of the Black Friars, probably the gloomiest place in the Old Town. The building is old and blackened with dusky little windowpanes unable to transmit or reflect light (118). The backyard where Tekla plays is infested with flies, rats, and spiders, and from a big black tarred dustbin in the corner flows a river of dark liquid (120). The room is so dark that the lamp has to be lit even in daytime. When Tekla is able to peer through the window to the street she sees only a big black building across the street (121).

When Tekla comes into contact with the children of the middle class in school images of *whiteness* predominate. Tekla envies these children their white faces and hands, and she learns to wash her hands in warm water and to drink vinegar in order to become like them. Whiteness is also associated with Tekla's confirmation, an experience that has a great and very decisive emotional impact on her, for the religious experience becomes intermingled with ideas of social equality and also leads to Tekla's sexual awakening. Thus, as the white bread of the confirmation ritual comes to symbolize the luxuries of the rich, so the dark red wine comes to represent the passions of the heart. The strongest single impression on Tekla is the symbolic kiss exchanged between the children on the day before the confirmation ceremony. With powerful color images Strindberg conveys Tekla's state of mind as she walks home afterward, moving like a sleepwalker. Black and white again predominate, but the one *red* image has a dramatic effect:

It had made a very deep impression on Tekla, so deep that she still walked homeward across the cemetery as if asleep. Darkness had fallen on the April evening and a mild south wind blew, rustling the twigs of the bare linden trees, among which the stars shone like tinsel on the boughs of a Christmas tree. She took one step at a time, holding her muff before her with both hands as if she were carrying a beautiful newly painted picture that she was afraid of smudging. Occasionally she held up her hands as though she wanted to look at a painting; she brought it closer, then held

it further away from her in order to get a perspective or to stamp
it into her mind, and when she then shut her eyes she could see
in the midst of a crowd of people a dark vigorous youth approaching her with outstretched arms; he encloses her in his rounded
arms, presses his face against hers so that she can see only a shock
of hair and two open eyes spurting fire into hers, and another soft
mouth breathes sweet scents into her mouth, and she feels a
slight pressure of warm silk on her upper lip. She embraces him
and feels her cold trembling hands being warmed by the Braban-
tine wool of his sweater; her cheek rests against a white, pleated
linen cloth, as white as the garments of the Savior in the Trans-
figuration, and in the middle of his breast shines a granite-red
drop of blood which is cold and presses hard against her temple
so that she wants to scream. But the pain is so lovely, and she
presses herself even harder against the sharp stone so that the
bone of her temple aches. Then she hears the Master's voice:
"Peace be with you." His arms release their hold, she reels back
as if awakening from a sleep, sees the red flame of the lamp resting over the beautiful dark head like the Holy Ghost over the
disciples' heads in Emmaus, sees the severe black faces staring
down from the wall with eyes rolling askew, and then the lame
verger comes and closes the stove door. She stops at the church-
yard gate and conjures up the vision once more from the beginning, she opens her coat and sniffs at the bodice of her dress from
which emanates a faint fragrance of lily of the valley, and she
bows her head to kiss the brown bombazine, but her throat strains
against her collar. But look! A white plant is growing out of her
left side with six little wrinkled bells on a pale yellow stem between two vivid green leaves, and it creeps up between her young
breasts and reaches toward her mouth to be kissed. And her breasts
tingle as though milk wanted to spout from them, and her legs
tremble so that she has to hold on to the great iron gates. (127–
128)

Whiteness, then, is a class symbol, a symbol of Tekla's
aspirations, and also a symbol of innocence and purity. Red
and white are introduced as sacramental symbols, but red,

we note, also suggests sensual passion, the ecstasy of love.

Lost in her reveries, Tekla is rudely awakened by a very dramatic incident, in which the images of *red* and *black* in combination seem to anticipate the darker passions that will soon engulf her, red and black being omens of evil:

At that moment she hears bugle blasts from up at the square —a ship's bell rings incessantly, incessantly—dogs are barking, boys are screaming, and then a noise comes rolling down the narrow street, a thin but hollow clattering like that of hammered copper; it grows louder and rolls on, approaches grandly, red as the glow from a fire, lighting up signboards and ornamental stonework and tiny windowpanes; it is getting closer to her, and now four black horses with fire in their eyes and fire in their harnesses come rushing past, and a blood-red coach with sooty men in gold helmets dashes by, and on the coach black serpents wind themselves around blood barrels with copper taps—while the bell rings, the bugles blow, and the fireglow dances about the coach. (128)

Images of *black* and *white* in combination fascinate Tekla because they represent what is most desirable to her: the dark-haired young man who kissed her, luxury and wealth, and—notoriety and attention. The last meaning is most evident in the description of a scene after the death of Tekla's mother. Sitting at her mother's deathbed Tekla observes the white label on the black bottle of medicine and sees in her mind the attractive combination of a white apron on the black woolen dress customary at funerals. She anticipates the attention that she will attract on her way to the funeral service. After the mother is dead Tekla immediately puts up white sheets before the windows, and then watches with a mixed feeling of pleasure and horror her dark figure against the white sheets reflected in the mirror (159). As the black casket is removed she finally feels free to begin her own life.

Dramatic color images are significantly absent in the account of Tekla's dull married life, but the scene at the waterfront of the trial of the witch brings back the images of *black* and *white*. The witch is dressed only in a white shift, her long dark hair falling loosely down her back and shoulders. She has a triumphant smile on her face as if to indicate her superiority to the crowd, telling them, as it seems to Tekla, "that the trial she was now about to undergo was a duel between herself and the Almighty, and that even if she should lose, she would still have enjoyed the honor of having struggled with him" (169). Tekla envies her, and thinks of the performance of an actress she had once seen in the role of the Goddess of Victory. When the executioner pushes the witch into the water the sun shines brightly on her pale face and white clothes, and as the waves close round her, her dark hair still floats like sea grass on the surface even after the white figure is no longer visible.

Sunshine and gentle colors set the tone for the happy and carefree day that Tekla spends at Sandemar with Ebba. But the dark youth is again present in Baron Magnus, and images of *red* and *black* again suggest ominous events soon to occur. As Tekla walks along the beach in the bright sunlight, she is forced to take a path that leads into the dark forest that always frightens her. A black woodpecker with a red throat is an evil omen, she feels (182). Having seen Ebba in the hut in the woods she returns to the manor where she accidentally discovers a book of black magic. Its colors are red and black (185–186).

There follows the dramatic scene that is an exact repetition of the waterfront scene in Stockholm. Tekla goes down to the lake to bathe with Ebba, but refuses to remove her clothes, because she is ashamed of the fact that her body is not as fine as Ebba's. Ebba jumps into the water and cries out: "Let us see now if I am a witch and can float" (189). She floats, her dark hair spread on the water like seaweed. Tekla immediately recalls the earlier incident, but concludes that Ebba could not possibly be a witch, when a cloud passing across the sun suddenly colors the white figure a ghastly blue under the greenish water. As a sea gull simultaneously cries out and the dinner *bell* is sounded in the distance, the combined force of all these associations overwhelms Tekla and she has a hysterical attack.

After the incident with Baron Magnus, Tekla is driven away from Sandemar. In the dark woods she curses God, her mother and father, and cries out for assistance from the devil against the powers that hide their light from her so as to lead her astray in the *darkness*. In a symbolic sense she now also abandons herself to the power of darkness (198). Significantly, it is the *blood* that she finds on what she first takes to be a stage that leads to her decision to go to Stockholm and turn herself in as a witch. Red and black in combination again spell her doom. But Tekla is deprived of her moment of triumph—the moment when *her* white figure and dark hair would signal her victory—for her attack of hysteria in prison, again brought on by her extreme suggestibility, demonstrates that she is a pathetic victim of forces beyond her control.

Having followed Tekla Degener's pathetic story to its unfortunate end, we are in a better position to appraise the significance of Strindberg's use of color imagery throughout the novel. We have already observed that Strindberg seems to use color imagery for two different purposes: for dramatic effect, and to lend a sense of inevitability to the events in the novel. It is primarily the latter, the sense of inevitability engendered as we witness the power that these color images associated with her past experiences have over Tekla, which sustains the psychological theme. For what Strindberg by this method has been able to project with remarkable dramatic force and logic are the inevitable links that tie the neurotic individual to his past. Tekla Degener is a woman whose past is constantly threatening to master the present, a victim of regressive impulses. Seldom, if ever, has a neurotic case history been rendered by a narrative art so uniquely and admirably adapted to the nature of the case.

~~⤍ 10. By The Open Sea

In his next novel, *I havsbandet* (*By the Open Sea*), Strindberg returned to the setting of the outer skerries which he had depicted with such loving care in *The People of Hemsö*. But *By the Open Sea* bears little resemblance to the earlier and so successful work, for although it may originally have been designed as a sequel to the tales from the outer skerries it grew into a powerful psychological novel, into what Strindberg himself called "a modern novel in Nietzsche's and Poe's footsteps," a book in a "new great Renaissance style." [1] A novel with a highly undemocratic and unsympathetic hero with the ambitions of an *Übermensch* and a Napoleon, with a skeletal plot, replete with learned allusions and obscure and unfamiliar symbolism, *By the Open Sea* was hardly calculated to appeal to the large public that had delighted in the skillful storytelling and good

[1] *Brev*, VII, 347; VIII, 54.

humor of *The People of Hemsö*. Strindberg spoke of the novel as "my most mature work, the one I set the greatest store on of everything I have written," but the sale of the book was disappointing.[2] But then he himself was beginning to recognize that he was growing away from the large public, and that the novel, "the sum of my observations on life up to age 42," was too learned and too esoteric to win a large audience.[3] Strindberg was embarking on an inner journey into the deeper recesses of the self, a journey on which few were willing to follow him.

To this day there are widely divergent views as to the merits and the meaning of the novel. Some regard it very highly, others find it very unpalatable. I am inclined to share the opinion of the former. *By the Open Sea* is a powerful psychological novel, a bold attempt to depict the progressive breakdown of a mind and to explore the workings of the unconscious. The inward turning that had begun in *The Son of a Servant* is completed, for we are no longer dealing with the outer manifestations of the self in its dealings with the world but with consciousness itself. The events that take place really occur in the hero's mind, or are of interest only in terms of their impact on that mind. The characters do not possess independent life: they are projections or images of the hero's unconscious mind. The world of external reality no longer appears in its quality of otherness, as an objective reality, but only as a mental image. Which is another way of saying that Strindberg has become a Symbolist. In his efforts to delve more deeply into the workings of the mind he has been forced to abandon naturalism altogether and resort to symbol and image.[4] The last half of the novel and

[2] *Ibid.*, VIII, 192.

[3] *Ibid.*, pp. 126, 128, 129.

[4] According to Gunnar Brandell, Strindberg wanted to give the French translation of *By the Open Sea* the subtitle "conte symboliste" (*Strindbergs Infernokris* [Stockholm: Bonniers, 1950], p. 212).

the last chapters in particular represent the heights of Strindberg's achievement as a psychological novelist, particularly if the symbolism is fully understood. With their powerful archetypal images they convey a strong feeling of the extent to which Strindberg's exploration of the unconscious has deepened, and the extent to which the darker knowledge so forcefully repressed in *Tschandala* has been integrated.

With regard to the development of the major theme in the novels, *By the Open Sea* marks a definite intensification of the conflict both between the self and the others and between the warring aspects of the self. Thus the threatened self in defense proclaims its absolute autonomy, only to be brutally convinced of its utter dependency, as the ego succumbs to the combined pressures of the superego and the unconscious. Although the novel signifies a return to the aristocratic and Romantic individualism heralded at the end of *The Son of a Servant*, this standpoint, too, is tested and found wanting.

Romantic individualism had been given a strong impetus in 1888 by Strindberg's discovery of Nietzsche. In the spring of that year, Georg Brandes gave a series of lectures in Copenhagen introducing the German philosopher to the Scandinavian public. The following year he published an article in the magazine *Tilskueren* outlining Nietzsche's ideas as he interpreted them. It bore the title "Aristocratic Radicalism." [5]

In this article Brandes, in sympathy with Nietzsche's views, pays tribute to the latter's worship of the higher man, the genius, the solitary individual, whose needs for happiness are extraordinary, and who has to create his own values. The criteria of this "Renaissance man" are spiritual: superior intellect, strength of will, asceticism, love of beauty. He has to dwell in solitude, on lonely heights or isolated islands, for

---

[5] Georg Brandes, "Friedrich Nietzsche—En Afhandling om aristokratisk Radikalisme," *Tilskueren* (Aug., 1889), pp. 565–613.

he must at all cost avoid contact with the mass men of the lowlands, whose needs are elementary and biological (reproduction, food) and who are guided by their herd instincts. The Renaissance man must also beware of the snares of any system of morality which tends to further the growth of the collective at the expense of the superior individual. Democracy, socialism, and communism are developments of a Christian slave morality and hence to be rejected.

The Romantic ancestry of this aristocratic radicalism is very evident, and in Scandinavia it can be traced back to Kierkegaard and his cult of the individual, and to Ibsen's early Romantic plays like *Brand*. The introduction of Nietzsche's philosophy of the *Übermensch* marked the rebirth of a well-established attitude. Thus Strindberg's own experiments with this point of view are part of a trend, also manifested by Ibsen in his late plays about tortured solitary giants pursued by demons (*Rosmersholm*, *John Gabriel Borkman*, *The Master Builder*), by Heidenstam, by Hamsun, and others.[6]

Strindberg's enthusiasm over Nietzsche was also boundless—at least to begin with! It is reflected in a letter to Heidenstam in May of 1888: "Buy yourself a modern German philosopher whose name is Nietzsche. G. B. has been lecturing about him. There is everything to be read. Don't deny yourself the pleasure. N. is a poet too." [7] This enthusiasm may be explained in part by Strindberg's feeling that Nietzsche had formulated the very ideas he himself was propounding.

In view of the rather ambivalent treatment afforded this new point of view in *By the Open Sea* we may well wonder what happened between the inception of the novel in the

---

[6] Strindberg seems, in particular, to have found a kindred spirit in the young Knut Hamsun. Witness his enthusiasm over the latter's *Fra det moderne Amerikas Aandsliv* (1889) (*Brev*, VIII, 25–26).

[7] *Ibid.*, VII, 91.

fall of 1889 and its completion during the summer of 1890.[8] Did Strindberg's enthusiasm suddenly wane as was its wont? Or did he begin to suspect that Nietzsche was a madman? Or did he perhaps want to disassociate himself from a fashionable trend? We do not know the answer, but we do know that Strindberg suddenly paused in the middle of the novel and was unable to continue for about five months, having left the hero of the novel at the height of his power. Nor do we know whether Strindberg's instinctive need to reverse the trend of the hero's fortune in midstream had again reasserted itself and thus led to a reexamination and consequent distrust of the whole philosophy represented by the hero. His letters give no indication of what problem he had encountered. What is significant is that in two letters to Georg Brandes on April 12 and 22, 1890, he says he is merely experimenting with a new point of view. Brandes had chided Strindberg for his too great readiness to embrace new ideas, arguing that it is a sign of maturity to make firm commitments. Strindberg defends his habit by maintaining that it is a form of openness to experience that furthers growth, and insists that he is by no means "uncritical" in his acceptance of Nietzsche's ideas. Having found some of his own ideas formulated by Nietzsche, he says, he has only "adopted his point of view, and henceforth I plan to experiment with that point of view in order to discover where it might lead." [9]

Strindberg seems to have discovered that it would lead to disaster, for the novel dwells on the tragic dilemma in which the hero involves himself. The hero's moments of triumph are few and short-lived. Nevertheless, there is little

---

[8] The first seven chapters of the novel were already finished in November, 1889; then there followed an interval of five months in which the work did not progress. The novel was completed on June 7, 1890 (*ibid.*, VIII, 54).

[9] *Ibid.*, pp. 26, 35.

doubt that Strindberg is basically in agreement with his hero's individualism, with his ideological views. The author's ambivalent attitude is due to his insight into the psychological consequences of rigid adherence to those views. For this type of aristocratic individualism is likely to subject the faithful to the perils of a life of enforced isolation, that is, megalomania and paranoia, along with the inevitable resentment of the masses.

Nevertheless, judging from some of his comments about the novel shortly after its completion, Strindberg seems unaware of the extent to which the book indirectly condemns and invalidates this kind of Romantic individualism, for he states that the novel depicts "the persecution of the strong individual by the common people who instinctively hate the strong. Alone, persecuted from above and below, his soul deteriorates bit by bit." [10] This statement is only partly correct, for it neglects the fact that although the hero is victimized by the common people who are his instinctive foes, he is victimized most by forces within his own psyche activated by his isolation: repressed desires, unconscious feelings of guilt, primitive fears and anxieties. Some twenty years later, however, Strindberg seems to have read the novel in a different light, because he comments as follows: "Influences from Nietzsche's philosophy, but the individual goes to his defeat in his efforts to attain absolute Individualism. Introduces the 90's: Übermensch" (19, 148).

The reference to Nietzsche's *Übermensch* is interesting, for although Strindberg's hero may be patterned on the Nietzschean model, he differs from the prototype in one very significant respect. Whereas Strindberg shares Nietzsche's contempt for the mass man and his rejection of the Christian God, Strindberg's hero is, by comparison, an intellectual, a rationalist, who makes a definite separation between the life

---

[10] *Ibid.*, p. 58.

of the intellect and the "lower" life of the senses and the feelings. Nietzsche's *Übermensch*, by contrast, represents the ideal of the whole man; hence the stress on joy and freedom, on the freedom to create and to be, and on the freedom from guilt and fear through complete acceptance of life. Zarathustra is, we recall, envisioned as a dancer, the Romantic image of wholeness of being, of spontaneity.[11] Strindberg's hero, on the contrary, is self-conscious and split, exhibiting the typical Romantic conflict between reason and spontaneity.

The difference is significant, because it points to Strindberg's growing awareness of the weaknesses of a rationalistic psychology that ruthlessly represses the life of the feelings and the senses in the name of reason, sacrificing the integration of the total self for what might be termed ego satisfaction. This awareness makes *By the Open Sea* a significant psychological document, anticipating the rejection of the cult of the ego in the novels to follow. On the other hand, it is in the powerful symbolism that we must first seek the source of the compelling impact of this complex and ambiguous novel which gradually develops into an archetypal drama of genuine, primitive grandeur.

The hero of *By the Open Sea* is by profession a scientist. His name, Axel Borg, suggests his affinities with two other important figures in Strindberg's novels. Axel, we recall, was the name of the writer-detective in *The Defense of a Fool*, and Borg was the name of the tough-minded young medical student in *The Red Room*.[12]

---

[11] On the significance of the image of the dancer in modern literature, see Frank Kermode, *Romantic Image* (New York: Vintage Books, 1964), pp. 49 f.

[12] A letter of March 18, 1891, reveals the extent to which Strindberg identifies with his hero: "I am breaking up now so that what happened to inspector Borg won't happen to me. Noticed approaching symptoms of general breakdown: persecution mania, hys-

Basically a weak and effeminate man with an inordinate desire for power, Borg is constantly tormented by a need to assert his autonomy. He is so abnormally sensitive to pressure from others that he quickly becomes unsure of himself and is put on the defensive. Literally unable to be with others for any length of time, he has always sought privacy and solitude in order to restore his mental equilibrium. When the novel begins Borg has just accepted a position as a fishing inspector on an isolated and inhospitable island in the archipelago. Here he will try to realize his ideal of the autonomous individual, the superior man who assumes total responsibility for himself and his actions. Instead of imagining a point of support outside of himself "in God like the weak Christians," Borg seeks "the anchorage for his existence, the focus of the circle that reality formed about him in himself" (24, 55).

Borg's abnormal sensitivity to the existence of others is immediately apparent in the very first scene of the novel. In a dramatic incident during the sea journey to the island Borg's superior intelligence is pitted against the brute strength of the natives. In a dangerous moment Borg grasps the rudder and assumes command of the small craft. Aware of the fact that he is exposing himself to the ridicule of the fishermen, and that the awareness of their ridicule would undermine his faith in his own ability, he refuses to meet their glances. His eyes are burning, but they are averted. To one of the fishermen it appears as if the inspector's eyes "did not wish to receive anything from him, as if they wanted to refrain from any contact with anything which might disturb or soil" (9).

terical longing for the children; crying fits in the midst of company!" (*Brev*, VIII, 221). Nevertheless, in the novel the narrative point of view is complex. Most of the time, it is true, we regard the world from Borg's angle of vision, but at times we perceive Borg from the point of view of the omniscient narrator or the islanders (cf. Staffan Björck, *Romanens formvärld* [2d ed.; Stockholm: Natur och Kultur, 1954], pp. 84–86).

On the island surrounded by ignorant fishermen who are very hostile to him, common people with whom he finds it impossible to communicate, Borg's belief in his own superiority is put to the test. His attempts to teach the natives rational methods of fishing are met with ridicule. He knows that he is regarded as a fool, and that he is the most popular topic at coffee parties. To begin with he finds the situation somewhat comical, but gradually, as the ridicule turns into outright hostility, his mental equilibrium is disturbed:

It was as if a thundercloud of alternating electric current lay over him and irritated his nerve fluid, wanted to annihilate it by neutralizing it. He felt as if the thoughts of so many focused on him possessed the ability gradually to pull him down, to put pressure on his opinion about his own worth, so that the moment would come when he would no longer be able to believe in himself and his intellectual superiority, but that finally their view, that he was the idiot and they the sane, would seize hold of his brain and force him to agree with their opinion. (70)

The pressure of public opinion is a constant threat to Borg's autonomy. He is tormented by anxieties about the prospect of his adjustment or leveling, and his powerful but delicate mind fears the contact with others, because it may suddenly "go out of tune." "His thought mechanism suffered from contact with others, it became agitated, unreliable as the needle of the compass in the proximity of iron" (113–114). Wearied from the intercourse with commonplace minds, "the fine wheels of his thoughts" fail to move properly in their bearings. His sense of judgment is clouded, his refined and exquisite taste for beautiful things threatens to succumb to the vulgarity and banality about him.

Under these circumstances it is not surprising that Borg seeks solitude. His refuge is either in nature or in the sanctuary of his own room. On the edge of "the great solitariness" of the Baltic Sea, all alone in a boat at sea, or in the fog, he is at peace and harmony with himself, because he is in full possession of himself. Solitude is his element. After a brief encounter with other people he turns his steps to the sea "in order to revisit himself in solitude" (102). He often feels the need to leave the island "in order to be alone, to collect himself, to rediscover himself" (158). On one such occasion as he sails into the soothing and liberating fog his state of mind is beautifully evoked by Strindberg:

Here, where the eye was liberated from all impressions of color and form, he first felt the delight in isolation from the motley outer world. He had, as it were, his own atmosphere about him, floating along alone as if on another heavenly body in a medium that was not air but steam, more pleasant and more refreshing to inhale than the drying air with its unnecessary 79 percent nitrogen, which has remained without any apparent purpose when the earth's matter arranged itself from the chaos of gases.

It was not a dark, smoke-colored fog but light, like newly boiled silver, through which the sunlight was sifted. Warm, like padding, it formed a healing covering around his tired self, protecting from shocks and pressure. He relished for a moment this wide-awake repose of the senses without sound, without color, without odor, and he felt how his tormented head was refreshed by this security of not being in contact with others. He was sure of not being asked, of not needing to answer, not to speak. The apparatus was at a standstill for a moment, after all wires had been broken, and now he began to reflect in a clear and orderly manner on what he had experienced. (160–161)

As he returns to his room he also anticipates the pleasure of being his own master, of being able to select his own company among the great and kindred spirits in his books, and among his own impressions, for he has remodeled the shabby room in conformity with his own fastidious taste. Surrounded by beautiful and precious objects and by the symbols of his intellectual power, books, manuscripts, scientific instruments, prints, Borg feels at home, for his room is in fact a projection of the orderly structure of his own mind.

The first four chapters of the novel are fairly static, designed primarily to introduce the reader to the nature of Borg's mind and sensibility, to his background, his values. With the arrival on the island of two ladies at the end of chapter four, the pace increases, for through the simple plot involving a trivial love affair, Strindberg exposes Borg's inner conflicts and puts his values to the test. Borg has tried valiantly to suppress the natural man, particularly the "lower" instincts, but he is a man and soon finds himself bent on gaining the affections and favor of the young Maria. There is something much worse in store for Borg. In order to gain his victory he has to do what he detests the most: he has to "lower" himself, adjust himself, to the woman's level, and play the game of love. Why is this so difficult for Borg? Because it means that he has to do something that is not only contrary to his values, but also absolutely distasteful to his humorless mind.

Borg is a man who has been taught to worship logic and reason and to suppress the instincts and the feelings as residues of man's primitive ancestry. His world view is rationalistic: it puts all the emphasis on the conscious ego, on intellectual power. Sexual desire, being an expression of man's instinct for perpetuating the species, he regards as the lowest of the drives, and to be resisted by the man of intellect, who should live on in his works, not in his children. In Borg's hierarchy of human beings only those who are able to resist their animal needs and passions can rise to real eminence. He classifies people in three categories: the conscious, the self-deceivers, and the unconscious. In the first category he places the intellectuals and the thinkers, the skeptics who believe in nothing or nobody; in the second category he places those who are creatures of feeling or guided by their sexual desires, religious believers, prophets, sentimental do-gooders; in the third and lowest category he places those who are guided by their animal instincts, who lack ability to distinguish subject and object, more specifically, children, criminals, and women (63 f.).

Considering the unflattering position on the ladder leading to perfection which Borg assigns to woman, it is understandable that he should find it uncomfortable to play the childish game of sex, for it means that he has to lower himself to her level. The ensuing drama which ends with Borg in the role of the successful seducer would also have been a silly affair were it not for the fact that Borg's exaggerated and totally humorless concern about his own precious self makes it all absurdly comical. And this travesty of the war of the sexes proves on closer examination to harbor strong psychological significance.

Since Borg is totally lacking in spontaneity and genuine feeling, every move in the war of love requires intensive mental effort and causes him much weariness of mind. With his abnormally sensitive mind Borg is restlessly identifying with Maria, anticipating her actions and thoughts, constantly preparing strategic moves, either defensive or offensive. Borg is particularly defenseless in two respects. With a glance from her eyes Maria can either bestow strength on him or deprive him of it, thus causing him to go contrary to his will. Because of Borg's urge to possess her she can also make him step out of his chosen role and perform other roles, childish and undignified roles, of which he is ashamed.

When Borg at their first meeting finds Maria's "two, big, confiding eyes looking up to him with admiration and surprise" his sense of his own importance immediately grows: "he believed everything he said to be true, and he felt along with a rising estimation for himself new powers awakening and old ones growing in strength and endurance" (86). By the afternoon the positions of strength are reversed. Borg, having had to exercise his authority by threatening to have some of the wives of the fishermen arrested, suddenly finds Maria and her mother sympathizing with the underdog, and Maria, in particular, uses her feminine wiles in order to get him to change his mind. A moment after he has issued an order to send for the sheriff Borg suddenly feels "two soft, warm hands grasping his right hand" and "two big, childish eyes looking into his and a voice with the tone of a mother pleading for mercy for the life of her child" (92). The inspector tries to free himself and to turn his back on "the big eyes, the glances of which he could not endure," but Maria is adamant, and Borg finally relents and rescinds his order. As he returns to his room he admits that his defeat represents a betrayal of his principles: he has let his "sexual impulses govern him to the extent that he has let himself be fooled into an illegal action" (93). His main concern is that Maria will now believe that she has scored a victory over him which will upset the balance of power, and, in addition, that the people of the island will no longer respect his authority.

In relation to Maria he is now faced with the same dilemma that has troubled him in past love affairs. How is he to reconcile two irreconcilables: his vision of an ideal union as one in which the woman worships the stronger, that is, the man, with the fact that, as he puts it, "the only way to approach a woman is on all fours," that is, by adjusting oneself, or lowering oneself, to her level, a kind of dissimulation he finds distasteful. But he has decided to win Maria, and he has no choice but to play a role, don a mask. Within a few hours he is doing his very best, for conversing with Maria and her mother he voices assent to the most sentimental and egalitarian views. But in leaving the cottage, he literally has to shake himself because there he feels covered with dust, and when he goes down to the shore to recover himself, he finds that his old proud isolation has been broken, that "threads have been spun about his soul," that he is no longer free (101–102). Even so, the game must continue, and from now on he has to resign himself to leading two lives and thus guard his own self: "He had no choice but to make his person double, to split himself, to create a personality, comprehensible and amenable to her, to play a duped lover, learn to admire her inferiority, accustom himself to a role, as she wanted it, and then in silence to lead his other half-life in secret and by himself, to sleep with one eye closed and keep the other open" (103).

A few days later he has the opportunity to practice his role. In an inspired moment he is able to lift Maria to his own level, to make her see with his eyes, but only for a moment, for soon he is playing childish games that will make him more human in her eyes: imitating the bellowing of a bull, dancing like a Hottentot, singing songs. But while she bathes, he finds himself a niche in the rocks where he can sink into himself and let his brain rest, the delicate mechanism of his mind having become exhausted from the contact with the "confused thoughts of others."

The stress on Borg's childish behavior is of considerable significance, for it suggests that Maria, who is projecting qualities that Borg has sought to repress, is a symbolic figure. She may well represent another archetypal image of the unconscious, the anima. The anima unlike the shadow that we encountered in *Tschandala* is usually a figure of the opposite sex. The anima is basically a personification of the feminine nature of a man's unconscious. It usually manifests itself in dreams and fantasies in personified form or simply in a man's behavior, as in the irrationalities of a man's feelings. Since it is an unconscious image it is also unconsciously projected upon the beloved, determining the reasons for attraction or aversion. Compounded of feelings, it then tends to influence or distort the man's understanding, turning his head so to speak. Belonging to the world of feeling the anima has a predilection for everything that is unconscious, dark, equivocal, and at loose ends in woman, and for her vanity, frigidity, helplessness. Within the structure of the psyche it functions as a kind of bridge between the individual consciousness and the collective unconscious, unlike the persona that serves as the bridge between a man's ego-consciousness and the world. It is through the anima that the latent, unconscious contents of the psyche are projected. It is a natural index to our internal psychological situation, and as Jolande Jacobi observes: "The seeker after self-knowledge will do well to accord it the utmost attention." [13]

The anima can appear in many guises. In literature some of its most familiar manifestations are Kundry in *Parsifal*, Andromeda in the Perseus myth, Helen of Troy, Beatrice in the *Divine Comedy*, Dulcinea in *Don Quixote*. What is of particular significance is the compensatory quality of the anima in its relation to the persona. Thus if the persona, man's habitual outward role or attitude, is intellectual, his anima, or soul image, reflecting his inner attitude, is apt to be sentimental: "the more rigidly the mask, the persona, cuts off the individual from his natural, instinctual life, the more archaic, undifferentiated, and powerful becomes the soul image." [14] So long as the different aspects of the unconscious, that is, the shadow and the anima, are not integrated with consciousness, a man's unconscious life will be predominantly feminine.

Like the shadow the anima may appear in either a positive or a negative light: it may be a person's wise guide or

---

[13] Jolande Jacobi, *The Psychology of C. G. Jung*, trans. Ralph Manheim (New Haven: Yale University Press, 1962), pp. 111 f.

[14] *Ibid.*, p. 115.

inspiring Muse, a Beatrice, or it may be a witch or a demon leading him to the destructive darkness. Like the shadow it is usually activated in mature years when the extroverted orientation of consciousness characteristic of our adaption to the outside world is ending, and the equally necessary adaption to the inner world begins.

The concept of the anima helps us, I think, to understand the significance of Borg's relationship to Maria. She is his soul image, and "an index" to his internal psychological situation. Since Borg's role as the scientist and intellectual has forced him to repress all spontaneity, all naturalness, the full range of the life of the feelings, the appetites of the healthy, natural man, Maria appears in the compensatory role of the childish, capricious, and irresponsible female, guided by her feelings. Nothing disturbs Borg as much as Maria's lack of a dominant role or persona: to him she is just a conglomerate of roles and without any definite identity (114).[15]

Borg is, interestingly, not without his own feminine traits. In an ironic, but not unexpected manner, he who has been taught by his father to suppress all feminine qualities and to place woman very low in his estimation, is actually effeminate in behavior, as evident in his dress, in his love of jewelry and beautiful china. Nervous, high-strung, irritable, he is given to frequent irrational responses. If his cup of coffee is not of the right temperature it may upset him for hours, a remark or a gesture may unsettle him for days.

Since Maria represents all the qualities that Borg has repressed, aversion and attraction alternate in his attitude to her: theirs is a love-hate relationship. When Borg succeeds in seducing Maria it is a hollow victory, born of a desire to bring the affair to an end. When Maria leaves the island the following day he is relieved, and delighted to return to the

---

[15] In this respect she is very similar to Maria in *The Defense of a Fool*.

old routine and to his solitude, more convinced than ever that the life of the intellect can only be purchased at the cost of "fasts and self-denial." In his solitude he experiences feelings of euphoria, his self now free from all outside pressure, from all contact with vulgar minds. It is then that he makes the fateful decision that seals his doom: to stay on the island over the winter. For, having rejected his soul image, having failed to integrate the aspects of the psyche she represents, the floodgates of the unconscious are opened, and Borg gradually loses his sanity, regressing in stages to a state of infancy. The feelings he has rejected and repressed return in a destructive form.

In the beginning Borg is delighted at no longer being the prey to suggestions from the outside world, finding a great sense of relief in not having to adjust himself to the level of "the others," but his sense of being in full possession of himself soon wanes, and a rapid deterioration of his mind sets in. In his lonely and stuffy chamber the sound of the wind, the roaring of the waves, and the piercing sounds of the buoy make him nervous and tense. To close out the sound he puts little steel props in his ears, but the result is that his overactive mind begins to work under an even higher rate of pressure, and without control as unregulated thoughts give way to unregulated fantasies. Only drugs can put his mind to sleep temporarily.

Soon he begins to be tormented by paranoiac delusions. He feels that there is a conspiracy against him, that the people are spying on him. In lucid moments he does not believe that this is really so, "because he knew very well, that persecution mania was the first symptom of the weakness that accompanies isolation" (223). Nevertheless, since he really has been persecuted in his life and has proof of this, he tells himself he does not suffer from "sickly persecution mania."

Borg's condition gradually worsens. With the bleakness

of winter not even nature can afford him stimulating impressions. After a month's isolation his voice grows thin, so that he feels he is listening to a stranger. He resigns from his position. In the end, tormented by dreams and hallucinations, and physically weak from lack of food, he remains in bed.

But even before Maria's departure another archetypal figure has activated and projected other psychological conflicts within Borg. This figure appears in the guise of a preacher whom Borg himself has brought to the island, mainly as a generous concession to the ladies, who have a missionary zeal for the welfare of the souls of the fishermen. This is ironic, for Borg is a man who, in himself as well as in others, tries to bury the Christian faith, or any other type of faith for that matter, as superstitions born of primitive fear and thus unworthy of modern man and his enlightened scientific mind. Paradoxically, the preacher is instrumental in bringing to the surface Borg's own latent fears and superstitions and guilt feelings.

Borg is a man who feels superior to God. With his scientific knowledge, he is a Titan challenging creation, correcting its flaws, putting order into the chaos of nature. He enjoys the sense of power and self-aggrandizement which comes from his ability to create life and order out of the raw material of nature. He is a Prometheus rebelling against the Gods in order to build the kingdom of man. At times Borg even insists that "God is myself or in myself."

In some instances Borg's need to play God and to be worshiped as a God attains demonic proportions. In order to impress the people with his power he turns his scientific knowledge into magic performances. While he does demonstrate a desire to help the people, his greatest need is to gain power over them, even at the cost of frightening them. One such magic performance is very revealing and serves to precipitate Borg's ultimate downfall, for it puts the power he has sought into the hands of the preacher. The incident occurs in chapter eight.

With his knowledge of optical phenomena Borg creates a mirage. Using some boards and paint he erects what will appear as an Italian landscape when seen from the island. The effect is unexpected. The miracle is greater than he had bargained for. The crowds are frightened by the mirage, and so is Borg, who turns deathly pale at the sight! When the crowd turns to him as toward a God, he is frightened of his own power, "frightened as before a natural force that he had unleashed but could not control." When he tries to explain to the ignorant fishermen the principle behind the phenomenon they naturally do not understand him. So he begs—and this is the great irony—the preacher to explain the phenomenon, which the latter does, but in his own way, taking advantage of the situation.

That the preacher is a symbolic figure, a projection of Borg's unconscious mind, becomes quite evident in a scene in chapter nine, a scene that is one of the high points in the novel. Borg has taken a boat and rowed out to sea; he finds himself in a thick fog and is enjoying the pleasure of being alone, of recollecting himself. Having steered by the sound of the buoy, he suddenly finds himself in bright sunshine and in full view of the buoy, the solitariness of which he envies. After a moment he finds himself again in the fog, where he mysteriously encounters another boat of ghostly appearance. In it is the preacher. Between the two men "a close combat of minds" ensues, a confrontation deliberately sought by the preacher. The conversation between the two men reveals that Borg and the preacher are old schoolfellows, and that the course of the preacher's life has been determined by an unfortunate remark that Borg had let fall some twenty-five years earlier. But the preacher insists that he no longer hates Borg, because he has, as he puts it, left the revenge to God. Borg realizes he has to do with a formidable enemy: how formidable this enemy really is he does not even suspect.

What Borg does not realize is that the preacher is his own shadow, a projection of his own repressed feelings of fear and guilt. Like the anima the shadow clearly reveals its compensatory function in this case, for what it brings to the surface is the child in himself which Borg has so ruthlessly repressed. He who has tried to play God is now reduced to an infant searching for a father to hold his hand in the dark. The preacher ironically assumes this father role. As Borg's mind starts to deteriorate he gradually regresses and begins to feel the need for the spiritual comforts of his childhood faith. Dreaming that he is a stranded ship tossed on the waves, he suddenly feels that he is touching firm ground again as the preacher grips his hand. In a fit of remarkable insight Borg tells the preacher: "If you were a woman instead, I would return to life, because woman is man's roots in the earth" (236). But he has lost his roots forever, for the woman he loves is now engaged to another.

With a childish, entreating voice Borg then begs the preacher to tell him a fairy tale, which the latter does, telling him the story of Tom Thumb. Borg remarks on the benefit to be derived from listening to these old tales: "it is restful to sink down into the best memories from the time when one was a little animal and loved the useless, the unreasonable, the meaningless." Then he asks the preacher to recite the Lord's Prayer, in which he discovers a new source of strength. In the past he had found his "Archimedean point" within himself, in his own mind, not outside himself like the weak Christians, but now he too feels the need for a firm point, an imaginary magnet, outside himself, in God.[16]

---

[16] It is interesting to note that Strindberg's friend, the Swedish poet and novelist Ola Hansson, with whom he corresponded fre-

"Give me a few more hypotheses," he cries, "above all the firm point outside of me, for I am completely loose" (238). He now fears "empty nothingness" suffering from "Horror vacui" (238–239).[17]

In the final stages of his insanity, as Borg suffers from hallucinations, nightmares, delusions of grandeur, and ideas of persecution, and Strindberg makes increasing use of symbolism to convey a feeling of what is taking place in Borg's mind, an additional archetype of the unconscious makes its appearance. This is the *child* archetype, here represented in the form of the homunculus. The child archetype is, according to Jung, apt to make its appearance in a mind that has separated itself in an extreme manner from whatever is child-like.[18]

As he nears his death, Borg suddenly gets a longing for a child and begins to conduct experiments with his own sperm with a view to producing a child, a child that is to be his own creation, thus, as he puts it, solving "the problem of the homunculus" (235). During these last days he himself has become something of a child, and, being treated like a baby, Borg not only needs to hear the old prayer to a father in heaven, but also asks the preacher to tell him fairy tales, and, interestingly, the particular fairy tale he asks for is the story of Tom Thumb, a classic homunculus figure according to Jung. One of Borg's last actions is also related to the homun-

---

quently during the years 1888–1890, had just published a story about schizophrenia, precisely entitled *Arkimedes punkt* (Ola Hansson, *Husvill och andra berättelser* [Stockholm: Tiden, 1960]).

[17] Several pages of the novel were inserted after Strindberg had submitted his manuscript to the publisher. These are the pages describing the preacher's visit to the inspector's bedside (p. 236, line 9, to p. 239, line 11) (*Brev*, VIII, 65n).

[18] C. G. Jung, "The Psychology of the Child Archetype," in *The Archetypes and the Collective Unconscious* (New York: Pantheon, 1959), pp. 151 f., 304.

culus archetype. In his confused state he staggers down to the beach, where he finds a stranded ship. Some boxes containing dolls have been washed ashore, and Borg taking the dolls to be little children gathers them in his arms and brings them home to his cottage to warm them by the fire and to care for them, feeling that he has found something to live for.

But of all the symbols in the final chapters none is more powerful and moving than that of the sound buoy. For as Borg nears his dissolution the sound buoy, once the proud symbol of isolation and independence, a symbol of man's taming of the sea, changes its meaning and becomes a symbol of his predicament. In his dreams Borg now feels like "a sound buoy set adrift, drifting and drifting in order to seek a shore to be cast upon" (230). His mind has lost its power of reasoning, and he is without a self, without a firm point. He is completely "loose" as he tells the preacher. The sound buoy with its continuous and piercing scream, sounding through the violent storm "as if it were crying for help," seems to echo Borg's cry for an anchor for his lost ego.

In his dreams Borg manifests the desire to return to his origin, to the mother's breast, now the only refuge:

he now often woke after having dreamed that he lay like a child at his mother's breast. The soul was evidently regressing, and the memory of the mother as the origin, the link between unconscious and conscious existence, the solacer, the intercessor, appeared. Childish thoughts about a reunion in another existence came forth, and his first thoughts of suicide manifested themselves in the form of a compelling longing to be restored to the mother somewhere in another world, one in which he did not believe. (231)

The closing scene may also be said to represent a symbolic reunion with the mother. It is Christmas Eve, and Borg, now on the very brink of total madness, in a moment of lucidity manages to leave the cottage and find his way to the harbor. He finds a boat, casts off, and sets sail for the open sea. With his back defiantly turned away from the land where the Christians are celebrating their god Jesus, Borg, alone under the stars, takes his bearings, not from the star of Bethlehem, but from the star Beta in the constellation Hercules. In proud defiance he invokes Hercules as his god, "the god of strength and wisdom, who killed the Lernaean hydra with its hundred heads, cleansed the stables of Augeas, caught the man-eating mares of Diomedes, robbed the Queen of the Amazons of her belt, and brought Cerberus from the gates of hell, finally to perish through the stupidity of a woman who from sheer love, poisoned him, after he had in his madness served Omphale, the nymph, for three years." Hercules, who refused to bow to his enemies, who refused to beg for mercy, who could only fall by his own strong hand, who liberated Prometheus, the bringer of light—he is the ideal, not Jesus.

It is toward this "new Christmas star" that Borg steers, "across the sea, the Great Mother, in whose lap was kindled the first spark of life; the inexhaustible source of fertility and love, the origin and the enemy of life" (243).

There is a striking and highly significant combination of symbols in this closing scene, deserving of further comment. The mythical hero Hercules is combined with the sea as the symbol of the Great Mother. Many strands of meaning are interwoven here, and I try to unravel only the most obvious ones. The most obvious aspect of the Hercules legend is of course the struggle of a masculine hero against feminine bondage. This is also the aspect stressed by Strindberg. Persecuted by his wicked stepmother Hera, duped by his wife, enslaved by Omphale—such is the life of Hercules. But his father Zeus is always on his side helping him perform his labors.

Translated into the language of Jungian psychology the myth of Hercules takes on added significance, for here Hercules' struggle to free himself from bondage comes to represent not only the effort to break the power of a maternal culture and to establish a masculine culture, but also the effort of consciousness to separate itself from the unconscious and establish its autonomy. For the women in the Hercules myth all represent the Great Mother, the archetypal image of the primordial realm of the unconscious, and the hero's fight is "always concerned with the threat to the spiritual, masculine principle from the Uroboric dragon or serpent, and with the danger of being swallowed by the maternal unconscious." Hercules represents the ego, logos, consciousness, and light; for like Prometheus he is one of the conquerors of the darkness. Hence he is a god of wisdom, of the spirit, as well as of strength.[19]

Of great significance in this context is the scene in which Borg (who, incidentally, wears a bracelet embellished with the insignia of the Uroboros, the serpent biting its own tail) actually in a state of euphoria visualizes himself in the godlike role of one who has separated light and darkness. In his study, busying himself with the classification of natural phenomena, his occupation fires him with "the idea that it was really he who had reduced chaos to order, he who had separated light and darkness; that chaos had only ceased with the birth of the organ of consciousness, capable of distinguishing between light and darkness when they in reality were not yet separated." The idea literally intoxicates him, until he feels his self expanding, and his "brain cells growing, bursting

---

[19] The relationship between the myths of the hero and the development of consciousness has been analyzed by Erich Neumann in his book *The Origins and History of Consciousness* (New York: Pantheon, 1954), to which I am indebted. In Scandinavian mythology Thor plays the same role as Hercules in classic mythology, for Thor battles the Midgard Worm, the Cosmic Serpent or Uroboros of Scandinavian mythology (Joseph Campbell, *The Masks of God: Occidental Mythology* [New York: Viking, 1964], pp. 447 f.).

their shells, multiplying and forming new species of concep-
tions in due time to go forth as thoughts, falling like leaven
into the brains of strangers; transforming millions of them, if
not before, then after his death, into hotbeds for his thought
seeds . . ." (181–182).

We are now in a position to grasp the meaning of Borg's
final invocation of Hercules, as he sails across the sea to his
death. Borg is a man who has rigorously cultivated the masculine principle, logos, the spirit, while combatting the irrational, the life of the feelings, the unconscious. But now the
Great Mother, here symbolically represented by the Uroboric
sea, is reclaiming her own, as Borg's consciousness is about to
be extinguished, returning to its origin in the maternal unconscious, which is, significantly, represented both as the origin and the enemy of life or of consciousness. Nevertheless,
Borg's last act is one of defiance, of revolt against the inevitable.

To unravel all the interwoven strands of meaning in this
complex novel is a difficult task indeed. The action moves on
several overlapping planes, and, in addition, Strindberg's point
of view remains, as almost always, ambiguous. On the surface
level, the story of Axel Borg is obviously the story of a proud
and intelligent individual's defeat as a result of pressures both
from "above" and from "below," pressures from his envious
colleagues and superiors who have driven him into isolation,
and from the ignorant islanders who resent his intelligence.
On a deeper, psychological level, the story of Axel Borg is
the story of the divided self, a self in conflict due to an over-
emphasis on the rational faculties and a corresponding repression of the life of the feelings and the senses. On this
level, Borg is the agent of his own destruction, although here
again his defeat may be seen as the result of pressures from
"above," at least metaphorically speaking, for in the background there looms a father figure, whose teachings have

formed Borg's character and inculcated his extreme intellectualism. On a yet deeper level, finally, the story of Axel Borg is a primitive and archetypal drama, centering on the conflict between consciousness and the unconscious. It is here that the novel is most equivocal. On this level Axel Borg is no longer a mere scientist; he is a mythical hero, Hercules, defending the masculine principle of spirit and logos against the maternal unconscious. The ambiguity resides in the fact that this hero is simultaneously a weak and effeminate individual, who in the end is reduced to an infant longing for his mother's breast. How are we to resolve this contradiction?

The answer lies, I believe, in Strindberg's keen awareness of the antinomies of the Romantic self, an awareness he had already demonstrated in *The Son of a Servant*. Like Ibsen in his last plays, Strindberg is dramatizing his belief that the cult of the autonomous self is accompanied by a yearning to overcome the separation that it brings, and that nemesis lies in wait for the man who purchases his spirituality at the price of cutting himself off from life.[20] Like Freud, who in this respect as in so many others follows in the footsteps of the Romantics, Strindberg in *By the Open Sea* dramatizes the unreconcilable conflict between those forces within the self which serve the ends of civilization and those that represent desires of a more primitive, biological origin. This conflict we shall encounter again, in a different form, in our next novel, *Inferno*.

---

[20] I have reference here to such late plays by Ibsen as *The Master Builder* and *When We Dead Awaken*.

⤙ 11. Inferno

THE 1890's were difficult years for Strindberg. After he had settled in Paris in 1894 for the purpose of making a name for himself in the world of science as he had already done in the theater, Strindberg underwent a severe mental crisis which ultimately brought in its wake a complete spiritual and religious reorientation and a period of intense creativity during which he wrote some of his greatest works. There is already a rich and varied literature relating to this so-called Inferno crisis. Eminent psychiatrists and scholars have analyzed the nature of the crisis and the factors that precipitated it.[1] I have no desire to add to this discussion

---

[1] The best study of this period is Gunnar Brandell's *Strindbergs Infernokris* (Stockholm: Bonniers, 1950). An excellent book, valuable in particular for its criticism of the efforts of German psychiatrists to analyze Strindberg as a schizophrenic individual, is Dr. Sven Hedenberg's *Strindberg i skärselden* (Göteborg: Akademiförlaget-Gumperts, 1961).

by offering a new or different interpretation. In this context I wish merely to consider *Inferno*, the first, and the major, prose work of the period, as a work of fiction, and to determine its significance in the development of our major theme, the quest for identity. Though *Legends*, the second volume to grow directly out of the Inferno crisis, includes the highly exciting but fragmentary experiment *Jacob Wrestling*, I do not deal with it here, for it is a much inferior work and adds little of significance.

Is *Inferno* a journal or is it a work of fiction? Strindberg's own remarks about the book throw little light on this question for they are as so often ambiguous. In a letter to Torsten Hedlund, his particular confidant during this period, he writes that he is planning to describe his experiences during the crisis in a book, "a novel if you wish to call it that." [2] A few days later he writes that he feels the call to become "the Zola of occultism" and that he is planning "a prose poem called *Inferno*. The same theme as in *By the Open Sea*. The destruction of the individual when he isolates himself" (28, 409). After completing the book he insists that it "is extracted from my journal and not fiction" (410). In chapter nine of the finished work he insists he is not distinguishing among certain figures in "this account, which is not a novel with pretensions to style and literary form" (MS, 119).[3]

In my own opinion *Inferno* is a work of art. It belongs to the genre I have called fictional autobiography, for although Strindberg has based his book on extracts from his journals he has ordered and interpreted events within a narrative structure, while retaining a sufficient degree of immediacy and complexity to produce the effect of a work of

[2] August Strindberg, *Från Fjärdingen till Blå Tornet: Ett brevurval 1870–1912*, ed. Torsten Eklund (Stockholm: Bonniers, 1961), p. 297.

[3] Unless otherwise indicated, all references to the text are from the translation by Mary Sandbach (London: Hutchinson, 1962).

fiction.[4] It is a "mad" book, but to regard it as a pathological document, as a product of a mind hovering on the brink of insanity, as evidence of Strindberg's mental illness, is to ignore the manner in which Strindberg has transformed his experiences into art. Nothing, in fact, testifies more eloquently to Strindberg's sanity than the aesthetic distance that separates him from the madman who is the hero of the novel. Below the mad and melodramatic surface is a very conscious effort to discover a pattern of meaning in previously isolated experiences.

In *Inferno* Strindberg's dramatic-mythical vision celebrates its greatest triumph, for it is his most melodramatic work of fiction as well as his most self-consciously mythical work. Never before or since has there been a more "literary" hell in fiction. Not only does the narrator enliven the proceedings with his histrionic skill, like a veritable magician appearing in shifting guises, but he also projects his various roles in mythical form. Rebel and penitent, fool and martyr, saint and sinner, rationalist and visionary, alchemist and chemist, he is also Prometheus and Oedipus, David and Job, Napoleon and Faust, Orpheus and Dante. The consequences are twofold.

On the one hand, the hero's histrionic antics serve to lessen the horror of the experiences he is undergoing. The admixture of the ludicrous and the serious produces an effect of grotesque tragicomedy. The discrepancy between the particular experience or event and the hero's exaggerated response, either intellectual or emotional, is so wide that the effect is often laughable. As in *The Defense of a Fool* we as readers are placed in a situation where we are watching the hero's theatrical performance, while behind the scene we perceive the author in the guise of the experimental psychologist observing the poor madman's grotesque act.

---

[4] Cf. Brandell, *op. cit.*, pp. 224, 226.

On the other hand, while the hero's repeated tendency to view his experiences in a mythical light may appear as a sign of his megalomania, it is also a manifestation of his need to make some sense of his experiences. His efforts are not very successful, for they tend to involve him in contradictions and ambiguities, which he is unable to resolve or to hold in balance. But behind the hero's pathetic efforts we perceive Strindberg's dialetical mind pitting two points of view against each other, and thereby testing their validity. It is this inner dialogue couched in mythical terms which gives *Inferno* its dramatic (as distinct from its melodramatic) impact. The tension is between meaning and meaninglessness, and the hero's dilemma arises from the fact that the point of view that seems to provide meaning carries the implication of guilt, while the point of view that issues in meaninglessness carries the implication of innocence.

Approached in this light *Inferno* may be regarded as an experiment with points of view. An older point of view has been tested and found wanting after it has produced sterility and a sense of guilt. I hesitate to use the word despair for although Strindberg's hero has the symptoms of Kierkegaard's "sickness unto death," his vacillations between proud revolt and impotent anguish are so frequent that a sense of despair is absent. As Strindberg's own remarks indicate, it is the Romantic individualism of *By the Open Sea* which is being abandoned. The cult of the intellectual *Übermensch* and of the autonomous ego is again questioned as Strindberg searches for the missing "Archimedean point" in a hesitant return to religious belief. The experimental nature of this hesitant return to faith is also reflected in Strindberg's remarks about *Inferno*. Thus he writes in a letter to Torsten Hedlund of August 18, 1896: "As a test I am therefore taking leave of the natural sciences." [5] And in the epilogue to *Legends* he

---

[5] Strindberg, *op. cit.*

speaks of the year 1894 as the year in which he, he says, "as a matter of principle left my skepticism, which had threatened to devastate all intellectual life, and began as an experiment to adopt a believer's viewpoint." Having done so, Strindberg says, "there emerged the new spiritual life which has been described in *Inferno* and in these *Legends*" (28, 399).

If *Inferno*, as Strindberg himself suggests, is based on the same theme as *By the Open Sea*, that is, the destruction of the individual when he isolates himself from the world, it differs from the earlier novel in two respects. It treats the hero's experiences in a tragicomic vein, and it rescues him from his incipient destruction by disclosing the path pointing the way to a meaningful pattern. In the earlier novel the ego disintegrated when it failed to face and resolve the anxiety that threatened its autonomy. In *Inferno* the experiences that produce the anxiety are integrated in a meaningful framework, and thus the ego autonomy is restored, With the new vision a new self is about to be born.

But before we consider the growth of this new vision, let us explore the melodramatic and tragicomic surface of the novel in some detail.

It is not to make light of Strindberg's experiences during the Inferno crisis, or to doubt that he actually suffered mental and physical anguish, that I suggest that *Inferno* to a great extent reads like the tales of Edgar Allan Poe, that it appears derivative and literary. We know that Strindberg upon re-discovering Poe in the late 1880's felt that there were pro-found affinities between the two of them. We might also recall Strindberg's remark in a letter of 1888: "this genre (Edgar Poe) will be that of the next ten years." [6] Remarks to the same effect are often repeated in following letters. In 1889 he writes to Ola Hansson: "If you knew what I have experienced since I read E. P.—experienced—because I have

---

[6] *Brev*, VII, 212.

noticed it." [7] In one letter he even seems to suggest that he is a reincarnation of Poe (who died in 1849, the year of Strindberg's birth). Strindberg's new direction toward the occult undoubtedly received a strong impetus from the tales of Poe, a writer in whom he may well have recognized a kindred tendency to blend rationalism and mysticism. *Inferno* bears a strong stamp of Edgar Allan Poe in both its narrative technique and its atmosphere.

Thus we note that the protagonist of *Inferno* is cast in the role of the solitary outsider, "the orphan ego," like Poe's William Wilson an "outcast of all outcasts most abandoned." [8] Again and again in his tales Poe pursues the theme of loneliness, of homelessness, and of alienation. "Poe liked to quote la Bruyère (or was it Pascal?)," says Harry Levin, "to the effect that most of our ills spring from our inability to be alone with ourselves—a maxim which "The Man of the Crowd" exemplifies and which *The Lonely Crowd* has latterly confirmed. The dread of loneliness, the terror of the night, the anguish of being isolated with one's demon—or raven—the prospect at which other men blanch, Poe made it his business to contemplate." [9] Homelessness, Levin asserts, was a precondition of Poe's genius: "It is what made him so poignant a voice from the depths, what makes him so percipient a witness to the gropings of modern man. It is what drives him to polar extremes, frees him to search for the absolute, and abandons him to the infinite." [10]

We have already observed Strindberg's obsession with the theme of loneliness. In *Inferno* it culminates. The narrator voices his feelings about being an outcast with exag-

---

[7] *Ibid.*, p. 229.

[8] Harry Levin, *The Power of Blackness* (New York: Vintage Books, 1960), p. 142.

[9] *Ibid.*, pp. 162–163.

[10] *Ibid.*, p. 127.

gerated pathos: "And now a beggar, a branded man, an outcast from society. . . . Whipped, played out, hunted to death,
I slunk along the boulevards like a night-bird and crept back
to my hole among the pest-ridden" (MS, 31). "Isolated once
more, driven out by this accursed enemy of mine" (67). "I
wept like an abandoned child who is scared of the dark" (86).
"I am like a pelican of the wilderness. I am become as an owl
of the waste places" (144). "Silence and solitude encompassed
me, the stillness of a desert, solemn, terrifying" (23). "Alone,
absolutely alone" (84). "Vae soli! Woe to the solitary, a
sparrow on a roof!" (86).

Like Poe's heroes the narrator of *Inferno* is also the sole
actor on the stage, confronted by demons and chimeras.[11]
These take many forms: vampires, mysterious sounds, pressures over the chest, angina, electric shocks. This produces
an atmosphere of dread, of claustrophobia. Haunted by pho-
bias of persecution the hero seeks vainly to escape his con-
finement. The settings of his adventures are also replete with
the customary Gothic trappings.

The Hotel Orfila, where Strindberg's hero experiences
nights of terror, does not unexpectedly look "like a monastery," having about it "an atmosphere of mysticism" (49).
There he is confronted with mysterious letters (52), strange
piano music (65, 68), electric currents, clatterings and bang-
ings, vacuum pumps sucking at the heart (92). The Doctor's
house in Ystad has the appearance of a Buddhist monastery
(98), and again there is electricity (in the bedstead) (99),
and vampires groping for his heart in the night, thunder and
lightning (99). The narrator complains of feeling "like a
wild animal in a cage" or as if he were "locked up in a prison"
(25, 26). He feels lost in a labyrinth from which there is
no escape (96).

Characteristic both of Strindberg's narrator and of Poe's

---

[11] *Ibid.*, p. 154.

heroes is also the eagerness fostered in solitude to confront
the unknown, to pursue knowledge even if it is only to be
attained at the price of destruction.[12] A restless and morbid
curiosity drives the hero to journeys into darkness, to the
very brink of the abyss. Poe, we recall, was fascinated by
various occult phenomena, such as mesmerism, a fascination
springing from a desire to extend the limits of consciousness.
There is also in Poe a fascination with disease and death,
a morbid interest in suspended animation and in the sensations experienced by the dying.[13]

In *Inferno* there is a similar accent on necrophilia. As
the hero enters the hospital at the beginning of the novel
he brings along two newly purchased white shirts to be used
as shrouds, for he feels that his death is imminent (he is
actually troubled by burns on his hands from chemicals used
in his experiments). At the hospital he feels surrounded by
specters and toasts their death's-heads (26). Later he reads
them what he calls "the lovely little pamphlet" *The Delight
of Dying* and conducts experiments in order to "reconnoitre
the borderland between life and death." He lies down on his
bed, uncorks a bottle of cyanide, and drifts into unconscious-
ness. Alas, something always happens that restores him to
consciousness! (84).

The most significant similarity between Poe and Strindberg has to do with narrative method. Poe's tales are studies
in the grotesque, and their grotesque effect is achieved by a
subtle combination of the ludicrous and the burlesque with
the fearful and the horrible. "The common denominator" in
Poe's method, says Harry Levin, is his "extremism, which not
infrequently sets up its tensions between the sublime and
the ridiculous." In particular, Poe presents a curious blend
of the mystic and rationalist, being "an intuitive poet at one

---

[12] *Ibid.*, p. 107.
[13] *Ibid.*, p. 154.

extreme and the most rationalistic of critics at the other."
He might also, as Harry Levin suggests, have aptly described
himself in the portrait of the master detective Auguste Dupin,
as "the Bi-Part Soul . . . a double Dupin—the creative and
the resolvent." Poe's double mind spins its yarns in order
to disentangle them.[14]

I have already suggested that the curiously theatrical
and grotesque impact of *Inferno* is due to a similar tension
between the sublime and the ridiculous or between the fearful and the ludicrous.

A beautiful example of this kind of grotesque naturalism
is the description of the Hôpital de Saint-Louis in Paris,
where Strindberg was seeking a cure for his burned hands,
having as we recall brought along two new white shirts to
be used as shrouds, anticipating imminent death:

The bell sounded for lunch, and at the table I found myself among
a company of spectres. Faces like death's-heads, faces of the dying.
A nose missing here, an eye there, a third with a dangling lip,
another with a crumbling cheek. Two of the individuals at the
table did not look ill at all, but their expression was sullen and
despairing. They were master thieves of good family who, thanks
to their powerful relatives, had been let out of prison on the
grounds of illness. A nauseating smell of iodine took away my
appetite; my bandaged hands obliged me to seek the assistance
of my neighbors when I wanted to cut bread or pour myself a
drink. In the midst of this delightful company of criminals and
those doomed to die there moved our kind mother, the Matron,
in her austere habit of black and white, dealing out to each of us
his poisonous draught. I toasted a death's-head in a mug of arsenic;
he toasted me in digitalis. It was lugubrious and yet one had to
be grateful. Grateful, for anything so ordinary and at the same
time so offensive! (26)

In the following passage the emphasis on hygienic and
anatomic details lends a macabre note to the hero's descrip-

---

[14] *Ibid.*, pp. 134–136.

tion of his preparations for death. Diabolical machines have been placed in the adjoining room, but he refuses to flee, proudly facing the inevitable:

I made my preparations for the night. I had a bath and made sure that my feet were spotlessly clean, a thing to which I attach great importance, as my mother had taught me when I was a child that dirty feet are a disgrace. I shaved and sprinkled perfume on the shirt I had bought in Vienna three years earlier for my wedding. . . . A condemned man's last toilet.

From the Bible I read those psalms in which David calls down the vengeance of the Eternal upon his enemies. (91)

In the next passage it is not only the hero's tendency to magnify minor discomforts into major afflictions that lends a grotesquely comic note, but the sheer number of afflictions listed. Thus his room, referred to as "the roseate chamber," because it is painted in a delicate pink and white, is suddenly transformed into a chamber of horrors:

The floorboards rocked beneath my feet, the chair was tottery, the table wobbled, the commode swayed, the bed creaked and the rest of the furniture shook when I walked about the room. The lamp smoked; the ink-pot was too narrow, so that the penholder got inky. This was a country mansion that reeked of dung, filth, sulphuretted hydrogen, sulphate of ammonia, and carbon disulphate. The hubbub from the cows, the pigs, the calves, the hens, the turkeys, and the doves went on all day long. Flies and wasps annoyed me by day and mosquitoes by night. (127)

Here also the scientific exactness with which the particular chemical stenches are noted creates a comic effect.

Purely comical is the effect engendered by the hero's response to another affliction, a dish of calf's brains and browned butter, this being the dish that the hero detests above all. His mother-in-law serves it to him with the best intentions:

"I've got something especially good today, just to please you," she would say.

And then she would place before me calf's brains and browned butter. I would realize that she had made a mistake and eat it, but with a reluctance that an affectation of enjoyment could ill conceal.

"You are not eating anything!"

And she would replenish my plate.

This was too much. Formerly I used to ascribe all my misfortunes to female malice; but I recognized that this woman was innocent and told myself it was the devil. (130)

Much of *Inferno* is infected with this black humor, and the examples could be multiplied. To accentuate this fact is, I repeat, not to indicate any doubt that Strindberg's own experiences in Paris were authentic. I do not for a minute doubt that Strindberg suffered from prolonged attacks of anxiety, both neurotic and ontological, during these years. What I am stressing is that in *Inferno* this anxiety is represented in a tragicomic vein.[15] Strindberg was at the end of his endurance: his hero is not. Which means that the artist has triumphed over adversity.

To couple Strindberg's *Inferno* with Henry Miller's *Tropic of Cancer* might seem a frivolous enterprise to some. That Henry Miller himself would not think so is amply evident from his remarks about Strindberg's novel in *Tropic of Cancer* and elsewhere. There are actually many affinities between Strindberg and Miller. Both are autobiographical novelists, and both are writers in revolt against the world about them, ultimately pledging their allegiance only to the self. Between *Inferno* and *Tropic of Cancer*, in particular, there are many similarities: the savage black humor, the

---

[15] It is also to register my disagreement with Gunnar Brandell's conclusion that Strindberg in *Inferno* has described "in the first-person form, the experiences of a neurotic with claim to naturalistic exactness" (*op. cit.*, p. 226).

Parisian setting, the drama of the writer going through hell, the zero point of nihilism reached by the self when cut off from all social and traditional ties, the apocalyptic fervor, the feeling that the world as we know it is about to go up in flames.[16]

That it is the treatment of the Parisian scene in *Inferno* in particular which has fascinated Miller is quite evident in this eloquent passage from *Tropic of Cancer:*

After leaving the Pension Orfila that afternoon I went to the library and there, after bathing in the Ganges and pondering over the signs of the zodiac, I began to reflect on the meaning of that inferno which Strindberg had so mercilessly depicted. And as I ruminated it began to grow clear to me, the mystery of his pilgrimage, the flight which the poet makes over the face of the earth and then, as if he had been ordained to reenact a lost drama, the heroic descent to the very bowels of the earth, the dark and fearsome sojourn in the belly of the whale, the bloody struggle to liberate himself, to emerge clean of the past, a bright, gory sun-god cast up on an alien shore. It was no mystery to me any longer why he and others (Dante, Rabelais, Van Gogh, etc., etc.) had made their pilgrimage to Paris. I understood then why it is that Paris attracts the tortured, the hallucinated, the great maniacs of love. I understood why it is that here, at the very hub of the wheel, one can embrace the most fantastic, the most impossible theories without finding them in the least strange; it is here that one reads again the books of his youth and the enigmas take on new meanings, one for every white hair. One walks the streets knowing that he is mad, possessed because it is only too obvious that these cold, indifferent faces are the visages of one's keepers. Here all boundaries fade away and the world reveals itself for the mad slaughter-house that it is. The treadmill stretches away to infinitude, the hatches are closed down tight, logic runs rampant

[16] For an excellent essay on Henry Miller as an apocalyptic writer see George Orwell's "Inside the Whale," in *A Collection of Essays* (New York: Anchor Books, 1957), pp. 215–226, 246–256.

with bloody cleaver flashing. The air is chill and stagnant, the language apocalyptic. Not an exit sign anywhere, no issue save death. A blind alley at the end of which is a scaffold.[17]

Here Miller focuses on the ease with which Paris, "the very navel of the world," is transformed by Strindberg's abnormally heightened sensibility into an infernal charnel house. Alone in the world, cut off from the past, and terrorized by premonitions of the future, Strindberg and Miller both see their destinies mirrored in the very physiognomy of the city. The streets, the houses, the doorways, the signs, speak with a new language to those whose only refuge is in the streets, and the language is macabre. Names like "Hôtel du Tombeau des Lapins," or "Hôtel de l'Avenir" or "Impasse Satan" or signs like "Défendez-vous contre la syphilis!" suddenly seem filled with portents. Omens are everywhere in this city which as one of the cradles of civilization is also one of its "putrid sinks." [18]

We may, I believe, draw one significant inference from this brief comparison between Strindberg and Henry Miller, and that is that the vision of Paris as an inferno is not the product of a neurotic individual's very personal delusions but rather of the heightened sensibility of the modern alienated writer. The images are there, so to speak, but they do not always mean anything to us. To Miller and to Strindberg they are meaningful because they serve to express their condition and their apocalyptic vision of life. Paris serves as the ready-made inferno they need, as their objective correlative, to use a now hackneyed term. In this respect both have a mutual ancestor in Balzac, whose vision of Paris is also a blend of a Dantesque moral view with a Swiftian fondness for the grotesque.

---

[17] Henry Miller, *The Tropic of Cancer* (Paris: Obelisk Press, n.d.), pp. 213–214.
[18] *Ibid.*, pp. 214–215.

There is an important difference between Miller and Strindberg with respect to the manner in which they use the Paris setting. Miller makes Paris serve his own apocalyptic vision. His purpose is primarily expressionistic. Strindberg, as noted, does this also, but, in addition, he seems bent on finding a meaningful pattern in the sign language of the city, something that will throw light on the meaning of his destiny. Strindberg is, in other words, searching for self-knowledge, for an illuminating vision. Miller, on the other hand, manifests no such intention.[19] In this context, it is also interesting to note that Miller dwells on sex, while Strindberg sees symbols of guilt reflected everywhere. This indicates again that for Strindberg the quest for meaning is intimately tied up with the question of guilt.

One of the most striking features of *Inferno* is its conscious symbolism. In the development of Strindberg's art of fiction *Inferno* marks an additional step in the gradual transition from naturalism to symbolism. As in *By the Open Sea* the external world is largely a projection of the hero's mind, but what has been added is a conscious and deliberate insistence on an actual correspondence between the world and the hero's mind. In a sense this is a step backward, for it means that Strindberg's symbols have lost the rich and allusive quality they possessed in *By the Open Sea*. They have become signs rather than symbols, pieces in an allegorical tapestry. For this reason it would also be difficult to categorize *Inferno* as a work belonging to the Symbolist movement. There are superficial resemblances between Rimbaud's *Une saison en enfer* of 1873 and *Inferno*, but the differences are significant. While Rimbaud's work is visionary, exalted, musical, evoking a new and autonomous reality through the magic power of poetic images, *Inferno* is con-

---

[19] See Philip Rahv's essay on Henry Miller in his book *Image and Idea* (Norfolk: New Directions, 1949).

crete and earthbound and its symbols do not evoke a transcendental reality or suggest an intangible atmosphere. They
are instead concrete analogies for abstract qualities, harboring a moral or psychological significance to be explained and
analyzed.[20]

Strindberg's fantasies, like those of Poe, are materialistic.
The new poetic vision in *Inferno* may also aptly be described
as "a mysticism of everyday life," for it is based on the belief
that every banal incident in our daily lives may harbor deep
significance if we are able to perceive it. It fosters marked
exactness and precision of observation. Yet it is a form of
symbolism, for it stresses the transforming power of the inner
eye. Therefore the narrator can exclaim: "Clearly the spirits
have taken to realism just as we human artists have" (62).
Only we must be able to see that this realism is, in effect,
a kind of "superrealism," as Strindberg calls it in *Legends*.
The transforming power of the inner eye is the essential
quality in this Symbolist vision, the radically new element.
In the past Strindberg would have regarded such a vision as
a form of mental aberration, as delusion. That he has changed
his mind is evident in a letter to Hedlund: "Hallucinations,
fantasies, dreams, seem to me to possess a great degree of
reality. If I observe my pillow assume human forms, then
these forms are there, and if anyone says that they only (!)
exist in my imagination, then I say:—You say only?—What
my inner eye sees is more to me!" [21]

While these "hallucinations" are in part the products
of an abnormally heightened sensibility they are also the
products of a consciously working poetic mind which seeks
to connect hitherto disconnected and unrelated phenomena
and experiences into a meaningful pattern.

By employing the mode of the grotesque as well as a

---

[20] Brandell, *op. cit.*, pp. 220–221.
[21] *Ibid.*, p. 219.

conscious and deliberate symbolism Strindberg has created a considerable element of aesthetic distance between his own experiences and those of his hero. By projecting those same experiences onto a mythical plane he goes a step further, now seeking to impose some structure of meaning on an existence that appears without order or purpose.

Among the many mythical roles we may distinguish two main groups. To one group belong the great mythical heroes of the *Old Testament*, Job, Jacob, and David. To the other group belong the Promethean rebels against the Gods: Oedipus, Orpheus, Phlegyas, Prometheus himself, and Faust. For the sake of convenience I label the former the "Job roles" and the latter the "Faust roles." Although all the roles demonstrate the hero's megalomania, the Job role serves to emphasize his innocence, the Faust role his guilt.

He proclaims: "For between my fate and Job's there was assuredly some analogy at least. Was not I, too, afflicted by incurable ulcers? Had not poverty fallen heavily upon me, and my friends deserted me?" (65). And he feels that God has singled him out, "the righteous and blameless man," in order to put him to the test (125).

Like Jacob he is wrestling with unseen Powers attempting to frustrate his endeavors. Someone, he feels, is setting ambushes for him: "Where was he to be found, that I might wrestle with him?" (30). He says he wants a personal God so that he can challenge him and thus assert his own greatness.

Like David he calls down vengeance on his enemies who are persecuting him. Faced with them he recites the psalms of David, and prays for a sign from heaven, and is answered with a thunderclap.

Like Faust the hero is the great scientist who has sought to penetrate to the very heart of creation, conducting experiments in order to make gold. Having tampered with forbidden knowledge he is to be humbled and punished. He is assailed by doubts about having sacrificed his happiness on earth for a chimera, purchasing his knowledge at the cost of losing his dear ones, his wife and daughter.

Like Oedipus he has sinned from arrogance and hubris, "the one vice that the Gods do not forgive" (79). For he too has solved the riddle of the sphinx. "Listen to me, you Sphinx up there!" he shouts proudly, "I have solved your riddle and I defy you" (47).

Like Orpheus he has breathed new life into nature after it had nearly died at the hands of the materialistic scientists: "I had set myself up as a second Orpheus . . . and it was my task to bring her back to life" (79). Like Orpheus he is also punished by having his head torn from his body by the bacchantes, the women who have always persecuted him, and are now persecuting him, because he is the man "who had revived the dead natural sciences" (149).

Like Prometheus he is, finally, punished because he has revealed the secrets of "the Powers," the gods, to mortal man (140).

Whether in the role of Job or in the role of Faust the hero is attempting to find an explanation for his sufferings. The answers are, however, widely different. Let us consider the two major roles more closely in order to illuminate the fundamental difference.

In the role of Job the narrator voices his proud rebellion against the Powers who are persecuting him. Poor, ill, deserted by his friends, he is stoically bearing his sufferings for unknown sins. Why have these sufferings been imposed on him? he asks.

At an early date one explanation offers itself, an explanation that proves to have a persistent appeal to him. The notion is that his sufferings are a trial, that he has been selected for some higher destiny, that the Gods need him for some unknown purpose. "The idea again occurred to me," he says, "that Providence must have some mission which it intended me to carry out in this world, and this was the beginning of my education for it" (31). The Powers are chastising him in order to reform him, he is being instructed and enlightened by them (33, 36). Even his enemies who persecute him are guided by unseen hands who have his welfare at heart (90).

What is the purpose for which he has been selected? This major question remains unanswered. Is he like Job, "the righteous and blameless man, put to the test by the Eternal, in order to demonstrate to the wicked how well an upright man can endure suffering unjustly inflicted"? (125). Perhaps he is, but having studied Swedenborg he arrives at a different explanation. The demons pursuing him have a good aim, they are disciplinary spirits aiding the Powers in their efforts to realize their plans. "And what are these plans? The perfection of the human type, the procreation of the Superman (Übermensch), that rod of chastisement, established in a place of honour by Nietzsche but too soon worn out and cast upon the fire" (163). Now he can tell his compatriots all over Europe: "Be therefore comforted and be proud of the grace that has been granted you, all ye who are sorrowful, who suffer from sleeplessness, nightmares, visions, anguish, and palpitations. Numen adest. God wants you" (163).

In this manner he finds in his sufferings an explanation that helps to fortify his own pride. He is not unaware of this, and in darker moments he hears another voice telling him that the demons who are pursuing him are within himself, and that they are only to be destroyed by repentance. But these are night thoughts, the products of silence and loneliness, of moments when we hear our heartbeats and feel a weight on our chests. In the morning when the sun shines, the old arrogance returns, and "the courage to revolt rears up and we fling our challenge and our doubts at Heaven"

(165–166). In such moments he sees no reason to repent, for would this not be to repudiate Providence, the Providence that had directed (or misdirected!) his fate? (164). Why should he humble himself before God? He has sought him but found the devil. Is he to be blamed for that? And to humble himself before God would be an insult to God for it would mean dragging him "down to the level of a planter who rules over slaves." And to pray to God is out of the question, for "Will you arrogate to yourself the right to bend the will of the Eternal and His decrees, by flattery and by servility?" (167).

It is also in this spirit of revolt that the book ends. In a moment of satanic humor the narrator concludes that existence is totally absurd, that it is all a jest, and that the Gods make merry over our sufferings. Summing up his life with its twists and turns and ups and downs he asks if all is not a colossal jest:

In my youth I was a true believer and you made of me a free-thinker. Of the free-thinker you made an atheist, of the atheist a monk. Inspired by the humanitarians, I extolled socialism. Five years later you showed me the absurdity of socialism. You have cut the ground from under all my enthusiasms, and suppose that I now dedicate myself to religion, I know for a certainty that before ten years have passed you will prove to me that religion is false.

Are not the Gods jesting with us mortals, and is that why we too, sharing the jest, are able to laugh in the most tormented moments of our lives?

How can you require that we take seriously something that appears to be no more than a colossal jest? (164–165)

In seeking to lead a virtuous life he has involved himself in similar absurdities. Withdrawing from bad company he has been attacked by the demons of solitude. Having vanquished his evil passions by abstinence, he has fallen into

the sin of thinking himself superior to others. Shunning
women he has been tormented by dreams. But coming home
drunk after midnight he has awakened fresh as a young god
(167).

At the end of the book he appears ready to embrace
Catholicism, but concludes: "What then? And thereafter?
A new jest on the part of the Gods? For when we weep
scalding tears they roar with laughter" (173).

In the epilogue he suggests for a mement that these
words are unworthy and that they should be crossed out, but
they remain. He now sees himself in the role of the good fool,
a laughingstock because he had thought of himself as a
prophet but has proved an impostor. He insists, however, it
is the Lord "who has led this false prophet astray and caused
him to speak, so the false prophet can feel that he is blameless, as he has only been playing the part assigned to him"
(174). "Behold, my brothers," he says, "one human destiny
among many, and confess that the life of a man may well
look like a jest" (175).

There is tremendous power in the last pages of the novel
and they carry firm conviction. In his attempts to play on the
reader's sympathies by depicting his nightmarish torments
the hero produced only a melodramatic effect; in these later
pages in which a whole life is summarized he reaches the
heights of a black and satanic humor. These pages of *Inferno*
also anticipate the vision of existence which emerges in the
post-Inferno novels and plays, a vision well summed up in
this passage in the novel: "It may even be that in the recesses
of our souls there lurks a vague notion that everything here
on earth is but a masquerade, a semblance, an illusion, and
that the Gods make merry over our suffering" (151).

Considering the hero's view of existence, it is not surprising that he is unwilling to abandon the cult of the self,
though there are those who like his friend the Theosophist

argue that his problem is excessive pride and counsel the denial and mortification of the ego. The latter idea strikes the hero as "insane." "All that I know, little as that may be," he says, "springs from one central point, my Ego. It is not the cult but the cultivation of this which seems to me to be the supreme and final goal of existence." His answer to his Theosophical friend is: "to kill the Ego is to commit suicide. . . . For that matter," he continues, "to whom shall I submit?" This is of course the heart of the matter. He is not willing to submit to a party, or to an ideology or a faith, or to the Powers: "To strive for the preservation of my Ego in the teeth of all the influences that a domineering sect or party may try to impose upon me," he insists, "that is my duty" (80–81).

When coupled with the hero's delusions of grandeur this proud defense of the ego in the face of the absurdity of existence may well be said to represent the apogee of Strindberg's Romantic cult of the autonomous self. For underneath a new vision is gradually developing, a vision destined to undermine this worship of the autonomous self. It grows out of what in the symbolic-mythic texture of the book is represented as a conflict between love and knowledge. In this context we must consider the hero's Faust role and his ambitions as a scientist.

In the role of Job the narrator is searching for the meaning of his existence, in the role of Faust he is attempting to assess his most recent stage of development. In his quest for knowledge and power he has sought to achieve immortality as a scientist with grandiose ambitions to revise the natural sciences, to penetrate to the secrets of creation, and to eliminate the boundaries between spirit and matter. He has conducted experiments in alchemy attempting to make gold. But as his physical and mental torments increase in intensity he is gradually assailed by doubts. Has he not perhaps been tampering with forbidden knowledge? Has he not sacrificed his happiness for a chimera? Has he not sacrificed love in his quest for knowledge? Is he not guilty of hubris? Suppose his scientific investigations were pure folly?

Sitting in his armchair he opens his Bible at random and reads: "Thus saith the Lord, thy redeemer, and he that formed thee from the womb: I am the Lord, that maketh all things; that stretches forth the heavens alone; that spreadeth abroad the earth by myself; that frustrateth the tokens of the liars, and maketh diviners mad; that turneth wise men backward, and maketh their knowledge foolish" (85). In Viktor Rydberg's voluminous *Germanic Mythology* his eyes are suddenly glued to the following lines that seem to carry a message for him: "According to the legend, Bhrigu, who had learned everything from his divine father, became so proud of his knowledge that he believed it to surpass that of his master. For this the latter sent him to the underworld where, to humble his pride, he was made to witness many terrible things of which he had previously known nothing" (102–103).[22] After reading this passage he adds: "My own case precisely: arrogance, conceit, hubris, punished by my father and master" (103). He too has been sent to the underworld to be humbled: "No doubt about it. I was in Hell." His path seems clear: He must seek to curb his overweening ambition and quest for power through knowledge, and he must seek redemption for his sins.

As noted, the hero never really bows in humility before the Powers. He refuses to admit that he has been guilty of the sin of pride; he has not been the master of his destiny, for the Powers have guided him. He is realizing gradually that

---

[22] Viktor Rydberg's (1828–1895) *Undersökningar i Germanisk Mytologi* was published in two volumes, 1886–1889. Rydberg also translated Goethe's *Faust* (1876), a translation of which Strindberg was highly critical.

in his quest for knowledge he has sacrificed love, that his scientific ambition has brought him only sorrow and suffering.

Thus he insists in the very first chapter of *Inferno* that in his efforts to reach the summit of intellectual achievement he has been forced to choose between love and knowledge, and that in his willingness to choose knowledge he may have forgotten the innocent victims of his ambition. But simultaneously he says he feels freer than ever after having left his wife and children: "A feeling of spiritual purity, of masculine virginity, made me regard my past married life as something unclean." Marriage had stood in the way of his scientific studies, but like Buddha he had shown the courage to give up his wife and children when he was in the prime of life and enjoying the happiness of married bliss (43). But gradually he begins to realize that he has sacrificed "a life of happiness for myself and child too" for a chimera. Like Byron's Cain he begins to believe that knowledge is sorrow.

Despite his hesitations about the sacrifices involved in the quest for knowledge we recognize an attitude similar to Borg's in *By the Open Sea*. Intellectual excellence is only to be purchased at the high price that entails the repression of the life of the instincts and the feelings, the normal healthy appetites for sex, food, drink, companionship. A monastic life designed to preserve "spiritual purity" and "masculine virginity" is the prerequisite. Women are to be banished, not only women of flesh and blood but also woman as a symbolic figure, as a spiritual principle, for in either role woman serves to keep man chained to the earth.

Strindberg's letters from 1893, the year in which he met his second wife Frida Uhl, to 1896, the culmination of the crisis, also reveal his obsession with this conflict between love and knowledge. Strindberg portrays himself repeatedly as the eagle who wants to soar to the great heights of the spirit, and who is not to be fettered by any ties, particularly not by those of love which are the most intangible and yet the strongest. In his letters to his spiritual confrere his favorite project is also a monastery in which a higher and more beautiful human species is to be developed by a regime that involves a struggle against the animal in man: "the repression of the vegetative and animal functions in order to further the affective and the intellectual. The cultivation of the spirit through isolation and the shutting off of contact with the impure: emancipation from expensive and useless habits of living." [23] The purpose of the monastery, he says, is "the education of the superman and education means restraint on the lower instincts." The means to be sought are those needed "to liberate the spirit from bonds and elevate it above time and space," such as "the airplane (my invention), the private, not the airship; the telescope (without lens or mirror); etc. (see my Antibarbarus); the art of making gold and diamonds." No love or concern about humanity is to be advertised by the monastery, for all the emphasis is to be on the education of the individual. Sexual desires, the family, women, wine, and cabbage (!) are the obstacles to his own efforts to reach the heights, he insists, and adds that he is ready to break camp (this is 1894 and he was still living with Frida).

In a letter to Torsten Hedlund in the fall of 1895 Strindberg says that he is a misogynist like Buddha and the latter's great disciples, Schopenhauer, Nietzsche, and von Hartmann. He says he hates the earth because it fetters his spirit and because he is attached to it. And he adds: "Woman is for me the earth with all its glories, the bond that fetters; and all evil of the greatest evil I have seen, is of the female sex." And he wonders whether he will ever be able to mortify the flesh, young and fiery as it still is. He is in an impossible

---

[23] Strindberg, *op. cit.*, pp. 259–261.

dilemma for he cannot be without women. As a bachelor he falls prey to alcohol and prostitutes, the family ties him down.[24]

A telling shift in this attitude gradually emerges in *Inferno*. It involves the recognition already noted that in his quest for knowledge Strindberg has sacrificed love, but more important, the insight that the path to redemption and atonement leads through woman.[25] Woman is to lead him through inferno and purgatory and reconcile him to the Powers. We might recall that at one time Strindberg had regarded woman as a substitute for God, as an object for his religious worship. In this worship he had been bitterly disappointed and had responded by turning woman into a witch and a vampire. Now woman is restored to her role as an intercessor between him and the Powers, but she is not the same woman. She is emancipated from her sexual role and now appears as a representative of the feminine principle without whom man is somehow incomplete. She appears as a child, an older woman, or as an angelic, even androgenous creature. In the light of our previous discussion of the anima figure in *By the Open Sea*, it is clear that the women in *Inferno* are also anima archetypes. They belong to a very different category. They are guardian figures; their role is to integrate the divided self.

Before we consider these anima figures, let me note one final and extremely significant illustration of Strindberg's tendency to project the basic conflict of *Inferno* in a mythical form. I refer to an entry in the journal for May 3, 1897, which is reproduced in *Legends*. This date, incidentally, is

---

[24] *Ibid.*, p. 289.

[25] See also the letter of August 23, 1896, with the first plan for *Inferno*: "The same theme as in *By the Open Sea*. The destruction of the individual when he isolates himself. Salvation through: work without honor and gold, duty, the family, *consequently woman—the mother and the child!*" (28, 409). The italics are mine.

approximately when *Inferno* was begun. In this entry the narrator states that he has just discovered Richard Wagner's opera *Rheingold*. Praising Wagner as "a great poet" and wondering why he himself has not until now "perceived the greatness of this musician," he makes the interesting remark: "Moreover, *Rheingold* is written for me." He proceeds to quote the scene between the Rhinemaidens and the gnome Alberich in Act I, in which Alberich is told about the magic properties of the ring that can be fashioned of the gold in the river. The Rhinemaidens who guard the gold feel that it is safe, for one man alone can shape the gold into a ring, the man who has foresworn love: "Nur wer der Minne / macht versagt / Nur wer der Liebe / Lust verjagt." No man exists who is willing to forfeit a woman's love, they insist. Alberich who is racked by desire for love and has been chasing the maidens, surprises them by foreswearing love for the sake of power. Stretching out his hand toward the gold he curses love forever: "Das Gold entreiss' ich dem Riff, / schmiede den rächenden Ring: / Denn hör' es die Fluth— so verfluch' ich die Liebe!" (28, 313–314).

In this dramatic scene the powerful theme of the entire *Ring* is introduced, the conflict between the desire for love and the desire for power.[26] That Strindberg should have made this entry in *Legends* at the time when he began writing *Inferno* reveals the extent to which he was aware of a similar conflict in his own life, and also shows his unwillingness to project it except in a mythical form.

To return to the anima figures who help resolve the hero's conflict. There are four: his daughter, whom he calls Beatrice; his mother-in-law; a mother superior; and Séraphita.

The daughter is first introduced in the chapter entitled "Beatrice." In view of the narrator's identification with Faust,

---

[26] Cf. Ernest Newman, "The Rhinegold," in *Stories of Great Operas* (New York: Knopf, 1930).

when he feels the little girl's arms around his neck after a lengthy separation, he is ready at once to compare his experience to "Dr. Faustus's reawakening to an earthly existence, but sweeter and purer." In view of the passage quoted earlier in which he found special pleasure in his "masculine virginity" the lines that follow are interesting: "When a man loves a child he becomes a woman; he casts off his masculinity and experiences what Swedenborg calls the sexless love of those who dwell in Heaven. This was how I could begin to prepare myself for Heaven. But first of all I must expiate my sins" (MS, 113). The language is significant, because it points up the fact that the kind of reunion being prepared between the masculine and the feminine is a spiritual union, a psychological integration in the direction of wholeness.

Interesting, also, is the narrator's rejection of his wife, the sexual partner. He wants only the innocent child, and, as we soon discover, a mother figure represented by the child's grandmother. The extent to which Strindberg's development of this theme is based on his own marital conflicts at the time is made very apparent in Strindberg's correspondence with his mother-in-law and with his daughter Kerstin. In a letter of February, 1897, he says he longs for the company of a child rather than a woman, and that he is coming to Austria not to engage in a battle with his wife but in order to see his daughter, whom he refers to as "my Beatrice, who leads me through hell." [27] He calls her Beatrice, the guardian of love.[28] In a letter to Kerstin of March 21, 1897, he also refers to the writing of his book (*Inferno*) in which "you too play a part as Beatrice." [29] On April 29, 1897, he says that "*Inferno* does not work without Beatrice," and says he is visiting her in his

---

[27] August Strindberg, *Brev till min dotter Kerstin,* trans. Karin Boye and Ake Thulstrup (Stockholm: Bonniers, 1961), p. 59.

[28] *Ibid.,* p. 60.

[29] *Ibid.,* p. 85.

thoughts. The same phrase is repeated in a letter a week later. When the book is ready for publication he writes to Kerstin that in a few days she will be immortal in her role as Beatrice.[30]

Kerstin and her grandmother live in Austria, and it is to Austria that the narrator directs his steps in the chapter entitled "Beatrice." In Austria the narrator changes his description of inferno to some degree. The images grow more conventional. We are in Dante's inferno, and on Catholic ground. It is also here that the narrator begins to admire the beauty of Catholicism, the religion he is preparing to adopt at the end of the book when he contemplates entering a monastery. It is interesting that he describes this turning to Catholicism as a consequence of what he calls homesickness, a "homesickness for the Mother Church." Protestantism is considered an act of treachery against the mother religion (170–171).[31] The term "Mother Church" has a special significance for him (173). In this context we may also note the important role played by the mother superior of the Hôpital de Saint-Louis where he had been a patient at the beginning of his sojourn in Paris. From her he learned how wonderful it was to use the word "Mother," a word that had not, he says, "crossed my lips for thirty years" (26). And he describes his reaction at his parting from this motherly nun: "At our parting I had wanted to kiss the hand of our kind mother who, without preaching at me, had taught me the way to the Cross" (31). All these mother images are, I think, significant, for they too emphasize the narrator's concern with the feminine as a spiritual principle.

But there is another female figure in *Inferno*, and of still greater significance. Her name is Séraphita, and she is not a creature of flesh and blood, but an angelic and disembodied

---

[30] *Ibid.*, p. 115.

[31] A similar interest in Catholicism was expressed by Borg in *By the Open Sea* (24, 225 f.).

spirit. She is the central figure in a novel by Balzac bearing her name as the title. In the chapter entitled "Purgatory" the narrator tells us how he happened to pick up this novel by chance and registers the excitement with which he devoured its content. Thus he says, "*Séraphita* became my gospel. It caused me to renew my ties with the beyond to such an extent that life filled me with repugnance and Heaven drew me to it, so that I yearned for it with the irresistible yearning one has for home" (59).

Who is this Séraphita, and why does she play such an important role in *Inferno?* Briefly, she is a symbolic figure, a "luminous guardian" like Beatrice, representing the triumph of love over desire. The wisdom that she embodies is that contained in the writings of the Swedish eighteenth-century mystic Emanuel Swedenborg. In Balzac's novel, a symbolic and revelatory and prophetic book hardly enjoyable as a work of fiction, she guides a young intellectual from a search for knowledge motivated by the love of self and the world to the quest for divine wisdom, a quest inspired by the love of heaven. The man whose name is Wilfred is described as a man who has grown pale over his books, sick of knowledge, and who is now seeking absolution even if it will take him to the ends of the earth. Somewhere in Norway he meets a Pastor Becker whose glowing description of Séraphita makes him fall in love with her.

The Pastor's description of Séraphita emerges as an account of Swedenborg's doctrine (rather superficial, to be sure) and of the steps to be followed if man is to transform himself into an angelic spirit like Séraphita. The transformation can take place only through love, of which there are three stages: the love of self, the love of the world, and the love of heaven. Heaven is composed of angelic spirits like Séraphita. For the man of the intellect like Wilfred the road to heaven leads through love, a love inspired by a new science, a science that studies this world from the point of view of its correspondences with heaven. Ordinary science is shallow and superficial when compared to this divine science. "There is a supreme science, of which some men—too late—get a glimpse, though they dare not own it. These men perceive the necessity for considering all bodies, not merely from the point of view of their mathematical properties, but also from that of their whole relations and occult affinities."

Through his meeting with Séraphita Wilfred is reborn, finding a way out of his near madness through love and faith. Another of Balzac's heroes, Louis Lambert in the novel with the same name, comes to a less fortunate end, though he has affinities with Wilfred. Dedicated to the pursuit of intellectual perfection, straining his powers and faculties to an inhuman degree, Louis Lambert is a restless, tortured man, tormented by desire. He is split and divided. Half of him is dead. The study of Louis Lambert is a study of morbid degeneration, of a genius who gradually goes mad.

In a perceptive essay Henry Miller has argued that Louis Lambert is Balzac's double, his alter ego, in which he expressed his own restless and divided mind, and that *Séraphita* is to be considered as a companion volume to *Louis Lambert* (it appeared the following year), pointing the way to a new kind of wholeness, a bridging of the duality.[32]

Now we do know that the novels of Balzac had assumed a new significance for Strindberg in the 1890's. He had read Balzac much earlier, but not with the same degree of enthusiasm as in the 1890's. At age forty-one, he says, he has finally begun to read Balzac, whom he terms a writer for men.[33] He reads Balzac and finds all his surmises about life and people

---

[32] The discussion of *Séraphita* and *Louis Lambert* included here is based largely on Henry Miller's two essays "Seraphita" and "Balzac and His Double" in *The Wisdom of the Heart* (Norfolk: New Directions, 1941).

[33] *Brev*, VIII, 70, 97, 106, 156.

confirmed. He calls the novels of Balzac "my only company" and his "only reading." This is as early as 1890. The novels he read were in all likelihood the more familiar ones, the great realistic works like *Le Père Goriot*. At the time he was probably not familiar with the philosophical novels, the novels in which we meet Balzac the Romantic occultist. Therefore, when Strindberg discovered the latter during the Inferno period they must have struck him with great force, for they seemed to delineate some of his own problems, particularly the conflict between knowledge and love, which had left his own self split and divided and brought him to the verge of a mental breakdown.

A letter to his daughter Kerstin is revealing. Strindberg writes: "And when Frida-mama has devoured *Séraphita* she might also ponder *Louis Lambert* by Balzac. There she encounters herself and August-daddy too, and it is always good when bankrupt souls meet. That book, *Louis Lambert*, I got as a Christmas present from a friend here. It was the only volume of all Balzac's books to be found here, and that book is written for me and Frida-mama or *by* us both. Isn't it almost occult?" [34] *Séraphita* he had discovered earlier under similar "occult" circumstances. In a letter of December 17, 1896, he calls it "a wonderful book," adding, "The only danger is that one feels a complete stranger on earth and begins to long for the other side! But then that is what one ought to—." [35]

The major significance of the discovery of *Séraphita* is of course that it stimulated Strindberg's interest in the works of Swedenborg whose teachings were destined to provide much of the conceptual framework for his vision of life after the *Inferno* period. The works of the Swedish mystic help confer a meaning on his experiences and illuminate his di-

[34] Strindberg, *Brev till min dotter Kerstin*, p. 34.
[35] *Ibid.*, pp. 27–28.

lemma by opening up new avenues to knowledge, particularly
to the knowledge of the self. Thanks to Swedenborg he can
interpret the strange events that have befallen him on a
moral as well as on a psychological plane. "Swedenborg," we
read, "brought light to my soul, dispelled my doubts, my vain
speculations about my imaginary enemies the electrical ex-
perts and the practitioners of black magic." "*Arcana Coeles-
tia*," he says, "solved for me all the riddles of the past two
years," solved it by convincing him of the physical existence
of Hell, and that he had in fact passed through it. "Swedenborg," he continues, "explained to me the reason for my stay
in the Hôpital de Saint-Louis thus: Alchemists are attacked
by leprosy, which produces itching scabs like fish scales—my
incurable skin disease in fact. Swedenborg interpreted the
meaning of the hundred conveniences of the Hôtel Orfila:
They were the Hell of Excrement" (161). Swedenborg also
explained his physical torments, his acute anxieties, his palpitations, his electric girdle as sensations that befall victims of
what he calls *Devastation*. The experiences he has had are in
fact identical to those Swedenborg describes in his *Dream
Diary* of 1744, the latter's record of his own spiritual devastation.

The narrator of *Inferno* is at times very eager to identify
with Swedenborg whom he calls "his sublime countryman,"
and "Buddha of the North" (161). This is significant, because it suggests the narrator's growing insight into the roots
of his difficulties, the source of his guilt. Before his conversion
Swedenborg was a scientist, a man of overweening ambition
with an enormous desire for fame, who dreamed of far-
reaching discoveries and toyed with mighty cosmological
theories. His religious crisis in 1743–1745 seems to have
brought him a recognition of the devastating effect of this
desire for personal self-aggrandizement. As a result of the
crisis he came to regard egotism as hell, as synonymous with

ignorance, and as the chief obstacle to the search for real wisdom. Swedenborg gave up science and sought divine wisdom through love and piety.

Strindberg's situation is of course somewhat analogous, for he too had conducted bold experiments in an effort to reach brilliant new scientific discoveries, and he too had been beset by similar torments indicating that the Powers were trying to redirect his steps. Now Swedenborg was pointing to his only way to salvation: "to seek out the demons in their lair, within myself, and to destroy them by—repentance" (164). And Strindberg continues: "Balzac, as the prophet's adjutant, had taught me in his *Séraphita* that remorse is the impotent emotion felt by the man who will sin again; repentance alone is effective, and brings everything to an end." There follows then the soul-searching that I have already recorded, during which he gradually seems to convince himself that he ought *not* to repent. His feelings of guilt have been brought to the surface, but in the end he proves unwilling to assume the burden of guilt.

While the hero of *Inferno* insists to the bitter end that he is righteous and blameless like Job and that the Gods are making sport over us mortals, he has of course clearly revealed to his readers that his quest for knowledge has led to a state of creative impotence. He is only half a man, like Louis Lambert, having cut himself off from the real sources of creativity. He has one-sidedly cultivated the intellect and the Faustian will to power at the expense of basic humanity. Above all, he has revealed his lack of self-knowledge, his lack of insight into the fact that the root of his troubles lies in his abnormally inflated ego, in his perpetual desire for self-aggrandizement.

All this proves that Strindberg knows more than his hero, that he is dramatizing an inner conflict that he himself has already resolved. Strindberg knew that his scientific ambitions had led him astray, away from his real vocation, and deep down he was aware of his megalomania. He also knew that his skepticism had proved barren, that he needed a faith in something outside himself. He seemingly already knew this when he wrote *By the Open Sea*, for he let Borg drown in the sea of the unconscious while crying out for an Archimedean point, a firm anchor for the not so autonomous self. The hero in *Inferno* is groping for this Archimedean point, and it is evident that the cure for his ills will be found in a return to faith. He is unwilling to abandon the cult of the self, but he appears ready to embrace a new vision that will ultimately force him even to that step. He is now seeking a contact with "the other side," a belief that he is guided by a stronger power who is concerned about his spiritual welfare. In the language of psychology we might say that he is trying to integrate the unconscious self and the new knowledge that this brings. A new self is in the process of formation.

For the time being it is Swedenborg who acts as the spiritual mentor. He is, as the hero in *Legends* puts it, "my Vergil guiding me through Hell" (28, 294). This is not the time or place to launch into a survey of Swedenborg's unique vision of life, for it would lead us too far into the realms of metaphysical speculation. It suffices to say that Swedenborg's philosophy is a form of Romantic occultism which conceives of the things of this world as analogies and metaphors intimating the existence of a transcendental reality and the unity of all things. Since the transcendental reality is within man it means that Swedenborg stresses the affinities between the external world and the mind and heart of man, obliterating the customary distinction between the organic and the inorganic world and between matter and spirit. This is the most familiar aspect of Swedenborg's philosophy, the so-called theory of correspondences which has had such a strong influence on so many modern writers. The implications of the new vision are numerous. In this context I point only to three major ones: moral, psychological, and aesthetic.

In moral terms the new vision of life enjoins man to the search for a new kind of knowledge, the divine wisdom that is attained through the study of correspondences. The quest for knowledge is not to be motivated by a desire to further personal ambition but by a desire to know God. God himself becomes in fact identical with knowledge (MS, 172). Selfishness is the main obstacle to knowledge, synonymous with ignorance.[36]

In psychological terms the significance of this vision is that it opens up new avenues to self-knowledge. In view of the correspondence between inner and outer events the world becomes a set of signs to be interpreted as guideposts. Strange coincidences, mysterious events, unusual sensations, dreams, are no longer to be disregarded or considered as delusions but interpreted in terms of psychological significance.

The aesthetic implications of Swedenborg's vision of life are also far-reaching and significant. In essence, Swedenborg confers a new and elevated role on the poet by raising the function of the metaphor to the expression of the orderly universe, hidden to the scientist but revealed to the poet whose task is to work with likenesses. The poet then has access to a form of knowledge denied others.[37] And his work

---

[36] Cf. Vilhelm Ekelund, "Swedenborgs erfarenhet," in *På hafsstranden* (Stockholm: Bonniers, 1922). In another context Ekelund also suggests that *Inferno* might well be labeled a Swedenborg essay, the word "essay" here indicating a form of literature in which the experience of a book is described with the same concreteness and dramatic intensity that a great novelist would employ in depicting the conflicts between personalities in a novel (see *Prosa* [Stockholm: Bonniers, 1952], I, 54–55).

[37] For a discussion of the relationship between the Hermetic and occult tradition mediated by Boehme and Swedenborg and the Symbolist movement, see Frank Kermode, *Romantic Image* (New York: Vintage Books, 1964).

with likenesses is an act of religious worship, for seeing that the likenesses between things point to their common origin, thus revealing the wisdom and greatness of the creator as the source of the unity of things, to discover and to interpret analogies is a way of honoring God. By revealing that the reality of this world is only a sign language the poet intimates the existence of a higher reality, more beautiful and more perfect.[38]

By way of conclusion, let me sum up what I have labeled the Faustian theme in *Inferno*. In retrospect it is easy to see how closely Strindberg has projected his own destiny along Faustian lines. To begin with, his hero is a man whose thirst for knowledge has not been quenched by the sciences and who has consequently turned to alchemy and magic, seeking by such means to penetrate to the secret of creation. By using magic he has sold his soul to the devil. In his pursuit of knowledge and power he has also sacrificed love, abandoning his wife and child as Faust abandoned Gretchen.

But unlike Marlowe's Faust, Strindberg's hero is shown the path to redemption in the same manner as Goethe's Faust. He comes to the realization that in his overweening pride, expressed in his belief that his own unwearied striving can win salvation, he has been evil.

Like Goethe's Faust Strindberg's hero is rescued by women, not by a specific woman of flesh and blood, but by "Eternal Womanhood," "das ewig Weibliche," "the Mothers." Like Beatrice the women guardian figures guide him through purgatory.

Through the mother figures the Faustian hero is then brought to the realization that the truth is hidden behind appearances, that temporal things are but symbols intimating the existence of another, higher reality. In Goethe's *Faust*

---

[38] Karl-Åke Kärnell, *Strindbergs bildspråk* (Stockholm: Almqvist och Wiksell; 1962), pp. 278–287.

this realization is embodied in the often quoted lines from the last stanza: "Alles vergängliche / ist nur ein Gleichniss," ending with the lines "Das ewig Weibliche / zieht uns an."

This in turn brings the hero to the final insight that only the poet can express the harmony, the wholeness and oneness of existence, by revealing through the image the interaction of the microcosm and the macrocosm.

The wholeness or oneness intimated by the poet may well be interpreted as the integration of the previously divided self. What is the transcendental realm of the "Mothers" but the unconscious? That Goethe's *Faust* may well be interpreted in this manner has been convincingly demonstrated by George Groddeck.[39] Such an interpretation is perhaps even nearer at hand in *Inferno*, wherein the situation is couched in less symbolic language, and where the hero is left in a state of readiness to seek a new kind of knowledge, the knowledge of the self rather than the knowledge of the world, and is motivated by love rather than by the quest for power. Having sought to master the world by re-creating it according to his wishes or to transform it through magic, he is now ready to transform his own self, and art rather than science is his mode of transformation. The alchemist has become a poet.

The parallel to the so-called individuation process that Jung has found in the field of medieval Hermetic philosophy, or alchemy, is consequently strikingly illuminated in *Inferno*. For although alchemy is a product of a different age and differs greatly from the individuation process, both may be seen as attempts to lead man to self-realization, "the secret of alchemy" being, in fact, according to Jung, "the transcendent function, the transformation of personality through the blending and fusion of the noble with the base components, of the differentiated with the inferior functions, of the conscious

---

[39] George Groddeck, *Exploring the Unconscious*, trans. V. M. E. Collins (New York: Funk and Wagnalls, 1940), pp. 179–207.

with the unconscious." [40] The gold the alchemists sought was not really gold, but the elixir of life, the philosopher's stone. By seeking to transform base metals into gold the alchemist was, like Strindberg centuries later, groping for a way to the transformation of the self.

---

[40] Jolande Jacobi, *The Psychology of C. G. Jung*, trans. Ralph Manheim (New Haven: Yale University Press, 1962), pp. 137–138.

◟ 12. *Alone*

Ensam (*Alone*) is the last in the series of autobiographical novels which Strindberg had begun with *The Son of a Servant* in 1886. As a work of art it is the most finished product in the series. Unlike the earlier novels, which often give the appearance of being hurried and improvised pieces of work, *Alone* is a perfect self-portrait, rounded, elegantly framed.

I have already expressed the view that Strindberg's novels often fail to move the reader. There is frequently something in the tone which alienates us. Strindberg's emotional involvement with his own characters is often undercut by reservations or by a clinical, analytical vision. Behind the agonies of the hero we glimpse the dispassionate author. Strindberg's tone of detachment often makes it impossible for us to respond with our feelings, appealing as it does primarily to our intellects. But in *Alone* Strindberg's defenses are down: he is without any of his habitual masks. He is neither the social rebel, nor the cynic, nor the innocently suffering martyr, nor the intellectual *Übermensch* storming creation: he is just what he was, a lonely, middle-aged writer living only for his art, a human being speaking with both compassion and a sense of humor and revealing a new and profound insight into his own situation.

In its restrained lyric-reflective tone, in its fleeting impressions of city life, in its mood of quiet resignation, *Alone* resembles the *flaneur* literature of the turn of the century, the novels of Hjalmar Söderberg and Henning Berger.[1] But Strindberg's novel is different in several respects. It lacks the decadent features of this *fin-de-siècle* literature, and the tone of resignation is blended with the sense of openness to experience so characteristic of Strindberg.

One hesitates to label *Alone* a novel, because it is so openly autobiographical, more like a writer's intimate journal or notebook. Yet it does have a fictional framework, and Strindberg himself thought of it as a novel. Writing to Harriet Bosse in April of 1906 he said: "Balzac's form of the novel attracts me the most now. The type *Alone*. Where you can explain yourself, elaborate, render human beings, observe them from within, in depth." [2] While this description does not fit *Alone*, as the novel hardly represents an attempt to render individual characters in depth, it points up the fact that Strindberg was searching for a new form of fiction in which he would be able to express his new vision of life with a minimum of artifice and invention.

[1] I particularly have in mind Hjalmar Söderberg's novel *Doktor Glas* (1905) which, incidentally, has recently been beautifully translated into English by Paul Britten Austin (Boston: Little, Brown, 1963).

[2] August Strindberg, *Från Fjärdingen till Blå Tornet: Ett brevurval 1870–1912*, ed. Torsten Eklund (Stockholm: Bonniers, 1946), p. 374.

In *Alone* the fictional element is very slight except in one important respect. The first-person narrator is a widower, which Strindberg was not, and he has a son who left for the United States with his mother at the age of nine, which Strindberg did not. The most significant departure from the actual situation is that the narrator is living alone, whereas Strindberg at the time he wrote the novel was still married to the actress Harriet Bosse, his third wife. This fact has considerable bearing on the manner in which the work as a whole is to be approached.

Alone was written over a period of three months, between March and June of 1903. The final separation between Strindberg and Harriet Bosse did not occur until June of 1903. This means that the little book may well be regarded as an experiment, an investigation and a test of whether the approaching solitude was to be endured or would spell disaster for him both as man and as a writer.[3] In the past Strindberg had repeatedly realized his inability to be alone for any length of time. With the imminent separation from Harriet Bosse he was envisioning loneliness as a permanent condition, mainly because during his life with her and their daughter he had divorced himself from his friends. Thus he wrote to her in July of 1902 after their first separation: "Because of your presence in my life all my friends have become immaterial and strange to me. And I feel absolute solitude approaching, awful and solemn."[4] When he proposed to her a year earlier he had asked her to be the woman through whom he would be reconciled to humanity. She was to save him from the monastery, return him to the living. With Harriet Bosse he had looked forward to a special kind of solitude, the seclusion

---

[3] Ola Östin, "August Strindbergs Ensam," *Edda*, LVIII (1958), 81–99.

[4] *Strindbergs brev till Harriet Bosse* (Stockholm: Natur och Kultur, 1932), p. 66.

within the family as a sheltered setting guarded by the tender walls of love from the threats of the outside world. But this beautiful dream is now shattered, and he is realizing that he must come to terms with life on his own.

In *Alone* Strindberg is envisioning the solitary life to which he now feels condemned, investigating the resources at his disposal. The result is a surprisingly positive book, surprising in view of the theme. In the earlier novels isolation consistently brought about a disintegration of the personality, awakening the demons of guilt and anxiety; in *Alone* the solitary life is regarded in a positive light, as a state that not only fosters growth and creativity but also provides a firmer sense of identity.

The reasons for this radical change of attitude are mainly to be sought in a decisive reorientation of values, in a new vision of life which has brought about a kind of rebirth. *Alone* is perhaps the best introduction to the world of the aging Strindberg as he entered upon his last and possibly best period of artistic creativity. In it we learn something about the writers and thinkers who were instrumental in shaping his new vision of life, his "nondogmatic" religion, his "Buddhism." We experience a sense of his newfound freedom, a freedom springing from hard-earned self-conquest and self-discipline, leaving him with a vast openness toward new areas of experience. Above all, we observe the ways in which he finds the raw material for his art in the most quotidian aspects of life. Lacking the distractions of social life, of travel, of the theater, he must draw entirely on his own resources in a life of seclusion. A glance, a gesture, a brief conversation overheard in a store, a painting, a scene glimpsed through a window, a tune played on a distant piano, all serve to stimulate his imagination and are transformed into dramatic material along with his own dreams and memories. *Alone* allows us a rare and precious glimpse into the dramatist's workshop, letting us partake of the creative process that was soon to fashion the strange world of the Chamber plays and the last novels.

The opening pages of *Alone* give vivid testimony to Strindberg's special feeling for the tense atmosphere that always exists between human beings and for the difficulties of communication. The narrator, who has returned to his native city after a ten-year stay in the country, is seeking to become reacquainted with his old friends after his long absence but is experiencing many difficulties. The years that have passed, new ties, new interests, now separate them from one another. Painful periods of silence ensue after a brief exchange of happy memories. Those who speak freely soon discover, in the narrator's vivid metaphorical language, that they "had bumped into submerged rocks, had torn at threads, stepped into newly reclaimed land, all of which they would have noticed, if they had observed the glances that armed themselves in defense and resistance, these pulls at the corners of the mouth when the lips disguised a suppressed word" (38, 123). Soon everyone is self-conscious, in a defensive position, buttoned up.

A few weeks later when they meet again the situation has worsened. Now everyone is prepared, having anticipated the questions and prepared the answers: "They came armed, and now it curdled like sour milk" (124). So they break up for good and go their separate ways. Those who continue end up in a total "confusion of tongues," quarreling about their mutual lack of understanding. " 'But you don't understand what I am saying!' was the usual cry of distress" (127). A social gathering is depicted as a battleground where everyone is trying to satisfy his need "to hear his own voice and to press his own views on others."

Had the novel continued in this vein it would have offered little new. This thoroughly disenchanted view of human relationships should be very familiar by now. But after the opening pages a new tone suddenly is heard, and it soon becomes apparent that Strindberg's point of view has shifted in a very decisive manner. He is no longer judging his fellow humans from a moral point of view, blaming them for their shortcomings. Instead he is expressing their despair, their despair over the inability to communicate with each other, their despair of being doomed to remain imprisoned within their separate selves. The tone is compassionate, it is the tone of *A Dream Play*: "Humankind is to be pitied."

What is more, Strindberg's narrator now seems inclined to blame himself rather than the others for his inability to establish meaningful relationships with them. He now puts the blame on his own abnormal sensitivity. He insists that he has never hated human beings: he has loved them deeply, but since the day of his birth he has been afraid of them. Easily wounded, he has taken even an innocent word as scorn (153). In society he has felt particularly insecure because of the increased exposure, the "larger target area" (146). Hence his need to place himself "in a defensive position" (187). To turn one's back to others is to let one's defenses down, for experience has taught him "that the back is the most vulnerable side, and that the chest is protected by large shields of bone designed for defense" (186). He also insists that he is so sensitive, so "skinless," that even a stranger who approaches him "appears stifling by his mental atmosphere" (200).

While freely admitting the degree to which this abnormal sensitivity has prevented him from being with others, Strindberg's narrator also reveals how he has suffered because of this. Among the most moving passages in the novel are those in which he describes how he rides in a streetcar in order to be in the same room with others, and how he squeezes himself into a tight corner so that he can feel the touch of another human being with his elbow (152).

We have observed how in the past those of Strindberg's heroes who have shared this abnormal sensitivity were placed in insoluble conflicts. When their excessive sensitivity drove them to seclude themselves and to shy away from human contact this brought dire consequences: attacks of guilt feelings and anxiety, even mental derangement. Unable to be with others they were equally unable to be alone. In *Alone* the dilemma has apparently been solved, and this is the most radical shift of point of view in the novel. The narrator is as sensitive as always, he is unable to be with others although he would like to be with them, he recognizes that he is doomed to be solitary and lonely, but—and this is the most important shift—he no longer fears being alone; on the contrary he regards it as a condition fostering growth and creativity.

To begin with, he feels a certain loss of strength, to be sure, but slowly a transformation begins to take place, and he finds that in place of the feared loss of the self his self attains a greater coherence. "By cutting off contacts with other human beings I seemed at first to be losing strength, but at the same time my ego began, as it were, to coagulate, to condense about a core. Where everything I had experienced gathered itself, was digested and absorbed as nourishment by my soul!" (128). Solitude is depicted as the condition under which the birth of a new self can take place:

This is finally solitude: to spin oneself into the silk of one's own soul, become a cocoon and wait for the metamorphosis, for that will not fail to come. In the meantime one lives on one's experiences, and telepathically one lives the lives of others. Death and resurrection; a new education for something unknown and new.

At last one is one's own master. Nobody's thoughts control mine, nobody's likes, caprices pressure me. . . . Now the soul begins to grow in newly gained freedom, and one experiences a great inner peace and a quiet joy and a feeling of security and self-responsibility. (145)

I have already suggested that the reasons for this new and strongly positive attitude to the solitary life are to be sought in the new vision of life which grew out of the Inferno crisis. *Inferno* itself was, as we have observed, inconclusive, but it marked a stage in Strindberg's gradual abandonment of the naturalistic view of life and in the development of what he was to call his "nondogmatic" Christianity, a strange combination of elements derived from the philosophy of Swedenborg, from Theosophy, from Buddhism, and from the Bible. It is this new religion with its emphasis on self-denial, on acceptance and resignation, on atonement and martyrdom, which has provided Strindberg with a new insight into the nature of the self and shown him the path to liberation from his too-rebellious self.

In *Alone* Strindberg speaks the language of those whose goal is a state of mystic selflessness, the language of rebirth. In *Inferno* he still spoke of his mysterious friend's teachings about the denial and mortification of the self as "an insane idea." "To kill the Ego is to commit suicide," he insisted (MS, 81). At the time he was seemingly unable to conceive of the denial of the self except in terms of power: as an objectionable way of humbling himself before someone else, a party, or a God. Now, only five years later, he speaks of his newly acquired religion and how it has given him a "complete education in self-conquest." The word "self-conquest" is new in Strindberg's vocabulary and most indicative of his radically new attitude to the self. The old attitude to the self reflected Strindberg's naturalistic vision of life as a struggle for power, the new reflects his efforts to broaden the basis of the self, shifting the emphasis from the conscious ego to the unconscious. His conception of the self now appears similar to that of Buddhism, in which the belief that the individual self is real and self-existent is the great delusion, the liberation from this delusion being achieved only when man ceases to cling to

his desire to assert his uniqueness or separateness.[5] The "cultivation of the Ego" has been succeeded by a mystic selflessness,
by Goethe's principle of *Stirb und Werde*.

Strindberg's new attitude toward the self is reflected in
various ways in *Alone*: in his attitude to knowledge, in his
attitude to art, and in his manner of viewing the world.

In the past Strindberg's heroes sought knowledge as a
way to power. They used knowledge as a way to aggrandize
themselves, either by debunking the knowledge of others, or
by inflating their own. In *Alone* the hero is seeking self-
knowledge. His readings no longer inspire him to solve the
problems of the world or give him clues to the nature of
things, they teach him about himself. Reading Balzac's great
human comedy he learns resignation, the acceptance of suffering. In Balzac's fifty volumes he has found himself; he says,
"I could make a synthesis of all the hitherto unresolved antitheses of my life" (147). Balzac, he says, has taught him "to
regard life with both eyes, while before I had only seen
through the monocle with one eye" (147). He credits Balzac
with having given him "a kind of religion, which I would like
to call nondogmatic Christianity" (147). In Balzac's world
he also discovered "how grief and pain somehow burned up
the refuse of the soul, refined instincts and feelings, and even
conferred higher skills on the soul liberated from the tormented body" (147–148).

The Bible, particularly the Old Testament, in the older
translations, provides him spiritual comfort. From devotional
literature he learns that suffering is a blessing in disguise
(157). There are times when he is in opposition to some of
its stern teachings, but he is no longer brooding about some
of the contradictions. He knows that faith is a healthy state
(160), and for this reason he will try to strengthen his faith,

---

[5] On the Buddhist conception of the self see Christmas Humphreys, *Buddhism* (London: Penguin Books, 1958), pp. 88, 119.

not question it. Unbelief is now seen as a sterile, parasitical, and negative existence. The unbeliever lacks "independent existence," because he is negative, and in order to be negative he must have the positive to negate (159–160). In the most difficult moments, however, not even Christianity is sufficient. Then only "a little Buddhism helps" (160). Its teachings are: "Desire nothing, demand nothing of human beings or of life, and you will always feel that you have received more than you could have demanded; and you know from experience, that when you have received what you desired, it was less what you had desired than the fulfillment itself which gave you joy" (160).

The quest for self-knowledge has had another important consequence. Strindberg's hero has learned to listen to the inner voice. Those messages from the unconscious, the language of the feelings, which he had previously rejected or repressed, or used as in *Inferno* to further inflate his conscious ego, are now received in a new spirit. There is a new openness to the hitherto repressed aspects of the self. The hero examines freely his memories of the past, treating them, he says, like pieces in a box of building blocks, constructing various combinations. He welcomes dreams, because as he puts it: "In my dreams my inner being is mirrored, therefore I can use them as I use the shaving mirror: to see what I am doing and avoid cutting myself" (135).

It is this new openness to the inner voice which is the reason for his now being able to be alone. In the past any attempt to isolate himself from others led to his being pursued by the demons. Now he can be alone with himself, for no longer do the voices of the unconscious come to torment him. He still regrets that the solitary life should be his fate, but it no longer frightens him.

In the past loneliness had proved detrimental to Strindberg's creative abilities. Now it proves a most productive state, for along with his newfound freedom gained by self-conquest he has also gained an openness to the world. Having renounced the quest for power over the world he has gained a different kind of power, the power to transform it into art. Everything serves his dramatic imagination: the people he meets on his walks, a remark overheard on the street, a trip to the store, a gesture, a scene viewed through an open window. Without a life of his own he takes a keen interest in the lives and destinies of his neighbors, inventing little stories about them. He now lives fully only when he is writing. His desire to write sometimes overcomes him to the extent that his walks, which are not to be dispensed with, leave him impatient. When he gets home and sits by his desk, he is wholly and fully alive:

I live, and I live many times over the lives of the people I depict; I am cheerful with the cheerful, angry with the angry, good with the good; I crawl out of my own person, and speak from the mouths of children, of women, of old men; I am king and beggar; I am the most exalted, the tyrant, and the most despised, the suppressed rebel against tyrants; I hold all views, and profess all religions; I live in all ages and have myself ceased to exist. This is a condition of indescribable happiness. (155–156)

Thus the quest for identity has ended in a positive selflessness, in the mystic's conquest of time and the self, in an openness to the world. The only identity is the identity of the artist, who exists only in his created world, in and through his identification with others.

Alone also provides us with some vivid illustrations of the workings of Strindberg's imagination, of the ease with which he transforms the life about him into drama. The imagery of the theater is, in fact, so prevalent in the book, that the stage has become a metaphor expressing Strindberg's vision of the world as an illusory spectacle. Human beings are acting in the comedies and tragedies of life, they are masked players on an unreal stage.

A few snatches of a conversation overheard below his balcony sound to him like "the last repartees of a tragedy" performed in the house over a period of three months: the tragedy of a grocer's rise and fall. An ordinary domestic tragedy, to be sure, but the enactment of an old story which goes back to Sophocles. The store gives the impression of a theater, for the narrator's trained eye is familiar with the means that will provide the illusion of something being grander than it really is. He is also at his first visit "struck dumb by the elaborate mise-en-scène" that makes him suspect "that the owner has been on the stage." The grocer cannot refrain from "playing comedy," putting up a false front. On one occasion the narrator observes him being called to the telephone, ostensibly in order to speak to an important customer. But, the narrator remarks, "he had no luck in that I was an author of comedies and had studied both facial gestures and the art of repartee. Thus his face told me that there was no telephone conversation and his answer to a simulated speech that it was a comedy." As the customers fail to materialize the comedy gradually turns into a tragedy, and the narrator watches "the ghostlike" face of the grocer as the latter looks for customers through his window: "It was a frightful scene seeing him behind his arcade." After the bankruptcy the narrator looks with interest at some substantial bills which turn out to be sheer fabrication, commenting wryly on the poor grocer's plight in "having been forced to play this comedy for his clerk" (139–143).

On his perambulations through the streets of the city, the glimpse of a face or an interior seen through an open window awaken memories and stimulate his imagination.

One morning, while passing an open window, he gets a glimpse of the sordid interior of an old house. Behind the

Aspidistra he sees an old-fashioned writing table and beyond
it a square, white-tile stove with a dirty, black edge around
each tile. The wallpaper is dark. The interior spells nothing
but boredom, the life of people in narrow circumstances
"who torment themselves and each other." But it serves to
awaken the memory of another home, placing another destiny
in sharper focus, helping him visualize another "tragedy."
On his return he makes a first draft of the drama (163–164).

In the evening, after dark, when the lamps are lit, he
gets even richer impressions, complete "scenes from life."
One such scene is particularly vivid. It is again an interior
glimpsed through a window, but this time there are people
in the room. The first object that strikes the eye is an ala-
baster urn grown yellow with age. On the walls are family
portraits from many generations. In a corner by the couch
is a gaming table, and around it are seated four strange
figures playing cards. They do not speak, for their lips do
not move. Three of them are very, very old; one man is
younger. In the middle of the room a young woman is
crocheting, but without enthusiasm, only measuring the passing seconds with her needle. "Never," says the narrator, "have
I seen boredom, the loathing of everything, the weariness of
life so condensed as in this room." The four players, who are
compared to "mummies," seem anxious, as if waiting for
someone, casting occasional glances at the clock on the wall.
Are they waiting for someone who will alleviate their boredom, change their lives, bring something new? As if expecting to be interrupted in their playing any moment, they are
not really entering into the game, moving like mannequins.
The narrator will never know the answer to his question, for
as the eagerly awaited visitor appears, he is given a rough
shove by a passerby and continues on his way (164–166).

Sometimes the narrator is gripped by a longing for the
country, for the sea, the archipelago, but even this desire he
is able to satisfy without moving from his desk by the win-

dow. Between the curtains he sees a bay of the Baltic Sea, and with his telescope he can remove himself to the scene and experience all the delights of actually being there. He watches the flowers, the pine forest, a crow picking on the ground, a sailboat, but one day he observes "a whole little scene." A girl of ten, in a red tennis hat, arrives in a rowboat, and goes ashore carrying—an ax! He observes the playful antics of the girl, speculating on her motive without solving the mystery. The scene ends on a humorous note. A cow suddenly appears, and the girl stiffens with fear, too frightened to flee, until gathering up her courage she threatens the cow with the ax, whereupon the cow disappears. "Imagine," says the narrator, "being drawn into such dramas in the distance in one's own peaceful home" (174–177).

Sometimes his exclusive cultivation of the inner life makes him long for stronger impressions, and his wishes are no sooner uttered than they are realized. Troops appear in the field below his windows, first infantry, then cavalry, then artillery. In the beginning, the infernal noise of the firing is disturbing, but as he grows accustomed to the sounds, he finds them beneficial, he says, "because they prevent me from dozing off into eternal silence. And at the discreet distance at which I have the war games they seem like plays performed on my behalf" (178–179). Much that happens, he feels, seems intended for him alone as if "staged" just for him (192).

In the late summer, when all the wealthy and beautiful people have left the city, the poor and the unfortunate and the ugly give the city a different appearance: "the play" is "less beautiful," more grotesque. On his way to the fashionable Djurgården in his carriage the narrator is treated to a spectacle that reminds him of the paintings of Ensor.[6] The

---

[6] Strindberg is referring to the Belgian painter James Ensor (1860–1949), with whose grotesque paintings of masks he was evidently familiar.

streams of people moving about only faintly resemble human beings: they are cripples many of them, with crooked legs and broken backs, some on crutches; dwarfs with the backs of giants or giants with the lower frames of dwarfs; faces without noses, and feet without toes. He has seen such creatures in Gluck's opera *Orpheus in the Underworld*, but had believed they were exaggerated (179–181).

At Djurgården he unaccountably thinks of "a somber tragedy" from his youth, and as he ponders on the possible association between Djurgården and this tragedy, two of the figures in the drama suddenly materialize before him, leading him to further speculations about "the secret motives hidden in the depth of the soul" which had led him to expect them to appear (181–182).

In the outskirts of the park the great throngs have thinned, and people have arranged themselves in small groups on the lawns. But even here dramas are in the process of developing: "But here I was struck by the fact that three and three sat together; two men with one woman, the first act in a pastoral play that ends with the tragedy of the knife" (182).

The occult and mystical experiences Strindberg relates add to the atmosphere of unreality that permeates *Alone*. We have already encountered occult phenomena in *Inferno*, but in *Alone* they are related for a different purpose. They are no longer frightening, or signs to be interpreted, but intimations of the existence of another and higher reality. In *Inferno* Strindberg expressed the need for a new type of religion, one that would establish a contact with "the other side." These experiences are such contacts, correspondences. There exists a mysterious relationship among all things.

People whom the narrator thinks of intensely are suddenly "seen" on the street. In the silence of the house in summer his own thoughts become spoken words, and he seems to feel that he has telepathic communications with absent friends or enemies (177). Houses become electric-power stations, generating current from the tensions between human wills (177). Furniture placed on the street is like the intestines of human beings bared to the public (167). Long-ing one summer night, when his loneliness weighs heavy on him, to hear Beethoven, the "Moonlight Sonata" in par-ticular, "which to me has become the greatest expression of mankind's sigh for liberation," the "Moonlight Sonata" is suddenly played. This fills him with "the shudder that grips you when faced with the inexplicable," because though the music came from the house next door, nobody was there. The movement he longed most to hear, the Allegro, was repeated three times, thereby making the experience still more inexplicable (189–190).

Alone is a positive work, and it is Strindberg's most affirmative statement about the role of the writer. It comes as no surprise therefore that it should also contain a tribute to Goethe, the writer whose works, besides those of Balzac, are now his dearest company. In his younger days he had downgraded Goethe (as well as Shakespeare), regarding Kierkegaard's *Either/Or* as a finer work than *Faust*, but now he seems eager to identify with Goethe.[7] Having himself re-cently abandoned naturalism he now also seems eager to defend both Balzac and Goethe against those who charge them with being materialistic or pagan. Goethe, Strindberg says, "has many stages on his road through life" but, through Rousseau, Kant, Schelling, and Spinoza, he finally reaches his own point of view, the philosophy of the Enlightenment. But then there comes a time when "the pantheistic explana-tions" somehow fail Goethe. To the seventy-year-old man everything suddenly appears inexplicable and incomprehen-sible. It is then that he turns to mysticism and to Sweden-

---

[7] Cf. *18*, 390.

borg. Thus the Faust of the first part of the drama, who in his wrestle with God emerges as "a victorious Saul," in the second part becomes "a defeated Paul." "This is my Goethe!" says the narrator (197–198).

Strindberg's new tendency to regard the transforming power of poetry in a positive light is also reflected in the pleasure with which he quotes two passages from Goethe's *Aus meinem Leben,* both of which stress that the writer's function is to create a poetic image of reality. The writer's purpose is not to seek the realization of his poetic vision in the world, but to transform reality into the orderly universe of poetry. This ability to transform his life into poetry is a gift that nobody needed more than Goethe, whose nature was such that he tended to swing from one extreme to the other. That art was the only means to integrate the violently antithetical strains of his own self, Strindberg too had come to realize (198–199).

The pleasure in reading Goethe, says Strindberg, in conclusion, comes from the light touch. "It is as if he could not take life really seriously, either because it lacked firm substance, or because it did not deserve our grief and our tears." And Strindberg goes on to praise "the undauntedness with which he [Goethe] approached the divine powers, with whom he feels a kinship; his contempt for fashions and conventions; his lack of ready-made views; his continuous growth and renewal, whereby he is always the youngest, always leading the way, ahead of his time" (199). This too is undoubtedly a portrait of Strindberg as he liked to see himself at this stage of his life.[8]

---

[8] In an article in *Samlaren* Walter A. Berendsohn maintains that despite Strindberg's desire to identify himself with Goethe his real affinities are with so deeply split an individual as Kierkegaard ("Goethe och Strindberg," *Samlaren,* 30 [1949], 118–128).

─ᐣ 13. *Black Banners*

Svarta fanor (*Black Banners*) is one of Strindberg's most powerful novels. It is also his most unpalatable
novel. Originally written in 1904 it was not published until
three years later. The closing pages of the first volume of
En blå bok (*A Blue Book*) give a vivid testimony to his
anguished state of mind as he was reading the proof in the
spring of 1906. "I *want to* write about happy and beautiful
things," he laments, "but I am not allowed to, I cannot; I
take it as a horrible duty to be truthful, and life is indescrib-
ably ugly" (46, 406–407). He seeks consolation in the book
of Job and in Plato's *Timaeus* and *Phaedo*, but finds them
too contradictory. Prayer alone, and the music of Beethoven,
sustain his spirit. "What is a poor human being to cling to?"
he cries. "What is he to believe?"

In an entry on April 16 he says: "Uncertain about
whether the book is a crime and ought to be canceled." But

this time he finds comfort in a passage from the book of Job in which the prophet is compelled to prophesy against his will. He adds, nevertheless, "it is a book of horrors" (407–408).

The significance of the novel gradually emerges against a background of color symbolism. Anxiously scanning for signs to guide him Strindberg shows a particular interest in colors, particularly the colors red, black, white, and blue. Flags predominate, and their colors have a spiritual significance, red representing passionate commitment to a cause or enterprise even at the cost of great suffering, black representing the sinful life from which he has now finally parted. In the light of this color symbolism he contemplates the titles of some of his books. Once he wrote a "red" book, *The Red Room,* in which he sought like the prophet Jeremiah "to uproot, to break down, to devastate, and to destroy"; now he is writing his "blue" book, his *breviarium universale,* a book of edification for the believers of all religions (404). Red and blue are quite clearly positive symbols, here indicating Strindberg's acceptance of both his youthful rebellion and nihilism and his newly regained religious faith as good stages in his development.

Black, on the contrary, is a symbol of evil, associated not only with flags but also with nightmarish visions of black dogs. In this sense *Black Banners* is a "black" book. It is a reckoning with the materialistic and atheistic world view to which he had himself once subscribed, with what he now derisively calls the "frog slough" (411). Atheists, writes Strindberg somewhere else, pledge allegiance to the black banner (174). But now he is no longer serving their cause, for he has come to realize that the "systematic adversities" he has suffered were caused by his own allegiance to the black cause. He too has been a black magician, but now he has atoned for his sins. Proof of the fact that he has been redeemed, rescued from spiritual death, he finds in some theosophical writings which inform him that redeemed black magicians have a firm belief in hell and are particularly adept at describing inferno and its horrors (413–415). In *Black Banners* Strindberg may be said to repudiate what we might call the middle stage of his life, the stage during which he turned increasingly to a scientific view of life.

Ostensibly *Black Banners* reads like an attack on the literary life, and like a *roman à clef*, because in his attempt to come to terms with the world view of the "blacks" Strindberg has subjected some well-known literary figures of the day to crude satirical treatment. Gustaf af Geijerstam and Ellen Key are easily recognized behind the masks of Zachris and Hanna Paj.[1] Strindberg has also been severely criticized for this rude treatment of his former friends. What has sometimes been overlooked is that Strindberg's point of view is more complex than it appears at first sight, and that a closer reading reveals that his reckoning with the literati is at least in part also a reckoning with himself.

But the real power of *Black Banners* has little to do with its topical satire. Its real power lies in its vivid evocation of the grotesque. This is also the quality that sets it so strongly apart from the mood and tone of *Alone*. In *Alone* Strindberg was in a meditative and conciliatory mood. The unreality of the world was evoked largely through the metaphors of the stage, although certain grotesque images were noted. In *Black Banners* the mood is different. In this novel the way to overcome the world is to insist not only on its unreality but also on its utter absurdity, on its grotesque and nightmarish quality. The longing for another and better realm of existence is intensified by a feeling of the horror of this

---

[1] Gustaf af Geijerstam (1858–1909) is a minor novelist and Ellen Key (1849–1926) a leader in the movement for the emancipation of women.

world. *Black Banners* depicts a grotesque inferno, an inferno
that in its concreteness and reality bears little resemblance
to the all too literary hell of *Inferno.*

The structure of *Black Banners* is vaguely reminiscent
of *The Red Room.* In *The Red Room* two worlds were contrasted, the world of the Bohemian artists and the world of
commerce and officialdom. In *Black Banners* the world of
the blacks, of writers and critics, is contrasted with the world
of the monastery, the spiritual retreat for those who seek
peace of mind.[2] In both novels a central figure serves to tie
the two worlds together: in *The Red Room* the young Arvid
Falk, in *Black Banners* the middle-aged writer Falkenström
who moves gradually from the literary life to the monastery.
Like Falk the latter may be considered a self-portrait, though
it ought to be stressed that as in *The Red Room* Strindberg's
point of view is not to be identified with that of any one
character in *Black Banners.*

But here the resemblance between the two novels ends,
for in other respects they are different from each other. If
we consider the particular elements from which they derive
their respective unity of structure the basic difference between
the two novels becomes immediately apparent. In *The Red
Room* we observed a thematic unity, the contrast between
innocence and experience, and a unity of tone, a tone of good
humor. In *Black Banners* the unity is derived primarily from
a particular atmosphere that permeates the novel, an atmosphere of the grotesque. *The Red Room* is fundamentally a
comic novel, whereas *Black Banners* is a study in black
humor, the humor of the absurd.

In his pioneering study of the grotesque in art and
literature Wolfgang Kayser maintains that its expression

---

[2] Both structurally and thematically *Black Banners* bears a striking resemblance to Aldous Huxley's novel *Time Must Have a Stop*
(London and New York: Harper, 1944).

basically assumes two forms, fantasy and satire.[3] Common to both forms is a distortion of the world, but whereas the satirical form, as its name indicates, distorts the world for the specific purpose of topical satire, the fantastic form seeks to evoke an atmosphere of absurdity or horror by means of an estrangement from reality, by making the familiar and natural strange, ominous, and unreliable. The satirical form seeks a fusion of disparate realms, blending the beautiful with the bizarre and the repulsive, the human with the animal, the organic and living with the mechanical; the fantastic form has a larger register. Fantasy too may fuse disparate realms but for a different purpose. It may transform harmless utensils and familiar objects into malevolent beings, it may make mechanical objects come alive, or it may transform human beings into puppets and masks, and life itself into a marionette play or a dance macabre—all for the purpose of evoking a feeling of estrangement from reality. It may also depict a world populated by monstrous creatures, particularly snakes, toads, spiders, nocturnal animals, various forms of vampires, bats, even plants if sufficiently monstrous in appearance. Like satire, fantasy may distort the size and shape of objects, of animals, of human beings. Frequently it depicts the progressive or sudden dissolution of personality as in the phenomenon of the double. Finally, it may take the form of a satanic humor that insists that life is a grotesque comedy, that we human beings are the victims of a divine joke.

Both major forms of the grotesque are present in *Black Banners*, and in ample measure. But as the novel progresses and shifts from the literary world to the monastery, the fantastic element leaps to prominence. In the first part the novel depicts a world in which human beings, caught up in the

---

[3] Wolfgang Kayser, *The Grotesque in Art and Literature*, trans. Ulrich Weisstein (Bloomington: Indiana University Press, 1963).

strife of animal passions or in the greed for power and money, have become transformed into animals or monsters. In the second part it depicts an estranged world in which all is illusory: characters who have become prisoners of the mask and lost their faces and souls; a dance macabre of sleep-walkers, ghosts, and living objects that suddenly acquire independent existence.

The total perspective in *Black Banners* is one we associate with the fantastic grotesque, a view of the world as an absurd place in which it is impossible to find one's bearings. This is also the aging Strindberg's vision of life, the refrain of *A Dream Play* and *The Dance of Death*, of the Chamber plays, and of the last novels. Foiled in his quest for a meaningful pattern in life Strindberg's major theme is that life is an absurd comedy. His perspective is essentially tragicomic, tragicomic because it never envisions any deeper meaning within an existence that appears without purpose. For Strindberg as for Kierkegaard the only way to redemption seems to lie in suffering, the suffering that comes from an intensified and impassioned feeling of the absurdity of human existence. An often repeated theme in Strindberg's letters during these post-Inferno years is also his belief, or perhaps it is only his hope, that life is so fantastic, so difficult, that it must be a mirage, a distorted image, which will be adjusted in another existence. Life appears to him dreamlike and inexplicable, a series of constantly transmuted and dissolving images. Death must be an awakening, life a long and horrible nightmare.[4]

The first chapters of *Black Banners* projects the reader headlong into a grotesque world. They depict a dinner at

---

[4] August Strindberg, *Från Fjärdingen till Blå Tornet: Ett brevurval 1870–1912*, ed. Torsten Eklund (Stockholm: Bonniers, 1946), pp. 338, 359, 370.

the home of a distinguished professor, to which the literary and cultural elite of Sweden has been invited. It is called a "ghost dinner" (41, 5), presumably in order to indicate the fantastic and unreal nature of the gathering. In these powerful chapters Strindberg achieves a satirical effect of Swiftian proportions primarily through the use of violent metaphors that fuse disparate realms of experience in the manner of the grotesque.

The diners are depicted as animals, the gentlemen facing each other across the table baring their teeth like angry beasts or like dogs with bones in their mouths (13). They are called "man-eaters" for they have murder in their hearts.

As they make their motions of eating in unison they are seen as mechanical toys, as puppets: "They nodded and drank, and drank and nodded, in a really Chinese way" (9). Occasionally they lift their masks a little (15). After a cutting remark their jaws stiffen as if frostbitten (9).

Ludicrous or repulsive metaphors are used in order to draw an unflattering picture of the elegant diners. The stains of perspiration under the armpits of the ladies are compared to marine charts and landmaps (14), a badly restrained yawn reveals a mouth with gold-filled teeth which "opens like a sleeping alcove with wall paintings" (11–12), and the bald heads bending over the table are compared to "the backsides of bathers" (8). As the diners finish their soup, they roll little bread balls in distraction, their hands compared to crabs crawling on the table (7).

But the fantastic element soon takes precedence over the satire. It may be observed, for instance, in the manner in which the innocent napkins left on the table after the meal are depicted: "the napkins, kneaded by nervous hands, brought to the mouth a hundred times, lay there twisted like intestines, like the windings of withered brains, like rag dolls,

Pulchinellas, forming faces, limbs of executed humans, just like the pillow after a sleepless night or a white handkerchief after a ball, or after a funeral with real tears" (19).

Most of all, it may be observed in the conversation, in the depiction of the atmosphere, and in the drawing of the central figure, the writer Zachris.

The words exchanged among the guests have assumed concrete physical form. They are represented as malevolent objects with a tangible and measurable impact. Since the guests are murderers, or at least what we have learned to call "psychic murderers," words are weapons in a psychological warfare, the aim of which is to insult or injure the enemy or to rob him of his dignity and self-assurance. Thus words have become bullets, daggers, missiles, spears, and poisoned arrows, and the man at whom they are directed staggers when hit until he can return the charge (18).

The atmosphere is tense and violent. This quality is suggested by frequent metaphorical references to overfermented vats, magazines for explosives, electrical currents, and safety valves (15, 25).

But in the figure of Zachris the grotesque images have found their sharpest focal point. He is *the* psychic murderer, a beast of prey, a psychological vampire. Without any definite identity, characterless in the bad sense of the word, he is depicted as a veritable chameleon, constantly appearing in the guise of a different animal. He is the sly fox, the roaring lion, the braying donkey, the burrowing gopher, the slippery eel, the crawling snake (26, 27, 50). He is a parasite and polyp sucking strength from his victims, but wasting away alone (50).

Zachris is also depicted as a ghost, meaning that he has no face. His face is a mask of rubber presenting a variety of faces. No one has seen his real face, because his eyes are not visible. They are hidden behind his green glasses, with which he was presumably born. When he has to remove and wipe his glasses he bends his head forward in order not to "reveal the mirrors of the soul." In addition, his mouth and teeth are hidden by a moustache. Like a magician he hypnotizes his victims with his glasses, or tricks them by constantly appearing in a new role (54–55).[5]

In his role as a vampire Zachris has had many victims. The novel concentrates on two: his wife Jenny and the writer Falkenström. He is also said to have destroyed the good name and work of a writer who had played an important role in the 1870's, the hero of *The Red Room*, Arvid Falk (154). (In another context, though, Arvid Falk is said to have been "resurrected from the dead" after having "steeled himself in the Bessemer ovens of Inferno," an interesting identification between Strindberg and Falk, [33].)

The marriage between Zachris and Jenny is depicted as a dance macabre. Like the marriage between the Captain and Alice in the drama *The Dance of Death* it is a state of infinite boredom relieved occasionally by backbiting, drunken orgies, and frenzied quarrels. Tied to each other by the invisible bonds of guilty knowledge, Zachris and Jenny are like two wild animals clawing each other within the narrow confines of a cage. They are struggling for power over each other, bent on psychic murder.

When Jenny, owing to the influence of the feminist Hanna Paj, makes an attempt to break away from Zachris, the latter decides to take revenge on his wife by destroying what she values most, her beauty. By tempting her to eat and drink so that she will grow fat and ugly he will be the master. He succeeds, because when Jenny realizes she has lost her beauty she also loses her desire to live. To add an extra measure of

---

[5] Zachris is evidently patterned on the model of E. T. A. Hoffmann's literary parasite in "Klein Zaches genannt Zinnober" (cf. also 46, 117–121).

horror to this psychic murder Strindberg then turns Zachris into a disgusting literary vampire who writes his novel of revenge as Jenny lies dying, stealing upstairs occasionally to spy on his victim, whom he suspects of writing a book exposing him.

Zachris fears to the very end that Jenny will unmask him, and his fears become a reality. Before she dies, Jenny appears in a fantastic scene that has the quality of a seance. During her progressive physical decline Jenny has undergone a tremendous change under the influence of her friend Kilo, who is closly connected with the so-called monastery. In this scene she appears before Zachris and some of his cronies like a sleepwalker, or a medium, like someone who has already passed over to the other side. Her eyes are veiled and she seems to be communicating with spirits, to be guided by unseen hands. Her former personality has dissolved: "Her whole person seemed disintegrated, and she became like a medium possessed by strangers, absentees, who occupied her in turn." There are those who feel she is simply enacting the role of Lady Macbeth, but she is not acting. Before her departure from the scene, which is a leave-taking of life, Jenny gives a speech in which she condemns the assembled literary men as a gathering of living dead, as psychic suicides and murderers: "I see you, although my eyes do not see. You are so far away and as small as dolls in a shopwindow; you are blue in the face like dead people; but that is because you are dead; you have committed suicide—he says—and one of you has committed murder. There he sits! If I live longer—if this can be called living . . . no, I am dead" (263). The man she calls a murderer is of course Zachris, her husband, who is also the only one who has really understood what Jenny was talking about.

But the portrait of Zachris is more nuanced than the description given thus far would suggest. Regarded from without, the portrait of Zachris is grotesque and satirical. Re-

garded from within, it is a portrait of a man in despair. It is
very evident that to a certain extent Strindberg has identified
with Zachris. This fact is significant, for it indicates that
Strindberg's indictment of this ambitious little writer is at
least in part an indictment of the values to which he had once
committed himself, that is, during his naturalistic period.

Thus we learn that a good deal of Zachris' behavior and
view of life may be explained or even condoned in view of
his marital difficulties. Before his marriage to Jenny he had
been married to a singer who first committed adultery and
then deprived him of his son, whom he loved above all else.
Having made a religion of love he then lost all illusions, and
"departed from the struggle with a world view so desperately cynical that he dared not express it without putting a
good-natured mask over his face" (93). This did not prevent
people from feeling the hatred and the contempt under the
assumed mask of benevolence and good will. Later he became
enmeshed in what Strindberg calls "Jenny's hell," which, it
is said, ought to excuse much of his unpleasant behavior to
others (49).

Strindberg seems to identify the closest with Zachris
after Jenny has come under the influence of Hanna Paj, here
of course seen as a representative of the kind of ideology
Strindberg abhorred, the movement advocating emancipation
for women. Experiencing first a sense of relief when Jenny
and the children leave him, Zachris soon begins to feel a great
sense of loss, of emptiness. In his solitude he becomes ob-
sessed with fear, haunted by specters from the past and feelings of self-disgust and utter despair. As he observes himself
in the mirror he sees a ghost, and he resigns himself to wait
for death. There is no longer anything to live for. Always a
parasite, he is without a self, without independent life:
"Zachris was a selfless jelly, an unorganized matter that lived
like a truffle on the roots of others. He had always lived the

lives of others, never his own, he had intermittently identified himself with a whole row of persons, performed roles, made types of himself" (211). He has no conscience, no sense of guilt: thus all he can feel is emptiness and despair. Only one thing can inspire him to live: the desire for revenge. He must write a novel in which he can write Jenny out of his life, "murder" her and her memory. The only way to begin a new life is to erase the old. As he returns to the writing desk he begins to live again, and so intensely that he is unaware of the passing of time.

Is this not a familiar situation? Is it not an almost exact reproduction of Axel's literary "vampirism" in *The Defense of a Fool?* When coupled with Jenny's critical indictment of the writer in her final speech this is indeed and indubitably self-criticism. Strindberg's conception of the role of the writer has changed: the new role is to act as an intercessor for a suffering mankind, expressing man's despair. In *Black Banners* we make the acquaintance of this new type of writer in the person of Falkenström.

Falkenström, too, has been exploited by Zachris, the latter having attached himself with particular force to the man who is described as the greatest talent among the contemporary Swedish writers. "Elegant, carefree, independent, unconcerned about ambition or social reputation, he had made a name for himself on his talent alone" (50). Having failed to dominate Falkenström by the usual means, Zachris has succeeded by gaining influence over Falkenström's wife and through Jenny, whom Falkenström admires.

Like Arvid Falk, the older Falkenström is a disillusioned idealist, but his cynicism and his depth of despair suggest that he has deeper affinities with the actor Falander in *The Red Room.* Life and experience have taught Falkenström "die grosse Verachtung" (51). Having always "dreamed of beautiful poems, he has only been allowed to see the ugly aspects of life" (72). He feels like one of the damned, unjustly condemned to grovel in filth and mud. Behind him he has three broken marriages.

Like Jenny, Falkenström is portrayed as a sleepwalker, a ghost. His appearance is due in part to drinking and late hours, but it is also a reflection of his suffering. He is depicted as "more like the dead than the living . . . like a corpse with extinguished eyes" (70). The features of his face have become "erased," his face just a spot of white with a few indentations (101).

In chapter nine Falkenström is portrayed in a moving and symbolic winter scene. Flanked by some dark spruce trees, darker than usual under the heavy winter sky, he sits on a bench in a secluded part of a city park. He has reached a state of utter despair; overcome by a sickness unto death, he is paralyzed by indecisiveness: "He really did not know where to go, because he had no place to go, had no goal, no interest in life, that could motivate him into action" (101). Passively he lets himself be covered by the pure white snow that is burying both him and his memories, making him invisible to passersby (102).

A brief scene of vivid dramatic intensity brings him into action. Visiting the area of town where his estranged wife and their two children are living, he looks up at the window and sees the children "fingering the window pane as if they wanted to get out, trapped like little birds, fluttering, bumping against the transparent unknown" (107). In the other window he sees his wife, depicted in the grotesque colors of an Ensor painting of masks: "With red hair, swollen eyes, and a mouth as if cut up with a razor, lips that always appeared bloody and gave him the idea that she sucked blood" (107). Depicted as a vampire, and a psychic murderer, her face has the complexion we anticipate, "the greenish white color as of someone drowned" (107). With a few determined steps

Falkenström is inside the apartment and a moment later there is a bleeding red sign of the cross in her face from a blow dealt her by his rattan stick. It furnishes only temporary relief from his suffering, because it quickly fills him with feelings of guilt and he flees the scene like a murderer.

Profoundly convinced of the fleeting and impermanent nature of existence, the impossibility of discovering any firm ground, that "love and hate, sorrow and joy, passions and interests, all was decayed and sliding," Falkenström pays a visit to the sensible Dr. Borg, whom we also recognize as a familiar figure from *The Red Room*. Lecturing Falkenström on the tyranny of sex, Dr. Borg tells him of a retreat for men called only the monastery, a place where weary men can gather strength to continue the battle for life. It is, he says, a nonsectarian institution although it has a tinge of religion, a religion without ritual (120–121).

The chapters depicting the life of this nonsectarian monastery are extremely important, because they introduce us to new facets of the personal and esoteric religion that sustained Strindberg's spirit in his later years. Evaluated from an aesthetic point of view most of the chapters are not very satisfactory, consisting as they do largely of dialogues or lectures on assigned topics. Many of the dialogues are as bizarre and abstruse as those gathered in the thousand pages of *A Blue Book*, which, incidentally, is subtitled "A Commentary on *Black Banners*" and dedicated to "Emanuel Swedenborg, the teacher and leader, from his disciple."

The two leaders of the monastery are Count Max and Kilo, two odd figures who seem to lack identity, resembling disembodied spirits rather than human beings. Both are students of Theosophy, and both are making an attempt to foster a revival of spiritual values after the previous period of materialism.

In *Alone* Strindberg concentrated very largely on the

self-conquest and self-discipline fostered by his new religious vision. In *Black Banners* the emphasis is on the metaphysical aspects, on the manner of viewing the world. The Romantic occultism of *Inferno* has been developed into a more systematic vision.

The dialogues, most of which are conducted by Kilo and Count Max, reflect a preoccupation with those mysterious experiences and occult phenomena that reveal the unreliability of our senses, our memories, and perceptions, the insubstantiality of matter, and the existence of a transcendental realm. The members of the monastery are actively engaged in gathering data consisting of seemingly inexplicable phenomena and strange coincidences. The limits of our knowledge are demonstrated, proving the existence of higher laws than those that human reason has developed in the form of a materialistic physics and chemistry.

The most interesting dialogues are those dealing with what is called "the mysticism of everyday life" (200). With Schopenhauer, whom he quotes, Count Max insists that matter lacks reality, that the world is a mirage, unreal, and insubstantial. This conception of the world obliterates the distinction between matter and spirit and between the ego and the world. Matter becomes a living thing, objects become animated. Furniture, clocks, musical instruments, potted plants, flowers, rooms, houses assume independent existence, reflecting the atmosphere engendered by the human beings with whom they are associated (185–195).

Not only the world of matter but the self, too, lacks substance. It too is an illusion. Among the experiences classified under the heading of the mysticism of everyday life are therefore included also those that reveal the mysteries of human identity. It is Falkenström who lectures on this topic, and his remarks are prefaced by a brief introduction in which he seems to voice Strindberg's own point of view. His readers have often misunderstood him, insists Falkenström, because they have felt that he has indicted them when he has in fact reacted against the evil in himself. His collected works are his biography, his confession. "It has, you see, seemed to me, already early in life, that my life was staged before me so that I would be able to observe all its facets. This reconciled me to my misfortunes, and it taught me to perceive myself as an object. When I now strike out against the irreligious in my little diatribe, I am including myself, above all, myself" (196).

In his lecture Falkenström discusses a phenomenon called "the irradiation of the soul," describing those moments when we have the strange sensation that the aspect of our psyche which we call the soul leads an independent life, that it may actually at times leave the body and act on its own. He admits that he is baffled by these experiences, which seem to obliterate the distinction between dream and reality, and suggests that for the time being only a systematic gathering and analysis of evidence will be able to illuminate their nature (196–197).

This mysticism of everyday life which plays such an important role in *Black Banners, A Blue Book*, and in the Chamber plays has religious and metaphysical implications as well as practical, moral, and psychological significance. The basic assumption of this mysticism, which is almost a naturalism, a method of observing everyday life more closely, is that it gradually points the way to a religious faith. Mysticism is a naturalism, but a naturalism that aims at transcendence. Falkenström quotes Talmud to illustrate what he means: "If you wish to learn to know the invisible then observe very carefully the visible (200). Through the careful study of the visible world we learn of its insubstantiality and come into contact with a transcendental realm. This *Anschluss an Jenseits*, this contact with the other side, is defined as the essence of religion, the religion of Swedenborg, and of Goethe (138). It strengthens our faith in a higher reality. And faith is a positive state, a state of strength. Apart from the belief in a transcendental realm it is not defined as a faith in anything specific, neither in God nor in a dogma. It amounts basically to a faith in a world that simply lies outside the domain of our limited reason, a richer and much more "oceanic" realm. The problem of faith in a personal God is never broached, and the religion we encounter in the monastery of *Black Banners* may well be described as a religion without a belief in God. Nietzsche had declared a few decades earlier that God was dead, and Strindberg had voiced his assent to this declaration. In *Black Banners* God is still dead, it seems, but religion has returned.

The conventional Christian dogmas are consequently handled in a practical manner. That hell exists we know independently of any belief in a dogma. We know it as a state of mind, as a moral and psychological condition (201–202). The dogma of Christ's expiatory sacrifice for our sins is explained in equally practical terms: try not to disappoint the man who helps you get out of your debts by involving yourself in new debts (202). The forgiveness of the sins of others is a commandment that is justified in psychological terms. As long as we hate our enemies we are under their influence, at their mercy. Only by forgiving them do we become free of them (205–206). Nevertheless, Falkenström himself is unable to forgive his archenemy, Zachris, for he wants to see justice done. As the one who has been unjustly attacked he wants to see his enemy destroyed. Only when Zachris is defeated, humiliated, will he (Falkenström) praise God and forgive the fallen man. That Falkenström's reckoning with Zachris is also a reckoning with himself, with his own past, is here clearly indicated. To forgive Zachris is to forgive himself and his own involvement in the age of perversity which Zachris represents, the age of materialism, of humbug, of false prophets, of advertising and exploitation (271).

The novel ends on an inconclusive note. Zachris carries on as before, while Falkenström seeks to practice the spiritual discipline of the monastery, and to gather observations of a metaphysical and occult nature like Kilo and Count Max, and like Strindberg himself in *A Blue Book*.

The last chapter of the novel comes as a surprise, for the man who has the last word is neither Zachris, nor Falkenström, nor Kilo or Max, but the sober and practical Smartman. We are again reminded of the ending of *The Red Room* in which the realistic Borg was allowed to sum up the situation. Smartman appears in a slightly different role, however, for he speaks only for himself, making no comments on the actions of the others. The "Review" is a summing up of his own life taking the form of a posthumous letter to his son. Calling himself a child of the age, he says he regarded life as a battlefield and existence as a war of survival. His aim was to gain power over others. Having gained this power he was filled with a sense of emptiness and silence, and in retrospect his life fills him with horror and despair. He compares himself to a wanderer who has reached a great wall, a mountain wall. His understanding tells him that there must be something behind it or at the top, but he lacks the strength and the hope and the courage to scale the wall. He has no future and regrets the past though he is unable to feel guilt. His state is one of total despair.

At the end of the letter Smartman addresses himself to his son, counseling him about how to live. Here his tone suddenly is much more positive, stressing the value of experience and of experimenting with points of view. As he speaks of the writer and the artist he suddenly seems to articulate a familiar note of openness to the future so characteristic of

Strindberg: "If you are a writer or an artist, you must live outside classes and estates, outside parties although defending the interests of your colleagues, seeking justice, following your genius. As a writer you have the right to play with thoughts, to experiment with standpoints, to test opinions, but without committing yourself to anything, because freedom is the vital element of the poet" (290).

Even this grotesque and disenchanted novel, in which Strindberg so strongly expresses his belief that the naturalistic view of life is bound to end in boredom, meaninglessness, and despair, somehow ends on a positive note.

⤙ 14. The Roofing Feast

Taklagsöl (*The Roofing Feast*) is Strindberg's most experimental, most modern work of fiction. Its uniqueness rests on the fact that it is the only work in which Strindberg like the modern psychological novelist seeks not only to record but also in some measure to retain the very "inwardness" of mental experience. Strindberg was always keenly interested in psychology, and, ahead of his contemporaries, he stressed the complexity of character and the importance of unconscious motivation, exploring hitherto uncharted areas of psychological experience. And he usually approached psychological problems in a strongly analytical fashion. This is at least true of his novels, and it explains why *The Son of a Servant* is not a psychological novel in the sense in which, say, James Joyce's *Ulysses* may be labeled one. Aside from a few of the opening chapters Strindberg's novel is much too discursive. Johan is a case study, and Strindberg approaches his mind from without, almost in a scientific fashion, aiming at objectivity. In *The Roofing Feast*, on the other hand, Strindberg seeks to convey the atmosphere of the mind, to create the illusion that we are capturing the very flow of consciousness, the fleeting thoughts and sensations registered by the human mind. It places Strindberg among the early experimenters in the psychological novel, and leads us to speculate on the question of how exciting a modern novelist Strindberg might have become had he chosen to apply himself more seriously to the craft of fiction. There is no doubt that he was utterly bored with the traditional form of the novel, that his restless, experimental, and improvisatory mind needed a new mode of expression. The psychological novel might well have filled this need, just as the cinema might have filled his need for a new dramatic mode of expression.

In *The Roofing Feast* Strindberg makes bold use of the monologue, with which he as a dramatist was very familiar. His letters to Schering, his German translator, indicate that he was toying with ideas of turning the drama into "a giant monologue," and that in fact, he had thought of ways of producing *The Roofing Feast* on the stage.[1] Nothing came of these plans. *The Roofing Feast* remained a work of fiction, fortunately we might add, because it thus became an interesting experiment in the mode of expression which we usually label the internal monologue.

Lest Strindberg be credited with a degree of inventiveness he did not possess, it should at once be noted that *The Roofing Feast* is mostly a somewhat structured monologue, and that Strindberg was not ready to dispense with the nat-

---

[1] "Writing *The Roofing Feast* was a great pleasure and I first planned it as a drama" (August Strindberg, *Från Fjärdingen till Blå Tornet: Ett brevurval 1870–1912*, ed. Torsten Eklund [Stockholm: Bonniers, 1946], pp. 381–383). A dramatized version of the novel was actually performed at Strindberg's own Intimate Theater in Stockholm in 1949.

uralistic framework of motivation. The man whose monologue is recorded in the novel is in a semiconscious state,
under heavy sedation. His eagerness to speak is motivated by
the effects of alternating injections of morphine and camphor.
Furthermore, Strindberg is still the omniscient author, arranging the stage, providing additional information about the sick
man, and on occasion observing the man from the point of
view of either the nurse or the doctor (the only other characters in the novel). The monologue is also broken up by brief
snatches of dialogue, though even these resemble monologues,
because the sick man is, in fact, delivering lectures and considered to be "raving." Finally, the monologue in *The Roofing
Feast* is not, strictly speaking, an internal monologue, since
the man is speaking aloud, but this seems of minor significance in view of the fact that his thoughts are of the kind
that would not normally be spoken, particularly not over a
period of days.

Even though Strindberg has seemingly found it necessary
to motivate in a naturalistic fashion his hero's compul-
sive and rambling loquaciousness, within the monologue
itself he experiments with techniques that we associate with
Symbolist literature, and it is in this area that the real novelty
of *The Roofing Feast* as a work of fiction rests. I am referring
here to the use of stream of consciousness to convey the illusion of a flow of associations unhampered by any logical
restraint; the use of the time shift to convey a feeling of the
meanderings of the mind between the past and the present
and the simultaneity of mental experiences; the use of symbols
and leitmotivs to provide structure and mood. In *The Roofing
Feast* Strindberg, the realist and naturalist, has come a long
way. He may have thought of his novel as a drama, but it is,
in fact, much closer to the conception of the novel as a poem,
a conception realized so brilliantly in Virginia Woolf's *To
the Lighthouse* and in James Joyce's *Finnegans Wake*. In his

efforts to convey the inwardness of subjective experience Strindberg has been forced like Joyce to become a Symbolist.[2]

But *The Roofing Feast* is more than an experiment. It is a very beautiful and profoundly moving work. Written in 1906 it belongs to the period in which the Chamber plays were conceived, and it shares the tone and atmosphere of these late works. The tone is one of resignation and acceptance. Strindberg's faith has given him a hard-earned sense of humility and compassion. He seeks to forgive his enemies, believing that he has demanded justice when he should have asked for grace. Life having become a bitter nightmare hardly to be endured, he hopes for death and a better existence in another world. The patient Buddha is invoked to teach men acceptance of suffering and the way to liberation. The atmosphere is one of unreality. Life is so absurd and incomprehensible that it must be an illusion. The brevity of happiness is starkly outlined against a backdrop of loneliness and suffering making the precious moments of joy stand out with painful clarity. The power of evil is of monstrous proportions. Nothing is real, nothing is as it appears to be: the world dissolves into props; character becomes a mask; human beings are either murderers or victims, but they are all marionettes in the huge comedy of life, engineered by the supreme and enigmatic artist, God.

The Roofing Feast develops and interweaves several of the predominant themes in Strindberg's later works. Although it is a short novel, only a detailed critical analysis can provide a complete picture of its intricate structure, its richness of texture, and its significance within the context of Strindberg's world.

---

[2] A chief characteristic of certain modern novelists is, as Leon Edel has observed, a bold attempt to "make words evoke image and symbol as the poet does," hence the effort to write what is in fact "Symbolist fiction" (*The Psychological Novel, 1900–1950* [New York: Lippincott, 1955], p. 7).

The man whose monologues are recorded in *The Roofing Feast* is by profession a curator. He is a learned man but also a hunter, a fisherman, an African explorer, a sailor. His appearance is exotic, southern. His beard is dark as is his hair, but his otherwise sunburned complexion is yellowish. He has been injured in an accident, and is just waking after a sleep induced by morphine. During the three days that have passed since the accident he has been talking incessantly. As he regains consciousness he notices a red cross on a white robe. This leads to associations with crusaders, Freemasons, the Swiss Alps, bottles of absinthe, trademarks, the English naval flag, and the signals of the navy, but his "inborn sense of order" is "plagued by the confusion of these images" and after the remark "But the Swiss coat of arms is a white cross on a red field, so it has been turned backward . . ." he lapses into sleep from the effort, while still verbalizing every idea originating in his feverish brain" (44, 7).

His first remarks concern a Graphophone. This primitive type of phonograph plays an extremely significant role in the novel, serving in effect to define and determine the structure of the monologue. A march played on the graphophone serves as a musical leitmotiv, which whenever it echoes in the man's mind channels his associations into a particular direction. The instrument itself becomes an image of the curator's stored-up memories. His memories are transcribed, as it were, and then played back. All that is needed is to release the catch and the past is unfolded. In this mechanical instrument Strindberg has found an appropriate metaphor for the pent-up and irresistible flow of the man's thoughts. Whereas the Graphophone and the leitmotiv of the march are intimately connected with the man's past, a recurring visual image is the connecting link between the past and the immediate present. A house is being erected on the adjoining lot, and in the mirror the sick man watches the growth of the scaffolding.

This slowly growing structure is the central symbol of the novel and has given it its title, referring as it does to the celebration that customarily takes place when the scaffolding is completed. The significance of the structure is that it serves to block the curator's view of "the green eye," the green lamp-shade in the window of his longtime enemy living in the house across the garden.

The Graphophone is associated with the most painful memories in the curator's life, his separation from his wife and child. It marks the end of his happiness and the beginning of his solitary life. For his son's fourth birthday he had purchased the Graphophone and a record. On one side of the record was a lively tune, a march. As it began a voice roared: "Falkenstein-marsch, Nachtigal-rekord" and then the march followed. The other side contained a clown's act, unfortunately in bad taste. The playing of the record caused a scene, and this was the last time the man was allowed to see his wife and child. All this we are told in the first monologue (7–13).

After a short sleep the second monologue begins. There is a brief account of the accident that has caused his hospitalization, then the sudden association of "Falkensteinmarsch! Nachtigal-rekord!" turns the curator's thoughts to the past and he describes his lonely life in his apartment after the final separation (15–19).

After another slumber and an injection of morphine the curator begins "to play back again like the Graphophone without the catch." For a moment he speaks of the garden and of the structure to be erected, then the question "Where was I? Yes: Falken-steinmarsch! Nachtigal-rekord!" begins a new chain of associations. This third monologue is a melancholy account of married life, the story of a family in the apartment below his own (20–31).

The curator sleeps until the next morning, then has a

conversation with the nurse in which it is noted that the structure outside is growing. After an injection of morphine the fourth and central monologue begins with the roar of "Falken-steinmarsch! Nachtigal-rekord!" This monologue is a flashback to the summer a year before the Graphophone incident, describing two weeks of happiness during a vacation in the archipelago. All the curator's pleasant memories are focused on these few idyllic days (35–59).

The fifth monologue begins after an interval of time during which the curator has been taken to the hospital and examined. Upon his return to his room he notices in the mirror that the house has grown, but that he is still able to see the top of his enemy's flagpole. Then "the roll of the brain phonograph began to move again, emitting all the last memories and impressions, but in strict order exactly as they had been transcribed." This monologue brings events to the moment of the final break, again punctuated by the roar of "Falken-steinmarsch! Nachtigal-rekord!" Then he tells of his lonely summer on the island in the archipelago preparing in vain for the return of his loved ones (61–65).

With events brought up to the present moment, the graphophone stops. The transcribed and orderly sequences of memory have been played back. The monologues that follow are fragmentary and disconnected without either temporal or logical sequence, consisting of random reflections on life, bits of scientific information, quotations from Luther and the book of Job, painful memories, confessions of guilt, cries of despair and pain, acute perceptions of happenings in the room. After a brief lecture on medicine to the doctor, who comments "it is like taking the stopper out of the soda-water bottle," the curator's monologue beginning "That's life" is reproduced in the form of stream of consciousness:

That's life . . . a masquerade with masks and dominoes; the masks are taken off after midnight! By the way, what time is it?

Why have you taken away the mirror? At least I don't see it; but then I escape the green eye; but then there's that about Congo; I've never hunted humans, although I have collected brains; it was some devil—yes, it was the green eye who spread that about; I laughed at first, thought it smart, clever; then I went along with it; finally I told it myself and even believed it; but every time I looked for a practice as a doctor it worked against me; it was the cannibal people were afraid of; that's what happens when you lie about yourself; but I couldn't take it back then; I would have been a liar; can't a lie ever be taken back? Of course it can; it can be forgotten, lose its bite, even become truth; once when I needed money I lied that I would get a fellowship the first of May; it was terrible; but imagine, on the first of May I got a fellowship I had never expected; the lie became truth, but wasn't truth. Of course a lie can be wiped away, since a terrible memory can be erased; energy is not indestructible, of course, only talk; if I throw a stone in the water, the rings cease when the resistance is greater than the power; in a stormy sea there are no rings; this lie, put out by Helmholtz or somebody, I've gone round preaching twenty years; when you're a child you believe everything that's said; they told me, when I was seven, that you could catch gray sparrows if you sprinkled salt on their tails. I tried, failed, but still believed it; maybe it's true; I've never tried it in an experimental way . . . I'm thirsty, give me a drink.—Your name is Sofia, and you made a fool of me with the raspberry bushes of knowledge.—You were a child, and you couldn't help it!—and you've forgotten it, you see! You do forget; Orfila says in his legal chemistry that the brain after death remains unchanged in its capsule and that it's like a lump of clay; our bodies come from earth, to earth they return; the god, Ptah, made man on a potter's wheel; that's why we're symmetrical, and so the portrait painter has difficulty with the face frontally; not even Rembrandt got the eyes right in the head! —Now I'm burning out" (68–69).

When the man ceases to speak, he is given a camphor injection and his monologue continues, actually in a more coherent manner, though Strindberg insists: "now chaos began, helter-skelter. His brain worked like empty millstones, threw sparks as if it wanted to catch fire" (69–72).

The last pages of the novel are somewhat disappointing. Having summed up his reflections on life in the line "Back and forth, everything falters, comes back, disappears, reappears," the curator, now in frightful pain, continues to speak for forty-eight hours, speaking "millions, millions of words, his whole life ebbing out in words; exactly as if he were closing the accounts" (77–78). With the exception of a few lines Strindberg has unfortunately chosen merely to paraphrase the man's words, reporting and not rendering his speech. This is a pity, for though it naturally would have been impossible for him to render millions of words in a short novel, a few concentrated pages of a stream of consciousness monologue similar to "That's life" might well have provided the illusion of a more intimate contact with the curator's inner thoughts and feelings.

But Strindberg's intensely exciting experiment with the monologue must be judged in terms of his artistic intentions and not in the light of the accomplishments of later and more skillful psychological novelists. His main intention was not to develop a new technique for rendering subjective states of mind, but to convey a vision of life, his own highly personal vision of the absurdity of human existence. Here the monologue serves his purpose admirably. One criticism of Strindberg's Chamber plays has been that they lack dramatic tension, dissolve into atmosphere or mere querulousness. In the Chamber plays things often happen too quickly, the characters—the young man in *The Ghost Sonata* serves as an example—rush through life with frantic haste. There is a brief moment of love and hope and happiness, and in the next scene there is already the inevitable dissillusionment when the nothingness and absurdity of life is unmasked. The consequence is that Strindberg's vision of life is often unconvincing in aesthetic terms, and he strikes us as a grumbling and pessimistic old man who does not give his characters a chance to discover life on their own. Only with great difficulty can Strindberg's pessimistic vision of the illusoriness of life and the brevity of happiness be rendered in a concentrated form, and the aesthetic failure of some of the Chamber plays, interesting as they may be as experiments with new dramatic techniques, bears this out.

But in *The Roofing Feast* the monologue, motivated by the curator's feverish state and his desperate need to make some sense and order out of life as he nears death, provides a natural vehicle for Strindberg's vision of life. The few idyllic moments in the man's life stand out in almost hallucinatory brilliance against the prevailing background of disorder, chaos, darkness. The curator's state of mind makes the summing up of bitter truths more convincing, because the unfortunate succession of events motivating them may be piled up rapidly without violating our sense of probability.

The Roofing Feast is the story of a marriage, but because of Strindberg's fondness for parallelism (an essential aspect of his dramatic technique) it becomes, in fact, the story of two marriages. Before his moving account of the inevitable denouement of his own marriage the curator accentuates his disillusioned view of the brevity of human happiness by his story of the fortunes of a newly married couple in the apartment below his own. The powerful impact of this narrative is due to the highly concentrated form in which it is told, a form in which a musical leitmotiv again plays a central role.

In telling this story Strindberg employs a technique that he had introduced in *Alone*. The curator like the narrator in *Alone* leads a solitary life, and in his solitude he gradually enters into the lives of his neighbors while remaining a detached observer, envisioning their lives by listening to the sounds of the house, snatches of conversation, tunes played on the piano, the cries of children, the popping of champagne corks, the ringing of telephones.

Without knowing either the actors or the stage the curator evokes a picture of a marriage simply by interpreting the sounds from below. He begins by describing his coming home one day shortly after the neighbors' wedding and hearing the sounds of the first ball. He hears piano music while still at the bottom of the stairwell, and there is an odor of fine tobacco in the darkness, emanating from three glowing spots, the cigars of three indistinct gentlemen in the hallway. From his own apartment he hears the music, the steps of the dancers, the laughter, the speeches, the songs, and, most important of all, the repertory of the Graphophone. The Graphophone again plays a significant role in the novel, now serving to create a mood. A new musical leitmotiv is introduced: a certain waltz, "Le Charme," is played numerous times during the night. The curator concludes that it is the young wife's favorite waltz (23).

The following day around noon he hears her play "Le Charme," but "softly, languishingly, like an echo of yesterday's ball" (23). The husband arrives in the evening, and his arrival is signaled by a loud yawn.

The Sunday dinners are family affairs: the parents are present, and *à quatre mains* is played after the meal, always beginning with Brahms's "Hungarian Dance." Sometimes there is dancing before the evening is over, and "Le Charme" is always played (23–24).

Gradually there is less music, more and more silence. The wife plays Wilhelm Petterson-Berger's "Summer Song," which the curator likes. The Sunday dinners are quieter. One day a new sound is heard: they are playing backgammon. The next sound the curator deduces from this activity: with a cry a new human being is born. Now there is a frenzy of sounds again, culminating at the christening (24).

"Le Charme" now returns, and the happy grandfathers announce their Sunday appearance with their particular repertory: Stradella, *Fra Diavolo*, student songs, Swedish folksongs (24–25). But soon the child is not sufficient to dispel the growing boredom and routine, expressed by yawns and infrequent conversations. The wife plays only rarely, "Le Charme" sounding now and then like "a sigh of loss over a vanished youth" (25). The grandfather who likes Stradella and *Fra Diavolo* evidently stayed too long on Sundays, for this repertory is suddenly missing (26).

The husband begins to stay away in the evenings, and the wife plays in a listless fashion avoiding "Le Charme." Finally one night she plays "Glädjens blomster i jordens mull," a melancholy Swedish folk song. Then a loud bang is heard and the cover to the piano is closed, and silence ensues. The husband comes home more frequently, but the yawns increase; the piano is not touched for three months; no guests arrive. The curator's final comment is: "The eternal silence has begun! Poor people!" (26).

Thus the story is told by means of sounds and chiefly by means of the musical leitmotiv. The curator's impressions of this anonymous marriage are, however, confirmed by his incidental visit to the apartment to make a telephone call. Since no one is in the apartment at the time, it is the physical objects, the furniture, the paintings, the photographs, the commonplace everyday things, that confirm his impression. Four years have passed, and by now "the cobwebs of boredom" have settled everywhere. He contemplates the study, which has something naked and abstract about it: no living objects, no plants, no color, no curtains by the windows. He observes the photographs, and understands why he has been unable to retain a clear picture of the couple's appearance. They have no identity; they are faceless, colorless. "There sits his wife, whom I have never been able to fix in my mind;

a *grisaille*, colorless, without nuances, who was not able to increase her repertory with a single piece, and therefore stopped playing for her husband who grew bored from listening to the same piece forever." The dining room presents the same "abstract, ash-gray devastation." The bedroom is a torture chamber with its frightful iron bedsteads, "the brasslike steam pipes, the engine room, the racks, the tenterhooks, the implements of torture, the iron maiden." On the tile stove sits a Buddha figure: "waiting, patient, wondering about the impatience of mankind" (26–29).

In this first story Strindberg makes use of the leitmotiv to convey the theme and create the mood. In the second story, the story of the curator's marriage, Strindberg employs a different technique: the dramatic use of contrasting moods. The brief idyllic moment, the short summer of happiness, is contrasted with the power of blackness, of evil. The dramatic atmosphere is here heightened by the effective use of symbolism in which color, as so often in Strindberg's novels, has a central function. The vampire motif so recurrent in the later works is also introduced.

A verdant little island in the archipelago is the setting. Here the curator once knew the full measure of happiness for two brief weeks with his wife and child. On this island with its cowslips, orchids, and lilacs, he lived "richly, fully, harmoniously, intensively." In some of the most beautiful passages he has ever written Strindberg etches in our memory a beautiful vignette of the Swedish summer:

I remember the Saturday mornings—one Saturday morning the gardener's boat put in at my pier; I got up at six o'clock; the sun shone freshly on the dewy grass; the boat lay at the pier loaded with all the splendor of summer; I bought new peas, fresh potatoes, radishes, asparagus, strawberries—and roses. Then I took my boat and inspected the pole hooks in the reeds beneath their window where they were still sleeping behind the blue curtains. When this was done it was seven; the baker's girl came with the coffee cake; the maid opened up the kitchen; the stove clattered and soon blue smoke rose from the chimney. The bedroom window was thrown up and I went in with my bounty, the bearer of offerings with his baskets, and strewed roses on them, on the white sheets and coverlets, on beautiful young bodies; I threw open windows in a handsome room with white furniture where the sea breeze swelled in and out amidst flowered curtains, the chirping of birds, the rustle of leaves, and the wash of waves. The child's crowing and the mother's laughter were interrupted by the maid who came in with the coffee tray. (36–37)

But this idyll is soon disrupted by the inevitable intrusion of the others, "the blacks." The house itself is haunted: a woman in black has been known to materialize for the workers in the field in the middle of the day, vanishing when approached. The curator has a scientific explanation for the phenomenon, but one noon he himself sees a lady in black accompanied by two little girls in red dresses hurrying toward the house, and then they vanish without a trace. He awakes in the night tormented by feelings of anguish. The songbirds are driven away by swallows of a particularly unpleasant variety, "small black falcons, voracious, cruel, fierce." Instead of the songs of the thrushes he has to listen to the piercing screams of the black swallows.

These forebodings soon spell disaster. A white yacht arrives. On board are relatives of the curator, individuals for whom he feels a pronounced aversion since they have always exerted an evil influence on his life. They are "the blacks": all dark-haired and with brown eyes.

The yacht begins to fascinate the curator's wife who misses the gaiety on board, a gaiety that is manifested not only by colored lights and the sound of glasses and trays, but also by the sound issuing from a great Graphophone playing " 'Le Charme'—imagine that" (43). Finally a meeting with the relatives is arranged, and to the curator's astonishment it is characterized by cordiality and friendliness. For the last time he experiences a moment of intense happiness, this time for two minutes,

which have remained in my memory as actually corresponding to our visions of the Isles of Bliss and peace on earth. The summer sun shone, the water lay blue, the wind stood still; the living-room windows were open; outside on the veranda and lawn ladies and gentlemen in light holiday dress were sitting and lying; flowers on the table, golden wine in the glasses with gilt rims; from inside Mendelssohn's "Caprice in B Minor" was heard, played by my sister-in-law; my small son was sitting on the knee of a cousin, whose spouse, somewhat on in years, was lost in gazing at my young wife's unusual beauty. My brother and I, hearing a piece of music that had played a certain role in our parents' home, exchanged a glance. Harmony, reconciliation were heard in our silence, enjoined or instilled by the powerful music. (46)

But soon "the masks were doffed and the family vampire began to bait and humiliate me at my own table." The warfare for the control of minds begins. The cousin who appears as a snake charmer worms his way into their lives, seeking to influence the curator's wife. With his vampire nature he seeks to take the curator's place in her life. Soon she is "murdered" and "poisoned," harboring the enemy's thoughts (48–49).

The inevitable end is rendered in a powerful symbolic form. As the quarrels between the curator and his wife increase in intensity, a storm begins to brew. The swallows are shrieking under the roof tiles, a tree is rubbing its branches against the wall of the house. Outside there is a flapping as of laundry or starched skirts, a sound that the curator is unable to explain at first, but when he looks out the window he sees a wild dance, a dance of "two white cloths pursuing each other, flying at each other, separating, searching each

other out again. It was two newspapers that had been forgotten on the veranda." When his wife appears she has seen,
for the first time, the dark lady with the two little girls in
red. The curator, listening to her, feels "the icy cold of death
running through his veins and tissues, as before the inexplicable." He goes to bed but is soon awakened by a veritable
cannonade, the banging of the outer door. Then something
happens which fills him with terror, and which he—for the
first time—is unable to explain: through the corridor a galloping sound begins, a galloping as if hundreds and hundreds
of human beings were running barefoot through the house.
He dares not open the door to find out the cause of this
disturbance and is prepared to "freeze to death from his shud-
ders of fear" (53–59).

The next morning the curator flees. Back in the city he
and his wife are briefly reconciled until the incident with
the Graphophone ends their relationship forever.

But the following summer he returns to the island, living among the memories of a vanished happiness, in vain
expecting his loved ones to return. The objects about him
convey his feelings of sadness and melancholy: the empty
beds in his wife's bedroom, the lilacs and the orchids that
have finished blooming, his wife's red slippers in a treetop
("a flying witch with her feet in the air, toes pointing inward; the winter snow, rain, and sun had faded them, twisted
them askew, horrible to watch"), the piano that refuses to
play, the creakings of the swing ("when it blew hard one
night it creaked and squeaked until morning as if it were
crying"): "Thus I lived with my dear shadows, a shadowy
life in the haunted house" (61–65).

In these poignant renderings of the dissolution of two
marriages Strindberg has written some of the most beautiful
and effective pages he ever produced. Too often he seems to
have believed that any writing when sufficiently suffused with
anger and passion could not fail to convince his readers. But

in *The Roofing Feast* his feelings of frustration and sorrow are not explicitly stated, but conveyed through poetic means. The drama of the marital conflicts and the pain and disappointments of the inevitable denouements are evoked by striking auditory and visual images. It is such writing that makes it possible for us to speak of *The Roofing Feast* as an experiment in Symbolist fiction.

As the curator's illness progresses and his monologues grow more and more fragmentary his utterances combine to form a vision of life in which we recognize some of the predominant themes in Strindberg's later works: the insistence on the unreality and absurdity of existence; the skeptical attitude to character and identity; the passionate desire for liberation from this life of suffering and guilt.

A leading motif is the image of human destinies hopelessly interwoven as in a web or a net. This motif recurs so often in the Chamber plays and in the last novels that it takes on the force and complexity of a symbol: "What a net, what a web are the destinies of human beings; all know each other, all are related or somehow entangled; one and the same bloodstream in so many rills; one single energy passing even through the bodies of our animals" (35). To assess guilt, to blame anyone for injuries one has suffered, is impossible, for everything is hopelessly entangled, impossible to unravel: "Every movement is dangerous for others, yet one must move; I am not guilty, and they are not: who is?" (35). The only conclusion is that we are all miserable, that no one is to be blamed for our misery: that we are all "governed by mysterious forces outside ourselves" (11). "There was a fatality that interwove human lives; there were destinies not to be escaped, consequently something predetermined, whether this lay hidden in birth, heredity, inherited traits, descent, or had its foundations in something unknown, which human beings were too cowardly to investigate" (52). The relationship of the symbol of the web to the notion of the unreality and absurdity of life becomes explicit in a somewhat hazy reference to Shakespeare's *The Tempest* and *Macbeth*: "It is all a web 'spun by the same thread as our dreams,' or 'a tale told by an idiot, full of sound and fury, signifying nothing,' says Shakespeare" (71).

The curator tries in vain to arrive at an understanding of the meaning of suffering, and the name of Job is invoked as so often in Strindberg's last works. But he is too tired and his conclusions are ultimately the same as Falkenström's in *Black Banners*, a resignation to the absurdity of life: "I must be very ill; I cannot hate any more, I don't have the strength; nothing bears touching; neither hatred nor love; today my enemies are friends and stick together, tomorrow they are enemies, divided, and then I can breathe" (77). As he hears the music from down below—"Le Charme" is suddenly heard again after a long absence—the curator reflects on the shuttle-like movements of life: "Back and forth, everything vacillates, comes back, disappears, reappears." His pain having become unbearable he cries out aloud, and as a consequence the music suddenly stops. When he notices this his resignation is transformed into rebellion, rebellion against the suffering of life: "Play more!" he cries, "I want the 'Summer Song'!— Two minutes of bliss for a life in hell! Two minutes, on the veranda, under the lilacs, the wife, the child, kinsmen, and friends, faithful servants, wine, music and flowers!" (78).

The curator's reflections on the nature of existence are accompanied by questions about the nature of character: "What is character? What is memory?" he asks. Strindberg here, as in *Alone*, proves firmly committed to the belief that it is our clinging to the illusory notion of the separate self which is the source of much of our suffering. Both *Alone* and *Black Banners* are exercises in self-sacrifice and self-conquest, the only ways to liberation.

As the curator's illness progresses and his monologues become more incoherent the illusory nature of the self, of character, becomes more apparent. Character is only a role, a mask, acquired in our daily existence, it may be doffed like a mask, sloughed off like a dry skin. While the stream-of-consciousness technique lends itself admirably to a rendering of this concept of the unstable ego, Strindberg again has not fully utilized the possibilities of this mode of expression. He merely reports to us what is happening:

At times new personalities seemed to grow in him, either endogenous remnants of ancestors or influences from everyone he thought of. He might thus be vicious and venomous and in the next moment arrogant and supercilious; then there appeared an old wise man, a child, a rudimentary woman. His own self disintegrated and his innate character was shown to be a mask behind which he had performed a role ensuing from an adjustment to the circumstances of life and according to the law of maximum development of mental powers. The whole canvas of education, schoolbooks, humanity, and newspapers separated itself into threads, and the little self he had embroidered was pulled out, disappeared. With disintegration of the self selfishness vanished, and he began to flow out, grasping about for what was nearest, the nurse and doctor, interesting himself in them, in their condition; with veritable amoeboid movements of the soul he threw out tentacles, fastening on their thoughts and feelings, as if to keep to sure ground. Then there was a lucid moment when he reasoned, arranged his affairs, settled his debts, gave orders, and asked them not to forget, above all not to forget what he was now saying. With the lapsing of memory he was worried by the fear that they would forget his orders; he identified them with himself. (79)

This observation ends with an insight also implied in the novel *Alone* a few years earlier: "With the disintegration of the self selfishness vanished," and the curator gradually begins to identify with everyone and everything about him, no longer having an identity of his own (79).

With loss of self comes a feeling of acceptance and liberation. The curator's tortured features comes to rest; he speaks of being tired and of wanting to sleep. The conclusion of the novel, which ends with the curator's death, is very beautiful. In the last pages Strindberg reintroduces the symbol of the growing building, and the meaning of the symbol suddenly strikes us with great force. The rise of the scaffolding, which the curator has anxiously observed in his mirror in his waking moments, has kept pace with his efforts to arrive at an acceptance of life. Once he has attained this state of acceptance the curator is free, no longer tormented by his feeling of guilt or hatred. Simultaneously, the rising structure finally blots out "the green eye," the symbolic embodiment not only of his own feelings of guilt but also of his enemy's violent hatred.[3]

Now, though it is February and there has been a light snowfall during the night, the curator says (and he is not dreaming!): "It is summer outside, oh, how green and beautiful." He is actually seeing the wreaths and flags on the newly finished scaffolding, and when he hears the cheers of the workers he smiles, thinking they are for him. "And thus he lay there, smiling as if he saw only beautiful things, green meadows, children and flowers, blue waters and flags in the sunshine" (81). Now the green eye is blotted out and forgotten, and therefore he has an unobstructed view of his beloved summer. In the symbolic action of the roof-raising feast as the vision of summer in the midst of the winter of life

---

[3] In a letter to Schering, Strindberg maintained that "the green eye" was designed to represent Baron Wrangel, Siri von Essen's first husband (*op. cit.*, p. 381).

Strindberg has found a haunting image not only of the liberation from the tormenting guilts and hatreds which imprison man within himself but also of his dreams of a happier, more beautiful, and less painful existence in another world.

⤙ 15. The Scapegoat

AMONG STRINDBERG's short novels *Synda-bocken* (*The Scapegoat*) has a particular claim to distinction. A work of great beauty and simplicity, it is also Strindberg's last work of fiction, published in 1907. It belongs to the period of the Chamber plays and A *Blue Book* which mirror the vision of the aging Strindberg just before his moving to the Blue Tower. Like the later drama, *The Highway*, it is his summing up, his last incarnation of himself as a man and as a writer, his final vision of life and art. Like the Chamber plays and A *Blue Book*, *The Scapegoat* is permeated by a tone of resignation and acceptance, by that curious blend of skepticism and faith which Strindberg called his "confession-less Christianity." Like Kierkegaard whom he so greatly admired, Strindberg finally envisions himself as the man of faith in the guise of the comic hero, reconciling himself to the absurdity of existence, its suffering and incomprehensibility, by a *credo quia absurdum*. Having struggled against his own overbearing arrogance and pride, he has finally gained a hard-earned humility. As a writer he now seeks anonymity, wishing to be in all humility "mankind's lawyer," existing only in his works in the manner of his beloved Shakespeare. Like Prospero in *The Tempest* Strindberg is seeking to rise above the sufferings, and the injustices, to forgive his enemies, by seeing life as unreal, as a dream, as a stage on which human beings are the masked players in the comedy of life. The frenzied metaphors of *Black Banners* are gone. In its classic simplicity and restraint, in its mythical perspective, and in its generosity of vision, *The Scapegoat* brings to mind the last and masterly short novels of André Gide and D. H. Lawrence, *Theseus* and *The Man Who Died*, respectively.

The fable is simple, and the protagonists are few. It is the new scenic asceticism of the Chamber plays transferred to the novel, as expressed in a letter to Adolf Paul in 1907: "try the intimate form; a trifling theme, thoroughly treated; few characters; broad viewpoints; free fantasy; but based on observation, on experience; well studied; simple, but not too simple; no large apparatus; no superfluous minor characters." [1] It is also remarkable how closely Strindberg in *The Scapegoat* follows his own program for dramatic composition as outlined in a manuscript from the turn of the century. An effective drama, he writes, "ought to operate with suggestions; contain a secret that the spectator learns to know either in the beginning or toward the end; an outburst of feeling, wrath, indignation; a reversal (*revirement*), a setback; a surprise; a punishment (nemesis), a humiliation; careful conclusion, either with or without atonement; a *quid pro quo*; a parallelism." [2] In view of these remarks it is not surprising

---

[1] Martin Lamm, *August Strindberg* (2d ed.; Stockholm: Bonniers, 1948), p. 352.

[2] *Ibid.*, p. 368.

that Strindberg should suggest in a letter to Schering that given some minor changes they might put *The Roofing Feast* and *The Scapegoat* on the stage, because "the secret of all my tales, short stories, fairy tales, is that they are dramas. When the theaters were closed to me for long periods of time, I got the idea of writing my dramas in epic form—for future use." [3]

The Scapegoat is set in a small Swedish town, a former health resort, now an idyllic and sleepy haven for pensioners, for widows and widowers. A river lined with sycamore trees flows through the town, which is situated in a kind of trough, surrounded by naked hills. No railroad leads to the town. The church, the city hall, the post office, the police head-quarters, and the local rathskeller are grouped around the central square. In this idyllic small town, cut off from the events of the great world, all seems quiet and peaceful, a last refuge for the old and the sick, but it soon becomes a setting for an old and ritualistic drama, the drama of the scapegoat.

The action in the novel is triggered by the arrival of a stranger, the young lawyer Libotz. Libotz is a man marked by fate, doomed to suffer for his own sake as well as for the sake of others, and those who come into contact with him feel constrained to further his destiny by tormenting him. He has had a difficult youth, and in spite of a flawless record in his service in the circuit court, he has been unable to find favor with his superiors or colleagues.

As a lawyer in the small town he is unsuccessful in his practice for some time, but one day fortune smiles on him, the customers begin to arrive, and slowly but surely Libotz becomes a moderately successful man. His position is extremely precarious, though, and when his father, the drunken

---

[3] August Strindberg, *Från Fjärdingen till Blå Tornet: Ett brevurval 1870–1912*, ed. Torsten Eklund (Stockholm: Bonniers, 1946), p. 382.

and bankrupt storekeeper, arrives in town and is arrested for disturbing the peace, the father's behavior and Libotz' attempts to arrange matters place him in a very unfavorable light in the eyes of the townspeople, who are, it seems, always eager to impute only the lowest of motives to him.[4]

A Sunday marks the beginning of Libotz' decline and fall. Having harbored some suspicions about the reliability of his assistant, a young man by the name of Sjögren, Libotz in examining the books discovers that Sjögren has embezzled funds and accepted bribes from the other party in lawsuits. Libotz makes the mistake of revealing his discoveries to his friend the sheriff, though he does not wish to bring any official charge against the young man. When he realizes that the sheriff is eager to do so, Libotz, always inclined to identify with the culprit, begins to defend Sjögren, insisting that he, Libotz, is the guilty one, since he has taught Sjögren the secrets of the trade. Two days later Libotz is presented a suit for slander, and charged with having falsely accused Sjögren of embezzlement. The innocent Libotz is brought to trial and fined. The townspeople take Sjögren's side, and Libotz finds himself the target of universal hatred. Moving about on the backstreets he tries to avoid the glances of disapproval directed at him. The newspapers begin to publish caricatures of him.

Although Libotz occasionally doubts his own innocence, and while the public image has been grafted onto him until he is no longer able to distinguish his own identity, he has faith in justice, and in the trial before the circuit court he is acquitted. This is regarded as a defeat for the city, and less from sympathy for Sjögren than from hatred of the stranger, invisible hands help Sjögren establish an office of his own to compete with Libotz. When Libotz is evicted

---

[4] A similar reversal of fortune with the arrival of the father may be observed in *The Romantic Organist* (1888).

from his lodging without explanation, he finally decides to leave the town.

A second major figure in the novel is the innkeeper Askanius, whose fate is a close parallel to that of Libotz. A stranger like Libotz he has traveled widely in his youth (he too has had a difficult youth!), and as a singer he has performed at the court of the czar and before the emperor in Versailles. Now he leads a quiet life in the small town, an upright, law-abiding citizen and restaurateur. In reality Askanius is a very subjective and domineering individual with delusions of grandeur.

His downfall is the result of his need "to show off" (44, 122). When Askanius shows off by displaying his knowledge of the seven wonders of the world, of the fountains at Versailles, and the glories of the czar's court, his weakness is harmless, but when his delusion of grandeur leads him to build a new and luxurious restaurant he gets into serious difficulties. There is an explosion on the opening night. After the restaurant has been repaired, his old customers are alienated by the luxury and the lack of intimacy. Nemesis has struck, and Askanius is driven into bankruptcy by his competitors. As a new Grand Hotel rises on the square Askanius becomes a broken old man. On the first of October, the day on which the new hotel is to open, he is found dead in his cellar, a suicide. This is also the day on which Libotz leaves town. With this vision of Askanius dead in his cellar and Libotz on the road, the novel ends.

There is a third figure in the novel, the sheriff Tjärne, who has been assigned a role seldom missing in Strindberg's later works, the role of the vampire. He belongs in the company of such figures as Zachris in *Black Banners* and Hummel in *The Ghost Sonata*. As a sheriff it is Tjärne's job to weed out secrets, to listen. From Libotz he learns about the tricks of the lawyer's trade, from Askanius the secrets of the kitchen.

When he finds it convenient to use these, he does so without scruples, though he is a friend of these men. A completely amoral individual, he becomes instrumental in the downfall of both of them.

Libotz is a familiar figure in Strindberg's gallery. He is the outsider, the stranger, Ishmael, the son of the servant.[5] His physical appearance already serves to set him apart: he looks like a foreigner. He has a low forehead, dark hair, a curled moustache, and a yellowish complexion. To Askanius he looks like a poor musician. His name points to a foreign extraction, Polish or Jewish. All his efforts to escape from his isolation and loneliness are destined to fail. Others seem to shun his company, because they are afraid of being drawn into his magic circle, of having their own destinies connected with his. For Libotz' destiny is to suffer.

Strindberg played many roles. One of his favorite roles was the pessimistic cynic, but the most persistent is the innocently suffering martyr. "The desire to be a victim is and remains the main point in his confession," says Martin Lamm.[6] Writing in a letter on April 2, 1907, Strindberg refers to his karma or destiny as being doomed to suffer innocently. He has the feeling that his whole life is a stage production to be both endured and depicted by him.[7] In *The Scapegoat* his life of suffering is summed up in the image of the innocent scapegoat.[8]

---

[5] Cf. the Hunter's last monologue in *The Highway*: "Here Ishmael rests, the son of Hagar, / whose name was once called Israel, / because he fought a fight with God, / and did not cease to fight until laid low, / defeated by his almighty goodness" (*Five Plays of Strindberg*, trans. Elizabeth Sprigge [New York: Anchor Books, 1960], p. 351).

[6] Lamm, *op. cit.*, p. 11.

[7] E.g., in a letter to Schering, April 2, 1907 (*op. cit.*, p. 379).

[8] The image of the scapegoat recurs in scene 5 of *The Highway*, where the Hunter says: "Execute yourself, as I did, as I had to do, when you made me into a scapegoat, onto whom you loaded all your guilt" (*Five Plays*, p. 336).

Since childhood Libotz has been ill-treated by all. In his father's store he was forced to cheat the customers. In school he was abused by the teachers. He once tried to hang himself but was discovered and brought back to life. Even this escape was denied him. But it is in the little provincial town that his sufferings reach their climax, and he is given an insight into the meaning of his destiny.

It is one of the paradoxes of his fate that Libotz, who above all desires integrity and beauty and happiness, should have become a lawyer, for as a lawyer he is surrounded by all the manifestations of dishonesty, ugliness, and misery. During the week, even on Sundays, people come to him for advice, unload their worries on him, unburden their sorrow, their disappointments, their hatred. He is not only a lawyer, he is a physician. The accumulated misery has left an atmosphere in his office which chokes and stifles, and the breath of his clients has formed a covering of dust on the windows so that he can only glimpse the street outside (153). As he listens to the problems of married couples he has to live through the torments of years in a matter of hours. While the man and his wife sometimes change their minds, Libotz is crushed. "It was as if he had lived ten years of a dreadful marriage; he seemed to have aged in these three hours, his face had become thinner and his skin had dried; this is how closely he assumed the sufferings of others" (159–160).

His own difficulties as well as the sufferings of others, along with the hatred to which he is subjected, finally leave lasting marks on him: his complexion grows sallower, and sallower, till people are repelled by his ugliness. Through occupying himself with people's evil thoughts, "these attached themselves to him like burrs" (170). Finally he comes to see himself with two selves: his own self and his public image. When his clients appear he reads in their eyes a "secret understanding with this crook created of their depravity and grafted onto him." He begins to regard this other self as a person with independent existence. When the town's newspapers begin to publish caricatures of him this divided self becomes more and more disturbing. He is terrified of his own image, wondering if he is really such a hypocrite that he cannot discover himself, and when he looks in the mirror he begins to find similarities to the newspaper images. He begins, in effect, to lose his identity, living a role that has been forced upon him (172).

It is, of course, the mythical role of the scapegoat. Libotz is made to bear the blame for others or to suffer in their place. Like the goat in the ancient Jewish ritual Libotz is sent into the wilderness on the Day of Atonement after the sins of the people have symbolically been laid upon him.

When Libotz is leaving town, significantly enough on October 1 (the Jewish holiday Yom Kippur, the Day of Atonement, usually falls in the neighborhood of this date) he overhears two citizens of the town refer to him in passing: "Look, there goes the scapegoat!" He finds the remark to be made in all innocence, but true, and he thinks of the Old Testament ritual, and reflects: "It was certainly not a grateful or a glorious role, but then Christ had carried the same ignominious burden, and it was supposed to mean something 'which we were not able to grasp.' " He thinks of him as "the serum animal" carrying the poison of evil, a role he accepts without bitterness. Leaving the town on foot he proceeds on the highway, "toward new vicissitudes, which he surmised but no longer feared" (200–204).

If Libotz as the outcast and martyr is another of Strindberg's self-portraits, this portrait achieves an added significance if viewed in the light of certain remarks about the life of the writer made in the contemporary *A Blue Book*. Libotz is Strindberg's image of the writer who is intimate with all human suffering to the extent that he no longer has a life of his own, but becomes an anonymous voice expressing the suffering of mankind. In this sense the writer too is a scape-goat.[9]

There is a newfound though hard-earned and precarious sense of humility in the older Strindberg. He praises the great anonymous writers, who hid behind their works: Shakespeare and the authors of the folk songs or ballads. In "Diktaren och människan" ("The Poet and the Man") he praises our fore-fathers who treated art under "the protective veil of the pseudonym," and the author of ballads, "who effaced his own self and only lived as the echo of a song. In that there was Christianity!" (47, 646–647).

The idea of the writer as scapegoat is most clearly pre-sented in Strindberg's many reflections on Shakespeare in *A Blue Book*. In "Diktarens självoffring" ("The Poet's Self-Sacrifice") Shakespeare is made to illustrate the thesis that "a real poet shall, ought to, or must, sacrifice his own self for his work." Although little is known about the great English writer, it is evident from his writings, says Strindberg, "what a stormy life he lived; there is hardly any wretchedness and filth he has not experienced, any passion he has not suffered; hatred and love, vengeance and heat, murder and fire; as a writer he seems to have experienced all" (46, 72). This de-scription of the poet as a man who sacrifices his life for his art is made apropos of an earlier and very personal sketch en-titled "Det oundvikliga" ("The Inevitable"), in which Strind-berg writes about a playwright who wanted to lead a life of purity and beauty, but who married an actress and then toured with her, she meanwhile performing in the nude in one of his plays. He was driven "down into the mud bath, as if he were forced to be dirtied by life, and in that particular way; as if he had no right to get an advance on heaven and

---

[9] An excellent study of Balzac's treatment of the same theme is William Troy's essay, "On Rereading Balzac: The Artist as Scape-goat," *Kenyon Review*, II (Summer, 1940), 333–344.

was not allowed to live a saintly life of purity. It is terrible, because it is inexplicable" (71).

In "Diktarens barn" ("The Poet's Children") Strindberg goes a step further in stressing the self-sacrifice of the great writer. "You are a writer and must produce reincarnations already here; you have the right to invent personae and at every stage speak the language of the person you are impersonating; you must make homunculi, practice autogamy." Shakespeare did this, "whether he consciously acted or life provided him with the parts." He is the cynical Hamlet, the misanthropic Timon, the jealous Othello, the murderous Macbeth, the loving Romeo: "Every villain may speak in his defense, and Shakespeare is his *lawyer*" (112, my italics).

Strindberg in his last works seems reconciled to a loss of identity, to anonymity, and to seeing his fate as a writer as one of suffering and self-sacrifice. The lawyer Libotz is a moving image of this vision.

But the significance of Libotz does not rest with his being a self-portrait and an embodiment of the aged Strindberg's view of the artist. The humble lawyer is one of Strindberg's great character creations, worthy of being placed beside those other great tragicomic figures of modern fiction, the heroes of Kafka and Beckett. In Strindberg's novels only Montanus in *The Red Room*, Carlsson in *The People of Hemsö*, and Alrik Lundstedt, the "romantic organist," are of the same stature. Interestingly enough, these are all comic heroes.

Strindberg has seldom been acclaimed for his sense of humor, but in many of his works he shows propensities for it, though it is often of a "dark" variety or a crude form of low humor. But in his last works, notably in *The Scapegoat*, he has attained the vision of life which Høffding has called "the great humor," the vision of Shakespeare's *The Tempest*, of

Cervantes' *Don Quixote*. humor as a way to acceptance and reconciliation.[10] This is the humor of the absurd and the paradox, the humor of Kierkegaard and Kafka, a humor tinged with tragedy. That Strindberg should have exhibited this type of humor in his last work of fiction is one of the most surprising aspects of his literary career.

As Wylie Sypher has pointed out in a perceptive essay, our sense of the comic has undergone a change. It is no longer low comedy or the comedy of manners, but "existential comedy," absurd comedy, a comedy that attempts to give a total perception of human existence. The comic is the irrational, the inexplicable, the nonsensical, the irreconcilable, inherent in the human situation.[11]

It is Kierkegaard who is responsible for the notion that only religious faith or comedy can encompass the absurdity of the human situation: the Knight of Faith, whose *credo quia absurdum* transcends the irreconcilables, and the comic hero on the threshold of faith with his recognition of the discrepancy and contradiction of his existence because "God is all, whereas man is nothing." In placing humor as the last stage before faith, and higher than the ethical (to which tragedy belongs), Kierkegaard expressed his sense of relatedness between the saint and the comic hero. His man of faith is often the comic man, for his life is a contradiction: he has an incognito; he does not make a show in the world; no one should know that the infinite moves within him. With his stress on suffering, and on the pathos of man's insignificance before God, Kierkegaard also pointed to that admixture of the tragic and the comic, of laughter and pain, which is our modern sense of the comic. His comic hero is the absurd hero

---

[10] Harald Høffding, *Den store humor* (Copenhagen: Gyldendal, 1916).

[11] Wylie Sypher, *Comedy* (New York: Anchor Books, 1956).

of Kafka and Beckett, pathetic, bungling, unheroic, a bit of a fool, the outsider trying to belong, trying to get in touch with "authority." [12]

As Sypher points out this modern sense of the comic is high comedy, and its social function is to instill a greater sense of humanity through humility, charity, and tolerance. In its recognition of the absurdity of the human situation it is related to Prospero's final acceptance of the incompatibilities of life when viewed from the perspective of infinity, where life has become a dream. It leads to forgiveness and endurance through a godlike charity of understanding.[13]

In view of Strindberg's renewed interest in Kierkegaard during and after the Inferno period there is every reason to believe that the portrait of Libotz is patterned closely on Kierkegaard's view of the religious man as the comic hero. As Martin Lamm has pointed out, Strindberg is returning to the philosopher who had affected him so profoundly during his youth because he is "convinced of the necessity of suffering, that to man existence must appear irrational and paradoxical, that faith itself must be founded on a paradox, on the 'absurd,' as the concluding words of *Legends* express it." [14] In a reflection in *A Blue Book* entitled "Credo quia (etsi) absurdum" Strindberg admits that he is unable to grasp or explain the doctrine of atonement through Christ's expiatory sacrifice, but regards this inability as a flaw in himself and not in the teachings. Using an illustration from mathematics he argues that one must often believe what is contrary to reason: "*Credo quia absurdum,* that is, I must believe (a fact) precisely because it is incomprehensible to me = ab-

---

[12] Søren Kierkegaard, *Concluding Unscientific Postscript* (Princeton: Princeton University Press, 1941), pp. 447–468.

[13] Sypher, *op. cit.*, pp. 250–255.

[14] Martin Lamm, *Strindberg och makterna* (Uppsala: Svenska Diakonistyrelsens Bokförlag, 1936), p. 40.

surd (to me, but not to others). If I were able to grasp it, the emergency exit or shortcut of faith would not be needed. This is the sacrifice, not of my reason, but of my common sense and my pride" (215–216). This is a very accurate description of Kierkegaard's concept of faith. Another reference to Kierkegaard in A *Blue Book* is extremely pertinent, because it develops a theme used by Kierkegaard in his discourse on humor in *Concluding Scientific Postscript*, the theme that "before God we are always in the wrong" (47, 704).

If Strindberg's increasing feeling of the absurdity of existence brought him closer to Kierkegaard's paradoxical affirmation, to the faith that his sufferings must have some meaning, his skepticism, his growing feeling that we live in a "world of folly and delusions," that all is a dream, brought him closer to Shakespeare's great comic vision in *The Tempest*. During the years in which the Chamber plays and A *Blue Book* and *The Scapegoat* were written, *The Tempest* must have been one of Strindberg's most loved works, for he refers to it over and over. One may perhaps contend that Strindberg in his remarks on the play is trying to mold Shakespeare in his own image, that he is trying to make him into a "Buddhist," but then Strindberg always read in a most subjective fashion. Most writers probably do. In Shakespeare's work, and in *The Tempest* particularly, Strindberg found a tone of compassion and charity, of acceptance and resignation, which he had not been able to express in his own works, but which he was desperately striving to attain. We need only recall the figure of Falkenström in *Black Banners*, refusing to the end to forgive and forget, in spite of admonishments to do so.

In the essay on *The Tempest* in his *Open Letters to the Intimate Theater* Strindberg comments on "the charitable and conciliatory tone" in this last play, Shakespeare's farewell to his public, "where he thanks them and ends with a prayer." *The Tempest* is "the poet's last confessions, view of life, farewell, thanks and prayer." Reflecting on Prospero's statement "We are such stuff as dreams are made on," Strindberg writes: "That is the way it really is when you get on in life; if you turn around and consider the things you have lived through, it is so dreadful that you 'hardly believe it is real,' and the best, which had a certain reality, gradually dissolves like smoke. Is it strange then if you begin to doubt the reality of reality?" In *The Tempest* Shakespeare has staged his conception of life as a dream, "this Buddhist-problem," as Strindberg calls it.

Strindberg concludes his remarks on *The Tempest* and the illusory nature of appearance by a reference to Prospero's charity and Caliban's atonement, stressing that it is more beautiful to be charitable than to take revenge, and quoting Prospero's last lines, his hope for grace and atonement. That, says Strindberg, is religion, and it is Christianity (50, 197–204).[15]

The spirit of *The Tempest*, its tone of high comedy as well as its cruder, low comedy, has had a profound influence on *The Scapegoat*, each of the two forms of comedy being embodied in a particular figure, the high comedy in Libotz, the buffoonery in Askanius.

Libotz is made an absurd comic hero by his pathetic, bungling ways, his way of responding to his sufferings by humorous resignation, his charity to those who have wronged him, his life of contradiction, his acceptance of the inexplicable.

Libotz' difficulties in the past have given him a disposition of meekness and shyness; he literally tiptoes about the

---

[15] For an English translation of this important essay, see August Strindberg, *Open Letters to the Intimate Theater*, trans. Walter Johnson (Seattle: University of Washington Press, 1966), pp. 199–207.

world so that he will not be noticed. All his efforts are designed to please; yet he fails to be accepted in the eyes of the world.

Askanius' final judgment of Libotz is typical. It is impossible that anyone could be such a fool: Askanius, being a man who plays a role, feels that Libotz is just acting the role of a fool, that he is a wolf in sheep's clothing. This is an opinion often shared by the townspeople who see in Libotz the shrewd lawyer hiding his real nature under the mask of humility and meekness. It is in this manner that the public image is grafted onto Libotz. To be a Libotz a man must be either a fool or a knave.

All his efforts seem pathetic, because they are doomed to fail. His professional tricks (the inflated title on the nameplate, keeping up appearances by seeming busy when in effect without clients), though his one way of emulating the ways of the world, fail. When he removes the title, the clients come. But when he tries to be a lawyer of immutable integrity, he is unsuccessful.

Being in his thirties and unmarried and lonely Libotz falls in love, but his romantic inclinations are again bound to fail, because he idealizes the object of his affections, Karin, one of Askanius' waitresses. The romance founders, because Libotz learns slowly to understand that they have absolutely nothing in common. His outings with the girl are the pathetic scenes of two people finding no basis for communication. The first week they speak at length about their backgrounds, the second week about the future, the third week they are already forced to talk about the things they talked about during the first week, until their few topics are exhausted. The comic climax to the affair comes on a Sunday walk, which ends with a luncheon. Libotz, surfeited with food on the warm afternoon, falls asleep and is replaced in Karin's affections by Tjärne, the sheriff.

But in spite of his sufferings Libotz is undaunted. Although his name suggests a derivation from Job (the man from Utz) he has none of the passion of Job, nor is he Jacob angrily wrestling with God. His is not a stoical but a humorous resignation.

His usual response is an infinitely sad laughter, and his remarks, though not amusing in themselves, become so because of the nature of his speech. Libotz evidently lisps and, like a child, has difficulty with certain letters of the alphabet. This has a comic effect. When a person steps on his toes he immediately has a consoling word for the culprit: "Kåss, de va inte falit!" Or, in answer to being blamed for his father's behavior: "Kåss i allan dar; ja, jag kan ju icke rå för det . . . så tråkit, så tråkit. . . ." Or another example of his speech: "Så komist, sade han sig själv; det där med kona slog mest an på henne. Si, stassbarn och fruntimmer, det är något säskilt. . . ." This speech defect gives Libotz a pathetic, childish, and innocent quality.[16]

The strength of Libotz, his humorous resignation, has its source in what Kierkegaard would call his "inwardness." The infinite moves within him, he is able to see his sufferings in perspective, his humor is the incognito of the religious man, for like Job Libotz communes with the Lord on his Mount Tabor, where he gains his strength to bear his heavy fate. He keeps his devotions secret for fear of being regarded a hypocrite.

After a particularly difficult experience, such as the arrival of his father, Libotz pays a visit to a mountain outside of town, where he speaks with God. "A strange sight it was to see this city man in his top hat up on the deserted mountain. He bared his head and murmured words, sometimes

---

[16] I have left these passages in the original Swedish because it is impossible to render them into English without distorting their relevance.

defiant and complaining, sometimes submissive. Then he covered his head, put his hands in his pockets, walked back and forth as if on his own floor; stood still, walked again, and finally descended after having bowed before the Invisible One" (44, 105–106). On his way home, it begins to rain and he receives the showers as a gift of grace.

His great inability is to understand "God's benevolence, when life was so cynically cruel that one was literally dragged helpless into the evil deed" (152–153). He is sorry to see that God does not help his faithful worshipers in their moments of temptation, and he does not understand why he himself against his will is always dragged into "these ambiguous situations," where he appears as a hypocrite. He consoles himself with the hope that he is not undergoing punishments but tests, "that his fate was Job's and he himself a fairly innocent man" (151–152).

His hope is to die, because he can expect nothing in this life, and his faith is that somehow his sufferings must have a meaning. As he leaves town and he hears himself referred to as the scapegoat, he is again faced with the inexplicable. But his response is a sad laughter, and the reflection: "Yes, verily, there are great differences between the fortunes of human beings, but why—'that one could not explain'—it was probably supposed to be that way" (my italics). Now he has at least a role, "not a grateful or a glorious role, but then Christ had carried the same ignominious burden, and that was supposed to mean something 'which we are not able to grasp'" (my italics).

In the innkeeper Askanius Strindberg has created another unforgettable character. If Libotz is the tragicomic hero, the hero of high comedy, with Askanius on the scene we are in the presence of the buffoon and the clown. Like Stephano, Trinculo, and Caliban, those three disturbing elements on Prospero's isle, Askanius injects a farcical note.

With his absurd dreams of power, his simplemindedness, his weakness for drink, he resembles these gentlemen. Like Caliban, Shakespeare's "mob man," Askanius is, "laughable, horrible, pathetic, unreachable by reason or by love," which also implies that he is by no means a simple figure.[17] Askanius is a character who continues to haunt the reader long after he has put the book down, for in addition to being a satirical portrait of man's persistent unwillingness to be himself, in his excessive pride and dreams of power, he is an embodiment of Strindberg's detached vision of the utter complexity and mystery of the human character. Askanius is the characterless individual, the man whose character is a mask, a mask that is never fully removed.

To this we must add that Askanius is also, like Libotz, a mythical figure and a self-portrait. The role he is enacting is that of Proteus, the god who has the power to change his form and appearance at will. Which is also a way of saying that he is another facet of Strindberg's portrait of the artist. In his portrait of the protean Askanius, Strindberg, I believe, has sought to express a feeling often reflected in his last works, the dread that he as a writer, as a man of many masks, lacks identity, lacks a self, that he too is a "fabricated" character, because he has dissipated himself in too many roles. It is perhaps best expressed in an entry in A Blue Book, in which Strindberg, commenting on Goethe's admission to Eckermann about his being forced to play so many roles in his long life, observes: "A long life brings the danger that the many roles begin to get entangled, just as when the wigs and costumes of the actor get into disorder when moving. The personality becomes a whole wax cabinet of figures that take on life, and one sees oneself like the Indian god with a hundred heads and arms" (47, 681).

---

[17] Francis Fergusson in his introduction to Shakespeare's The Tempest (New York: Dell, 1961), p. 16.

Askanius is a portrait of the characterless individual acting in the comedy of life. To the world he presents the mask of the correct, sober, and law-abiding citizen and innkeeper. He leads a quiet life. No one knows him intimately, since he does not encourage intimacy.

But there are moments when Askanius lets the mask fall. Under the influence of a few drinks he undergoes a transformation. The taciturn man becomes loquacious, suddenly "testing all the synonyms of the language." At such times he appears in many roles, "turning himself inside out, rising out of the graves of the past in new guises" (*44*, 119).

His major weakness and the cause of his ultimate downfall is his need "to show off," for in his moments of intoxication this need expresses itself in an urge to confess, to reveal secrets. He seems gripped by a demon, and his heart becomes an open book. At two o'clock in the morning he may surprise his listeners "with confessions of forbidden actions, which ought to have led to the penitentiary" (119). From revelations of the secrets of the kitchen to hints about mysterious events and crimes in America the path is short.

Thus that atmosphere of hidden crimes and secrets which also permeates the Chamber plays is evoked. This atmosphere is intensified by the presence at these drinking bouts of the sheriff Tjärne, a man whose whole existence is bent on gathering information. Unlike Askanius, Tjärne can drink all night long and yet remain sober, and unlike the volatile innkeeper, Tjärne has "no facets, as we say, but was always the same" (120). He gives the appearance of taking an interest in everything and everybody "while having himself ceased to exist." Like other such vampire figures in Strindberg's later works, Tjärne is compared to a snake. He is "a tall, thin person with too small a head; like a snake created he seemed able to go through holes, if only he could get his head in" (120). Askanius regards Tjärne as his friend and as a wonderful person, but Libotz, who knows that Tjärne is "a psychic murderer" who will someday "murder" Askanius (142), has a different opinion, deploring the tendency of Askanius to make "homunculi of full-grown people" and to re-create them "in his own image." But even Tjärne has a secret that he is hiding from the world. He has a wound that those who know refrain from touching: a somewhat doubtful paternity.

Since everyone has secrets that may be unmasked, the conversations and the drinking bouts have a tense atmosphere. To converse becomes an art of tightrope-walking, a delicate balancing act. As Askanius in his need to make himself interesting proceeds to further revelations, and Tjärne becomes more and more aggressive in his attempts to unmask the innkeeper, the man who suffers is Libotz. Libotz sits with lowered eyes, because he "was able to leave his own self, to identify with others and that is why he bore the sufferings of all" (131). When Tjärne wonders what Askanius has really done, Libotz answers: "One should not inquire into the past of people . . . because every human being has to suffer for his actions, and when he has suffered enough, he is forgiven" (132).

Tjärne has to be satisfied with the secrets of the kitchen, and this is sufficient for him to destroy Askanius. After Nemesis has struck, and Askanius is already a defeated man, his need to make himself interesting grows. He now grows into a demonic and grotesque figure.

The climactic scene occurs on a Christmas Eve. As Libotz and Tjärne go for a walk they see "a spooky vision," Askanius playing a game of billiards, alone in his fully illuminated but deserted restaurant. They pass, but later return to find Askanius sitting alone with a hundred empty tables around him, drinking a bottle of champagne and listening to the invisible orchestra playing a march.

Although a broken man, Askanius is still capable of surprising his listeners with his performances. When he suddenly gets up and begins to direct the imaginary orchestra, they experience "a new incarnation of the dignified man, and it frightened them like the apparition of an unknown person in a room with closed doors" (183). When the drinking begins, Askanius gives "one of his Proteus performances, he shed skin, character, and face every tenth minute, sometimes he seemed to speak in his sleep, even dream." One minute he is in Versailles, the next moment in Brooklyn, New York, again hinting at mysterious events. In one of his "endless monologues" he dwells on the nature of character and fate: "Let us now assume that a man's character is his fate, but character is inborn, then my fate is also inborn, and then I am without guilt, am I not?" He comments on how little human beings really know about each other: "they think they know each other, but they know nothing." He says he does not know if Tjärne is really an honest man, or if Libotz really is what he appears to be (184).

As Askanius becomes so personal, a secret fear quickly permeates the atmosphere: "they became afraid, one of the other, and meanwhile their faces changed, as if they wanted to protect themselves from attack, making themselves ready to parry an assault, smiling in the wrong place in order to counteract an expected sharp word." But Askanius "sliced alive, despairing, was guided by a longing to commit psychic suicide, dragging the others with him into the abyss, but only in order to land on top, to feel himself remarkable, sublime in his fall." He feels the need to say something that will place him in a frightful light, so that the others will be compelled to admire him. Just as he is preparing his great revelation, preceded by the speech "Gentlemen, I know with whom I am sitting at this table, but you do not know . . . who . . . I . . . am!" his great scene, prepared for so many years, is spoiled by the entrance of a waitress, who informs him that his wife is ill (182–186).

As Libotz and Tjärne leave, Libotz asks: "Who do you think Askanius is?" Tjärne answers that Askanius is just an ordinary innkeeper with great vanity, and that his secret is not much of anything; as a boy he probably stole apples or spent three days in prison on a charge of drunkenness. Libotz asks: "Do you really believe that people are that simple?" The question is left unanswered (186–187).

Askanius continues to prepare "his great scene" (190) every Saturday night for some time, but without success, for Libotz always intervenes to protect him, "if there really existed a dangerous secret, which one could never know" (190). But one day Askanius undergoes a sudden "character change." His old "character mask" from the inn returns. He disappears from sight and is said to be busy in his cellar inventing a new liqueur. On the first of October he is found dead in his restaurant. Like a statue, white as marble, he is found sitting in the middle of the dining room, while the orchestrion plays an infernal music. His last message is scrawled on the mirrors with a diamond. It contains the old refrain: "People are not what they seem to be" (203).

A final ironic note on the utter subjectivity of the absurd innkeeper is injected into this last remark: "People are not what they seem to be," for as Libotz learns from a passerby as he is leaving the town, the motto on the mirror was followed by the ludicrous remark: "T——e (supposed to be Tjärne) is a decent man, but L——z (supposed to be you), he is suspect." When Libotz learns that Askanius, to affirm this conviction, has given some money to Tjärne, "his only friend in this life," he can only respond with a "Gosh, how strange!" a pathetic resignation before the utter mystery of human nature.

As a portrait of the characterless individual Askanius is

satirically drawn, yet he remains a complex and fascinating figure. Some of the reasons for this complexity have already been suggested, but the main reason is the fact that his identity is allowed to remain a mystery, for, given the allusions and suggestions with which the novel provides the reader, we are led to suspect that Askanius is not the simple figure the sheriff believes him to be. Like Libotz he is a stranger, an outsider, and like the lawyer he is enacting a role. A number of factors serve to set Askanius apart from the small and conventional world in which he lives: his mysterious background; the fact that he once was an artist; his name; his great subjectivity, including his unusual ability to transform himself, to shift roles and mask.

Askanius like Libotz is a wanderer figure. He has spent a good part of his life traveling all over the globe, to Russia, to France, to America, to Egypt. In his youth he was a singer, and performed at the courts of the great emperors and kings: before the czar and before Napoleon III at Versailles. When he tries to impress his friends he always speaks of the glories of these places. Now he no longer sings, but he reads a great deal and plays the piano.

His name is interesting. It actually sounds Swedish, but it is not, and Strindberg makes a special point of bringing this to our attention. When Tjärne speaks about foreigners in a derogatory manner, Askanius, "the man with the Roman name," (93) casts a dark glance at him. Askanius is a Latin name, the name of a great warrior, the son of Aeneas, who in the epic accompanies his father on his journeys, later becoming the founder of Alba Longa, and, indirectly, of Rome. And so Askanius, too, has a mythical ancestry.

"Askanius was no ordinary person," we read, "because along with his good qualities he harbored the greatest subjectivity, craving for power, and egotism" (126). Strindberg continually stresses Askanius' "selfishness and subjectivity"

(165). He is "the subjective man" (191). This quality is very apparent in his inability to see his own contradictory position, in his inability to distinguish a friend from a foe, in his eagerness and need to impress others with his greatness. His mask hides a great pride and a desire for power. He is "a filled balloon tugging at the ropes to rise" (164). He is the little man, who wants to be big.

But Askanius' most significant trait is expressed in his "Proteus performances," in his ability to transform himself, to "shed skin, character, and face every tenth minute" (183). Askanius too is "a veritable chameleon."

These are traits and allusions that give us a clue to the ancestry of Askanius, to the mystery of his identity. Askanius is a comic version of the Napoleon figure, which is, as Nils Norman has shown in his excellent article "Strindberg och Napoleon," a recurring symbol in Strindberg's works both before and after the Inferno crisis.[18] Strindberg seems to have felt a particular affinity with Napoleon, and, as Norman observes, several of Strindberg's heroes have traits of Napoleon, among them Borg in *By the Open Sea* and Alrik Lundstedt in *The Romantic Organist*. During the Inferno crisis Strindberg, who often spoke of being a reincarnation of a great figure out of the past (once it was Edgar Allan Poe!), seems to have come to the conclusion that his sufferings were punishments for sins committed in an earlier existence, and argues that he had, in fact, been Napoleon in an earlier incarnation. In his speculations on the subject Strindberg pursues his supposed ancestry even further and asks in *Legends*: Who was Napoleon? Of whom was he a reincarnation? And he traces his incarnation to Ajax, concluding that he too (Strindberg) like Ajax had been punished because of his hubris: "I had sinned from pride, the only sin which the

---

[18] Nils Norman, "Strindberg och Napoleon," *Svensk litteratur-tidskrift*, 4 (1959), 151–170.

gods do not forgive." Against Napoleon, who here serves as a symbol of pride and arrogance, Strindberg places the figure of Christ with his humility, a humility to which Thomas à Kempis' *Imitatio Christi* had taught him to aspire (28, 310–312).

The idea of nemesis, which increasingly began to occupy Strindberg during the Inferno period, is, as Norman has also observed, intimately connected with the Napoleon symbol. As Napoleon's pride led to his downfall, and Strindberg's arrogance to his road to Damascus, so Askanius is struck by nemesis when his arrogance leads him from words to deeds.

In his article Norman restricts himself to a discussion of works and letters with actual references to Napoleon. His essay does not refer to any works after *To Damascus*. It would be easy to show that the Napoleon figure, metaphorically speaking, appears even after *To Damascus*, undoubtedly because Strindberg himself has not yet "settled his account" with the aspect of himself which it represents. To Strindberg Napoleon is more than a symbol of pride and arrogance: he is also a primary symbol of his ambivalent attitude to the artist, the artist who makes poetry of his existence, the artist who like another Proteus repeatedly appears in new transformations.

In this context it is interesting to note that in the dialogue between Pater Melcher and the Stranger in *To Damascus*, part iii, the Pater refers to Napoleon as a master of the art of transformation, in this respect only excelled by Kierkegaard. Napoleon, "the Emperor of the people, the Nero of Freedom, the suppressor of Equality and the 'big brother' of Fraternity," is called "the most cunning of all the two-headed, for he was able to laugh at himself, to rise above his own contradictions, to change his skin and his soul, and yet for every change be clearly aware of himself as a *new incarnation*, convinced, self-justified" (29, 357 [my italics]).

The qualities that are here extolled bear a striking resemblance to those used by Strindberg in his picture of the artist in *Alone*, in *Black Banners*, and in the already quoted "Diktarens barn" (see above, p. 276). The artist as the man of many masks and the metamorphic Napoleon have profound affinities.

But Strindberg's attitude to the artist, as we have already observed, remains ambivalent. The same freedom that is extolled in one work is feared in another. For the artist in his arrogance over his ability to transform himself into multiple guises, to play a thousand roles, may finally lose all sense of identity. He becomes the subjective artist, the poet who turns his own life and the life about him into literature. At times he is envisioned as a Peer Gynt figure dreaming of becoming an emperor but ending by losing his self.

The Peer Gynt theme is central in Strindberg's works, and there is no need to illustrate it extensively here.[19] It appears, for instance, in the tale of Alrik Lundstedt, "the romantic organist," whose vivid imagination leads him to play so many roles that he is in danger of losing all contact with reality. In the present context it is noteworthy that one of the roles in which Alrik imagines himself is the role of Napoleon. On his way to the conservatory in Stockholm he imagines that he is Napoleon rushing from the burning Moscow in his sleigh.

It also appears in the moving fable, "Jubal utan jag" ("Jubal without Self") in *Sagor* of 1903, in which an ordinary young man, Gustav Klang, becomes a famous opera singer, with the result that he repudiates his past, his family, and his friends, and assumes the name of Jubal. Like Alrik, Jubal plays the roles of "kings and prophets, patriots and demons" and believes himself, in his newfound self-reliance,

---

[19] Torsten Eklund, *Tjänstekvinnans son: En psykologisk Strindbergsstudie* (Stockholm: Bonniers, 1948), pp. 320 f.

"to be the person of whom he acted the part" (38, 96–97). But Jubal, too, meets his nemesis, in the guise of a woman, and one day her fame overshadows his, and he is forgotten. The story ends, appropriately, on a Gyntian note, for Jubal comes to realize (as does Peer Gynt in the famous scene with the onion) that he has no self, only to find it again when his mother (now a widow living in a hut high up in the mountains) calls him by both his names, Gustav Klang.

From the foregoing it should be abundantly clear that the ill-fated innkeeper Askanius belongs in the company of these artists troubled like Strindberg himself by their Gyntian selves. But Askanius is a richer and more complex, more double-faced figure than either Alrik or Jubal. Alrik is treated with humor, it is true, but only in the first part of the tale. In the second half, Strindberg unaccountably shifts his point of view (as he so often does), siding against the too playful artist. The story of Jubal is a moral fable. It has poetic justice, and Jubal never comes alive as a human being.

But Askanius continues to haunt us, for Strindberg's eyes peer behind the comic mask. The satirical portrait is not without compassion, and the last scene with Askanius stiff-backed like a statue in front of the silver bowl and the bottle of maraschino liqueur with the deadly cyanide, the music blaring around him, though grotesque, is also an image of heroic defiance in the face of a hostile fate. There is "a lofty expression on his regular features." For Askanius, too, is a victim. With this last image of Askanius imprinted on one's mind, one is left with the feeling that as a writer Strindberg is finally resigned to seeing himself as "the Indian god with a hundred heads and arms," and that like another Prospero he has at last accepted the responsibility for this Caliban of his own creation.[20]

---

[20] Of interest in this context is August Falck's descriptions of his evenings with Strindberg during the years of the Intimate Theater.

Thus both Askanius and Libotz portray different aspects of Strindberg the man and the writer. In the Napoleonic inn-keeper he has portrayed his own arrogance and pride, and his fears of losing his identity by too close an identification with his created world. In the lawyer Libotz, the martyr and scapegoat, he has portrayed his search for humility and resignation before the mystery of life, his longing for anonymity and self-effacement. It is a measure of Strindberg's complex vision that in this last novel he was able to create such an objective portrait of himself, a portrait suffused with humor and high comedy.

Referring to Strindberg's whiskey-drinking which usually began about eight o'clock in the evening and lasted until three or four o'clock in the morning, Falck writes: "The liquor made Strindberg tired, but at the same time infinitely clear in his thinking. Often when we drank together I felt that for Strindberg it was an act of liberation, like loosening the fetters of the will. Voices—heavenly or infernal—took shape within him, living their rich life before his clear vision, chewing on his bitter repartees" (August Falck, *Fem år med Strindberg* [Stockholm: Wahlström och Widstrand, 1935], pp. 77–78).

⌐ 16. Conclusion

The Scapegoat is the last of Strindberg's novels and, as is fitting, amounts to a summing up at the end of the journey. Like so many other modern writers, Strindberg has turned to an old myth in his search for the meaning of his destiny. In the myth of the scapegoat he has found the story that mirrors the role of the artist in the modern world, the artist whose destiny it is to be punished for being a practitioner of Christian morality in a world of fraud and deceit. Unlike the hero of classical myth, he is destined to remain a homeless wanderer, unaccepted and misunderstood, an Ahasuerus, not a Ulysses.

The quest for identity has ended in the affirmation of a form of nonidentity, a form of self-abandonment. For the artist is seen as an intercessor, as "mankind's lawyer," living in and for others, without an identity of his own. This does not imply a loss of self, because the *modus vivendi* of the writer is a paradoxical compromise: the loss of personal identity in return for a wealth of identities. The self that has been abandoned is merely the persona, or public self, which has been exchanged for a multitude of selves.

In *The Scapegoat*, as well as in *Alone* and in *The Roofing Feast*, the old conception of identity based on self-consciousness is recognized as a delusion, the real obstacle to self-knowledge. A condition of mystic selflessness now appears as the ideal, and while this condition might at first appear as a denial and a mortification of the self, a loss of autonomy, it has, paradoxically, become the source of a firmer sense of self. For what has been abandoned is not the self but self-consciousness, the consciousness excessively colored by anxiety and conflicting desires and ambitions. What remains is the anonymous self that has rejected all excessive claims for the self as a source of value and is therefore open to the world, ready to immerse itself in a variety of points of view.

This self-abandonment is also manifested in a reversal of the relative significance of personality and art. The Romantics invested heavily in their personality, and Strindberg is no exception to this rule. But after the Inferno period, it is art that matters, not personality. Fantasies, dreams, the web of illusions, those things that form the stuff of art, once having been regarded as escape routes from real life, are now avenues to self-knowledge. Art has, in fact, become a means of self-integration, a process whereby inner tensions and conflicts are objectified and reconciled and past experiences are integrated into a meaningful synthesis.

In Strindberg we are in effect confronted with a writer whose novels constitute a record of a remarkably successful self-liberation and self-integration, for to the extent that he wrote to unify his life, to give meaning to his destiny, and to transform the pain and suffering of existence into art of lasting value, he must be said to have succeeded. In retrospect, it seems proper to speak of Strindberg's search for identity as a remarkable case of autopsychoanalysis, at least if we insist on a close analogy between the process of aesthetic integration in a work of literature and the process involved in successful psychotherapy.[1]

The world, too, has become transformed in these last novels. The city that the young Arvid Falk once so boldly challenged, and from which the saddened but resigned Libotz is departing, is still the same world of moral corruption. But it has now become transmuted through and into art, transmuted into an illusory and unreal spectacle. As such it has also become endurable.

Strindberg's vision of the world thus remains essentially nihilistic, but the form of nihilism has changed. From a nihilism of revolt it has been transformed into a nihilism of pessimistic resignation, a nihilism of the Buddhistic and Schopenhauerian variety. Like A Dream Play, and like the Chamber plays, the last novels depict the world as a place of strife and misery for which no one is to blame, since suffering is intimately bound up with the very nature of existence. The paths to liberation from suffering are conditioned by the recognition of the illusory nature of the self and the world. The principle of individuality must be overcome through self-denial and self-conquest, and the primordial will, manifested in selfish desires, must be silenced. Only through art or disinterested contemplation is man able to harness the will and achieve the lucidity that will make him perceive the illusory nature of existence and so, temporarily, set him free.

---

[1] For an excellent analysis of the analogy between the aesthetic integration of a work of art and the integration of the self in psychotherapy, see Herbert Fingarette, The Self in Transformation (New York: Harper Torchbooks, 1965), chap. 6.

This is a disenchanted vision of life, and only cold comfort is to be derived from it. Life is to be endured, and art alone makes it endurable. But compassion and resignation have taken the place of indignation and revolt, and it is only too evident that this disenchanted vision of life has its source in a disappointed love of innocence and beauty and simple happiness. The long and torturous quest for cures from the ills of the self and the world, be they religion, science, socialism, evolution, woman, has ended in the recognition that there are no cures. In his last novels Strindberg is resigned, resigned not only to the absurdities of existence but also to the mysteries of human identity. At last, he is resigned to being what he was always destined to be: an artist.

Regarded purely as a work of narrative art, *The Scapegoat* marks a significant stage of development, the end of a progressive movement from the realism of the early novels to the symbolism and myth of the late novels. If *The Roofing Feast*, with its Symbolist techniques, is Strindberg's most advanced experiment in the psychological novel, *The Scapegoat* illustrates his efforts to find in the world of myth the pattern that will give order and meaning to experience.

Several conclusions emerge when we consider the nature of this development. One inescapable conclusion is that there exists a definite relationship between the progressive penetration of the psyche and the need to transcend the limitations of the realistic novel in the direction of symbolism and myth. A second conclusion is that there is a close relationship between autobiography and the psychological novel. Strindberg's novels admirably bear out the thesis, most recently advanced by Robert Scholes and Robert Kellogg, that the most brilliant contributions within the psychological novel have come from those autobiographical novelists who, like Joyce and Proust, have turned within themselves for the new reality with which to forge their art, and that consequently there exists a definite relationship between self-analysis and the presentation of the inner life in fiction.[2]

The third and most significant conclusion is that the progressive inward turning that is the most characteristic feature of Strindberg's development as a novelist is symptomatic of a larger trend in the European novel during the latter half of the nineteenth and the first part of the twentieth century. Either anticipating, or following in the wake of, a new philosophical orientation that focused on the investigation of not only the conscious but also the unconscious mind, the new orientation of Schopenhauer, Nietzsche, William James, Bergson, Charcot, and Freud, the novelists of the late nineteenth century sought increasingly to project the inner life, the world of introspection and feeling. Turning away from the social scene, and from what they felt to be a shallow and mechanistic conception of character, these novelists occupied themselves increasingly with the problem of human identity, with the complexities and contradictions of the self. In so doing, they quickly discovered that the naturalistic forms of fiction were not able to convey this sense of complexity, that in order to succeed they had to turn to symbolism, myth, and poetry, and to experiments with time and the interior monologue. While engaged in extending the scope of naturalism to the realm of the inner life, into empirical investigations of the psyche, these novelists, in the process, developed into Symbolists.[3]

I am referring, of course, to what we usually label the psychological novel, and I am suggesting that Strindberg's place is among those who were the progenitors of this type of fiction. He admired the great realists, Dickens, Zola, Bal-

[2] Cf. Robert Scholes and Robert Kellogg, *The Nature of Narrative* (New York: Oxford University Press, 1966), pp. 155–156, 193.

[3] For an account of this inward turning in the modern novel, see Leon Edel, *The Psychological Novel, 1900–1950* (New York: Lippincott, 1955), chap. 2.

zac, and began in their footsteps as a social critic, but as he
gradually shifted his attention to psychological and existential
problems, he also moved in the direction of Poe, Dostoevski,
Hamsun, and Henry James, the direction that ultimately produced Proust, Joyce, Kafka, and Virginia Woolf. It is also
significant to note that when Strindberg, during and after the
Inferno crisis, again labeled Balzac his master, it was Balzac
the Romantic transcendentalist to whom he turned, the author of *Louis Lambert* and *La Peau de chagrin*, not the author
of *Le Père Goriot*.

Skeptical critics might object that Strindberg is not to
be ranked with these illustrious modern novelists, suspecting
that I am merely trying to inflate his importance by association. After all, he did not seriously cultivate the novel as an art
form as he did the drama. Nothing could be farther from my
intention. I do suggest that any evaluation of Strindberg's
achievement and significance as a novelist must be made with
reference to this particular genre, the psychological novel.
For what really turns his novels into moving and significant
works of literature is not so much the manner in which they
convey his quest for self-discovery and self-integration, but
the manner in which this self-exploration is reflected in the
development of new modes of conveying the inner life in the
novel.

How are we to evaluate Strindberg's novels? The answer
rests of course with the individual reader, who is always the
final court of appeal. Strindberg's dramas have rarely found
favor with the large public: they have been admired for their
brilliant technique, their fanatic logic, their passionate intensity, their penetrating dissection of marital woes, but the same
audience has frequently left the theater mumbling something
about that "mad Swede." The reaction to his novels, at least
to the majority of them, is perhaps destined to remain luke-
warm or negative. Often intentionally self-therapeutic, they

will strike many as more liberating for their author than for their readers. Despite their occasional flashes of humor and wit, and their poignant evocations of moments of beauty and harmony, they seldom give pleasure or enjoyment. On the contrary, they often leave the reader with a sense of frustration. The fastidious will deplore their lack of decorum, their violent exaggerations, their brutal reversals, their nervous restlessness and tension. Frequently one-sided and prejudiced in their criticism of society and of human beings, they strike many as negative and destructive, and, often conveying an eagerness to debunk an idea before it has been sufficiently examined, they are judged superficial when considered as potential contributions to thought.

There are, though, many entries on the other side of the ledger, because Strindberg's vision is broader and more profound than is usually acknowledged. His keen sense of awareness of the evils of the world is balanced by a sense of compassion for a suffering humanity and by the lament over our lost innocence, our inevitable isolation from one another caused by the lack of love or by the masks stamped on us by society. And the theme of revolt, despite its negative and nihilistic nature, is motivated by a desire to protect the individual from those forces that attempt to rob him of his uniqueness and his integrity. There is in Strindberg's novels, as in the existentialist literature of our own time, a passionate hatred of injustice, of bad faith, of cant, of any codes of morality or behavior imposed by society without any clear justification, of any society that denies the individual his freedom to choose his ideas or his beliefs.

With respect to the craft of fiction, Strindberg's novels have been surpassed by the works of bolder and more polished novelists. But *The People of Hemsö* remains a masterpiece within the framework of the naturalistic novel, and *By the Open Sea*, despite the static early chapters, is a brilliantly conceived and executed psychological romance. It is, however, in the short novels that Strindberg celebrates his greatest triumphs as a narrative artist: witness his skillful use of bold dramatic contrasts in *Progress*, of color imagery in *A Witch*, of the intimate journal in *Alone*, of the monologue and of musical leitmotivs in *The Roofing Feast*, of myth in *The Scapegoat*. Within the format, each of these novels is a masterpiece.

Strindberg's claim to being considered a major novelist rests securely on his having produced in his novels, as in his dramas, a psychology better adapted to convey the split and disharmonic nature of modern man. Less a creator of life than a dissector of it, it is as an anatomist of the self in conflict that Strindberg the novelist demands our attention, because it is in this capacity that he has enriched our knowledge and our experience.

And that is why the thumbnail sketch of the writer Arvid Falk, the young hero of *The Red Room*, a sketch tucked away in *The Gothic Rooms* (1904), paints the most distinctive portrait of Strindberg the novelist: "He [Arvid Falk] experimented with standpoints. As a conscientious laboratory technician, he arranged control experiments, placed himself on the opponent's side by way of a test, checked the proofs against the original, tested the sum in reverse, and when the control experiment turned out negative, he returned to the tested point of departure." To others, we read, he might appear as a man "who finally came into conflict with himself," but this is not so; Arvid Falk would have been understood

had he used Kierkegaard's method. The latter invented personae and gave himself a new pseudonym each time. Victor Eremita is not Johannes Climacus; Constantin Constantius is not Johannes de Silentio, but all together are Sören Kierkegaard. Falk was a vivisectionist, he experimented with his own soul, always went about with open wounds, until he gave his life for knowledge; I

do not want to use the abused word truth. And if his collected
works were to appear some day, not a word ought to be changed,
but all contradictions be resolved in the joint Kierkegaardian title:
Stages on Life's Way. (40, 45-46)

Bibliography

THE WORKS OF AUGUST STRINDBERG

IN SWEDISH

Brev. Ed. Torsten Eklund. Stockholm: Bonniers, 1947–1966. 9 vols.

Brev till min dotter Kerstin. Trans. Karin Boye and Åke Thulstrup. Stockholm: Bonniers, 1961.

En dåres försvarstal. Trans. Tage Aurell. Stockholm: Bonniers, 1962.

Från Fjärdingen till Blå Tornet: Ett brevurval 1870–1912. Ed. Torsten Eklund. Stockholm: Bonniers, 1946.

Samlade skrifter. Ed. John Landquist. Stockholm: Bonniers, 1912–1927. 55 vols.

Strindberg's brev till Harriet Bosse. Stockholm: Natur och Kultur, 1932.

Vivisektioner. Trans. Tage Aurell. Stockholm: Bonniers, 1958.

IN ENGLISH

By the Open Sea. Trans. Ellie Schleussner. London: Frank Palmer, 1913.

Confession of a Fool. Trans. Ellie Schleussner. London: Stephen Swift, 1912.

Inferno. Trans. Mary Sandbach. London: Hutchinson, 1962.

Legends: Autobiographical Sketches. London, 1912.

A Madman's Defense. Trans. Evert Sprinchorn. New York: Anchor Books, 1967.

The Natives of Hemsö. Trans. Arvid Paulson. New York: Paul S. Eriksson, 1965.

The People of Hemsö. Trans. Elspeth Harvey Schubert. Stockholm: Bonniers, 1959.

The Red Room. Trans. Elspeth Harvey Schubert. London: Everyman, 1967.

The Scapegoat. Trans. Arvid Paulson. New York: Paul S. Eriksson, 1967.

The Son of a Servant. Trans. Evert Sprinchorn. New York: Anchor Books, 1966.

OTHER WORKS CONSULTED

Ahlström, Stellan. "Lawrence Durrell och Strindberg," *Svenska Dagbladet* (Stockholm), Sept. 29, 1964, p. 5.

Ahlström, Stellan, ed. *August Strindberg. Ungdom och mannaår.* Stockholm: Wahlström och Widstrand, 1959.

Ahlström, Stellan, and Torsten Eklund. *August Strindberg. Mannaår och ålderdom.* Stockholm: Wahlström och Widstrand, 1961.

Bennich-Björkman, Bo. "Fåglar och författarroller hos Strindberg," *Samlaren,* 83 (1962), 1–66.

Berendsohn, Walter A. *August Strindbergs skärgårds- och Stockholmsskildringar.* Stockholm: Rabén och Sjögren, 1962.

———. "Goethe och Strindberg," *Samlaren,* 30 (1949), 118–128.

———. "Strindberg's *Ensam*: A Study in Structure and Style," *Scandinavian Studies*, 31 (Nov., 1959), 168–179.

———. *Strindbergsproblem*. Stockholm: KF:s Bokförlag, 1946.

Björck, Staffan. "I marginalen till Hemsöborna," in *Strindbergs Språk och stil*. Ed. Göran Lindström. Lund: Gleerups, 1964.

———. *Romanens formvärld*. 2d ed. Stockholm: Natur och Kultur, 1954.

Boas, George. "The Romantic Self: An Historical Sketch," *Studies in Romanticism*, IV (Autumn, 1964), 1–16.

Borland, Harold H. *Nietzsche's Influence on Swedish Literature*. Göteborg: Kungl. Vetenskaps- och Vitterhetssamhällets Handlingar, 1956.

Brandell, Gunnar. *Strindbergs Infernokris*. Stockholm: Bonniers, 1950.

———. "Strindbergs monologer," *Svenska Dagbladet* (Stockholm), Jan. 22, 1955.

Brandes, Georg. "Friedrich Nietzsche—En Afhandling om Aristokratisk Radikalisme," *Tilskueren* (Aug., 1889), pp. 565–613.

Brandes, Georg, and Edvard Brandes. *Brevväxling med svenska och finska författare och vetenskapsmän*. Stockholm: Bonniers, 1939–1942. Vol. I.

Brustein, Robert. *The Theatre of Revolt*. Boston: Little, Brown, 1966.

Campbell, Joseph. *The Masks of God: Occidental Mythology*. New York: Viking, 1964.

Danto, Arthur C. *Nietzsche as Philosopher*. New York: Macmillan, 1965.

Edel, Leon. *The Psychological Novel*, 1900–1950. New York: Lippincott, 1955.

Ekelund, Vilhelm. *På hafsstranden*. Stockholm: Bonniers, 1922.

Eklund, Torsten. "Strindbergs I havsbandet," *Edda*, XXIX (1929), 113–144.

———. *Tjänstekvinnans son: En psykologisk Strindbergsstudie*. Stockholm: Bonniers, 1948.

Fairley, Barker. *A Study of Goethe*. Oxford: Clarendon Press, 1947.

Falck, August. *Fem år med Strindberg*. Stockholm: Wahlström och Widstrand, 1935.

Fingarette, Herbert. *The Self in Transformation*. New York: Harper Torchbooks, 1965.

Fromm, Erich. *Escape from Freedom*. New York: Rinehart, 1941.

Frye, Northrop. *Anatomy of Criticism*. New York: Atheneum, 1966.

Groddeck, George. *Exploring the Unconscious*. Trans. V. M. E. Collins. New York: Funk and Wagnalls, 1940.

Gustafson, Alrik. *A History of Swedish Literature*. Minneapolis: University of Minnesota Press, 1961.

Hallberg, Peter. "Strindbergs Kammarspel," *Edda*, LVIII (1958), 1–21.

Hamsun, Knut. *Artikler*. Oslo: Gyldendal, 1939.

Hansson, Ola. *Husvill och andra berättelser*. Stockholm: Tiden, 1960.

Hedenberg, Sven. *Strindberg i skärselden*. Göteborg: Akademiförlaget-Gumperts, 1961.

Heller, Erich. *The Artist's Journey into the Interior and Other Essays*. New York: Random House, 1966.

Humphreys, Christmas. *Buddhism*. London: Penguin Books, 1958.

Huxley, Aldous. *Time Must Have a Stop*. London and New York: Harper, 1944.

Jacobi, Jolande. *The Psychology of C. G. Jung*. Trans. Ralph Manheim. New Haven: Yale University Press, 1962.

Jacobsen, Harry. *Digteren og Fantasten: Strindberg paa "Skovlyst."* Copenhagen: Gyldendal, 1945.

———. *Strindberg og hans første hustru*. Copenhagen: Gyldendal, 1946.

James, Henry. *The Art of the Novel: Critical Prefaces*. Ed. Leon Edel. New York: Scribner, 1962.

———. *The Future of the Novel: Essays on the Art of Fiction*. Ed. Leon Edel. New York: Scribner, 1956.

James, William. *The Varieties of Religious Experience*. New York: Modern Library, 1902.

Johannesson, Eric O. "The Problem of Identity in Strindberg's Novels," *Scandinavian Studies*, 34 (Feb., 1962), 1–35.

———. "Strindberg's *Taklagsöl*: An Early Experiment in the Psychological Novel," *Scandinavian Studies*, 35 (Aug., 1963), 223–238.

———. "*Syndabocken*: Strindberg's Last Novel," *Scandinavian Studies*, 35 (Feb., 1963), 1–28.

Jung, C. G. *The Archetypes and the Collective Unconscious*. New York: Pantheon, 1959.

———. *Modern Man in Search of a Soul*. New York: Harcourt, Brace, n.d.

Kärnell, Karl-Åke. *Strindbergs bildspråk*. Stockholm: Almqvist och Wiksell, 1962.

Kayser, Wolfgang. *The Grotesque in Art and Literature*. Trans. Ulrich Weisstein. Bloomington: Indiana University Press, 1963.

Kermode, Frank. *Romantic Image*. New York: Vintage Books, 1964.

Kierkegaard, Søren. *Concluding Unscientific Postscript*. Princeton: Princeton University Press, 1941.

———. *Either/Or*. Trans. Walter Lowrie, rev. Howard Johnson. New York: Anchor Books, 1959. 2 vols.

———. *The Present Age*. Trans. Alexander Dru. New York: Harper Torchbooks, 1962.

Lamm, Martin. *August Strindberg*. 2d ed. Stockholm: Bonniers, 1948.

———. *Strindberg och makterna*. Uppsala: Svenska Diakonistyrelsens Bokförlag, 1936.

Langbaum, Robert. "The Mysteries of Identity: A Theme in Modern Literature," *American Scholar*, 34 (Autumn, 1965).

Levin, Harry. *The Power of Blackness*. New York: Vintage Books, 1960.

Lindblad, Göran. *August Strindberg som berättare*. Stockholm: Norstedt, 1924.

Lindström, Göran. "Strindbergforskning 1915–1962," *Svensk litteraturtidskrift*, 2 (1962), 60–81.

Lindström, Hans. *Hjärnornas kamp: Psykologiska ideer och motiv i Strindbergs åttiotalsdiktning*. Stockholm: Natur och Kultur, 1952.

McCarthy, Mary. "Characters in Fiction," *Partisan Review*, XXVIII (March–April, 1961), 171–191.

McFarlane, J. W. "The Whisper of the Blood: A Study of Knut Hamsun's Early Novels," *PMLA*, LXXI (Sept., 1956), 563–594.

Maudsley, Henry. *The Pathology of Mind*. New York: Appleton, 1880.

Miller, Henry. *The Tropic of Cancer*. Paris: Obelisk Press, n.d.

———. *The Wisdom of the Heart*. Norfolk: New Directions, 1941.

Miller, J. Hillis. *Charles Dickens: The World of His Novels*. Cambridge: Harvard University Press, 1958.

Neumann, Erich. *The Origins and History of Consciousness*. New York: Pantheon, 1954.

Newman, Ernest. *Stories of Great Operas*. New York: Knopf, 1930.

Norman, Nils. "Strindberg och Napoleon," *Svensk litteraturtidskrift*, 4 (1959), 151–170.

Nyborg, Eigil. *Den indre linie i H. C. Andersens eventyr*. Copenhagen: Gyldendal, 1962.

Östin, Ola. "August Strindbergs Ensam," *Edda*, LVIII (1958), 81–99.

Poulenard, Élie. *August Strindberg: Romancier et nouvelliste*. Paris: Presses Universitaires de France, n.d.

Printz-Påhlsson, Göran. "Krukan och bitarna: Strindberg och 1800-talets romantradition," *Bonniers Litterära Magasin*, 33 (Dec., 1964), 740–754; 34 (Jan., 1965), 12–28.

Ribot, Théodule. *The Diseases of Personality*. Chicago: Open Court, 1891.

Rieff, Philip. *Freud: The Mind of the Moralist*. New York: Anchor Books, 1961.

Rinman, Sven. "En dåres försvarstal," *Svensk litteraturtidskrift*, 2 (1965), 63–75.

———. "Strindberg," in *Ny illustrerad svensk litteraturhistoria*. Ed. E. N. Tigerstedt. Stockholm: Natur och Kultur, 1957.

Sartre, Jean-Paul. "Strindberg, vår 'fordringsägare,' " *Dagens Nyheter* (Stockholm), Jan. 28, 1949.

Scholes, Robert, and Robert Kellogg. *The Nature of Narrative.* New York: Oxford University Press, 1966.

Smedmark, Carl Reinhold. *Mäster Olof och Röda rummet.* Stockholm: Almqvist och Wiksell, 1952.

Stenström, Thure. *Den ensamme: En motivstudie i det moderna genombrottets litteratur.* Stockholm: Natur och Kultur, 1961.

Sypher, Wylie. *Comedy.* New York: Anchor Books, 1956.

——. *Loss of the Self in Modern Literature and Art.* New York: Vintage Books, 1965.

Troy, William. "On Rereading Balzac: The Artist as Scapegoat," *Kenyon Review,* II (Summer, 1940), 333–344.

Werin, Algot. "Filosofen som blev Strindbergs moraliska stöd," *Svensk litteraturtidskrift,* 23 (1960), 101–102.

——. "Karaktärer i Röda rummet," in *Synpunkter på Strindberg.* Ed. Gunnar Brandell. Pp. 78–93. Stockholm: Aldus, 1964.

Whyte, Lancelot Law. *The Unconscious before Freud.* New York: Anchor Books, 1962.

Wheelis, Allen. *The Quest for Identity.* New York: Norton, 1958.

Index of Proper Names

Fictional characters are not included. Titles of books are indexed under the name of the author except for Strindberg, whose works form separate entries.